ETHNIC CHALLENGES BEYOND BORDERS

ST ANTONY'S SERIES
General Editor: Alex Pravda, Fellow of St Antony's College, Oxford

Recent titles include:

Craig Brandist
CARNIVAL CULTURE AND THE SOVIET MODERNIST NOVEL

Jane Ellis
THE RUSSIAN ORTHODOX CHURCH

Y Hakan Erdem
SLAVERY IN THE OTTOMAN EMPIRE AND ITS DEMISE, 1800–1909

Dae Hwan Kim and Tat Yan Kong (*editors*)
THE KOREAN PENINSULA IN TRANSITION

Jill Krause and Neil Renwick (*editors*)
IDENTITIES IN INTERNATIONAL RELATIONS

Jaroslav Krejčí and Pavel Machonin
CZECHOSLOVAKIA 1918–92

Iftikhar H. Malik
STATE AND CIVIL SOCIETY IN PAKISTAN

Barbara Marshall
WILLY BRANDT

Javier Martínez-Lara
BUILDING DEMOCRACY IN BRAZIL

Joseph Nevo
KING ABDALLAH AND PALESTINE

William J. Tompson
KHRUSHCHEV

St Antony's Series
Series Standing Order ISBN 0–333–71109–2
(*outside North America only*)

You can receive future titles in this series as they are published by placing a standing order. Please contact your bookseller or, in case of difficulty, write to us at the address below with your name and address, the title of the series and the ISBN quoted above.

Customer Services Department, Macmillan Distribution Ltd
Houndmills, Basingstoke, Hampshire RG21 6XS, England

Ethnic Challenges beyond Borders

Chinese and Russian Perspectives of the Central Asian Conundrum

Edited by

Yongjin Zhang
Senior Lecturer
Department of Political Studies
University of Auckland

and

Rouben Azizian
Lecturer
Department of Political Studies
University of Auckland

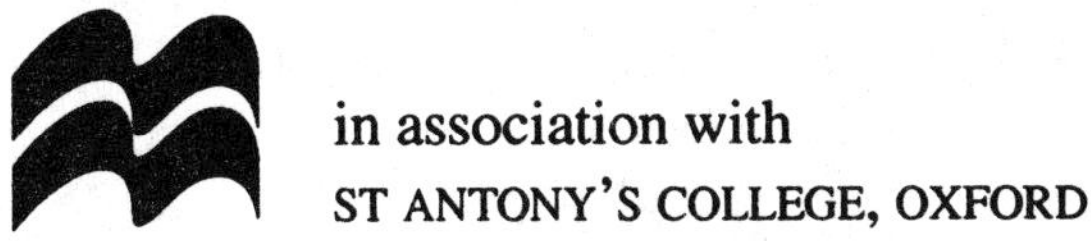

in association with
ST ANTONY'S COLLEGE, OXFORD

First published in Great Britain 1998 by
MACMILLAN PRESS LTD
Houndmills, Basingstoke, Hampshire RG21 6XS and London
Companies and representatives throughout the world

A catalogue record for this book is available from the British Library.

ISBN 0–333–69467–8

First published in the United States of America 1998 by
ST. MARTIN'S PRESS, INC.,
Scholarly and Reference Division,
175 Fifth Avenue, New York, N.Y. 10010

ISBN 0–312–21037–X

Library of Congress Cataloging-in-Publication Data
Ethnic challenges beyond borders : Chinese and Russian perspectives of the Central Asian conundrum / edited by Yongjin Zhang and Rouben Azizian.
p. cm. — (St. Antony's series)
Includes bibliographical references and index.
ISBN 0–312–21037–X
1. Asia, Central—Foreign relations—1991– 2. Asia, Central–Politics and government—1991– 3. Ethnicity—Asia, Central. 4. Asia, Central—Economic conditions. 5. Asia, Central—Strategic aspects. 6. China—Foreign relations—Asia, Central. 7. Asia, Central—Foreign relations—China. 8. Russia (Federation)—Foreign relations—Asia, Central. 9. Asia, Central—Foreign relations–Russia (Federation) I. Zhang, Yongjin. II. Azizian, Rouben. III. Series.
DK859.57.E86 1997
958'.0429—dc21 97–25618
CIP

This book is printed on paper suitable for recycling and made from fully managed and sustained forest sources.

10 9 8 7 6 5 4 3 2 1
07 06 05 04 03 02 01 00 99 98

Printed in Great Britain by The Ipswich Book Company Ltd, Ipswich, Suffolk

To Jessie, Sophia and Tamara

Contents

Part III Economic Agonies

Part IV Strategic and Security Issues

Acknowledgments

The editing and publishing of this book is truly a project of transoceanic collaboration. The idea was first conceived in 1995 by two of us, one Chinese and one Russian, working in the Department of Political Studies of the University of Auckland. We have subsequently obtained support and co-operation from Chinese and Russian scholars for this project and have been able to arrange to receive the manuscripts of their original research from China and Russia. They are then edited, and where necessary, translated in the Southern hemisphere. The editorial board of St Antony's-Macmillan Series has generously agreed to include this volume in the Series.

In undertaking such a transoceanic project, we have incurred many debts. Our greatest thanks go to the contributors to this book. Without their contribution and co-operation, the publication of this book would not have been possible. We owe thanks in particular to the two co-ordinators, Dr. Guangcheng Xing of the Institute of Eastern European and Central Asian Studies, the Chinese Academy of Social Sciences, and Dr. Sergei Lounev of the Institute of Oriental Studies, the Russian Academy of Sciences, for their patience and persistence in securing the desired contributions. We are also grateful to them for the hospitality extended to us when we visited their respective institutes in 1995 and 1996.

We would like to express our gratitude to The Staff Research Fund of the University of Auckland for providing part of the necessary funding for this project. The Department of Political Studies of the University of Auckland has always been very supportive to us. We would like to acknowledge all the help and encouragement we have received from our colleagues there, in particular, Andrew Sharp, the Head of our Department. We would also like to thank Leslie Holmes of the University of Melbourne for his suggestions of publishers, and Nick Tucker of the University of Reading for painstaking editorial assistance.

Alex Pravda, the general editor of the St. Antony's-Macmillan Series, and Tim Farmiloe of Macmillan have both been sources of valuable advice and assistance. We are very grateful to them for that.

Finally, our thanks are due to St. Antony's College, Oxford University, which offers Yongjin Zhang Senior Associate Membership for his sabbatical in 1997 and provides an ideal environment for the final editing of this book.

Y. Z. and R. A.

List of Contributors

Alexander Akimov is Head of Department of Economic Studies of the Institute of Oriental Studies, the Russian Academy of Sciences. One of his most recent publications is *World Population: Looking Ahead* (1992).

Rouben Azizian is Lecturer in the Department of Political Studies, University of Auckland. Before joining the University of Auckland, he was with the Soviet and Russian diplomatic service. He regularly publishes on Russian foreign policy as well as on ethnic. He is the editor of *Economic Prospects for the Soviet Far East* (1990) and *Fortunes of Russians in Australian History* (1991).

Vladimir Fesyukov is a former Deputy Director of Gosteleradio of the USSR. He works now in the system of Foreign Broadcasting of Russia.

Andrei Kortunov is currently Chairman of the Board of the Moscow Public Science Foundation. Prior to that, he served as the Deputy Director of the Institute of USA and Canada Studies, the Russian Academy of Sciences. He is the author of many books, including *The Disintegration of the USSR and the Politics of the USA* (1993), and *Russia and the Reforms of the UN* (1995).

Gengchen Liu is Senior Research Fellow of the Institute of Eastern European and Central Asian Studies, the Chinese Academy of Social Sciences. He specializes in studying nationality problems in the former Soviet Union and Central Asia. His most recent publication includes a contribution to *Studies of Nationality Problems of the Soviet Union* (1996).

Qingjian Liu is Senior Research Fellow of the Institute of Eastern European and Central Asian Studies, the Chinese Academy of Social Sciences. He specializes in the studies of the Soviet economy and economic reforms in Russia and the former Soviet republics. His publication includes *The Soviet Economy: A General Survey* (1990), and most recently *The Development of Siberia and the Russian Far East and International Economic Cooperation* (1996).

Sergei Lounev is Leading Research Fellow of the Institute of Oriental Studies, the Russian Academy of Sciences. He has written extensively on Asia, including *India and the United States: Interstate Relations* (1987), and *Diplomacy in South Asia* (1993).

Algis Prazauskas is Head of Department of Political Studies of the Institute of Oriental Studies, the Russian Academy of Sciences. He is the author of *Ethnicity, Politics and State in Modern India* (1990) and the editor of *Interethnic Conflicts in the Eastern Countries* (1991).

Alexander Salitsky is Senior Research Fellow of the Institute of Oriental Studies, the Russian Academy of Sciences. He is the author of more than 30 books, including *China's Open Policy: the Experience of the 1980s* (1989) and *The Economic Links of China and Hong Kong in the Post-War Period* (forthcoming).

Gleryi Shirokov is Senior Research Fellow of the Institute of Oriental Studies, the Russian Academy of Sciences. He had previously served as the Deputy Director of the Institute. His many published works include *Industrial Revolution in the Eastern Countries* (1980) and *Developing Countries in the World Economy* (1988).

Zhuangzhi Sun is Research Fellow and Deputy Director of Department of Central Asian Studies of the Institute of Eastern European and Central Asian Studies, the Chinese Academy of Social Sciences. He is author of many articles on Central Asia in leading Chinese journals including *The New Socio-political Development in Five Central Asian States* and *On the 'Unification' of Former Soviet Central Asia and Its Prospect.*

Alexander Umnov is Leading Research Fellow of the Institute of the World Economy and International Relations, the Russian Academy of Sciences. He had published extensively on Russian foreign policy and the Middle East and Central Asia. His most recent work is *Iran: the Failure of the 'White Revolution'* (1996).

Guangcheng Xing is Assistant Director and Senior Research Fellow of the Institute of Eastern European and Central Asian Studies, the Chinese Academy of Social Sciences. His recent publications include *The Rise of Central Asia* (1993) and *China's Relations with Newly Independent Central Asian States* (1997).

Yongjin Zhang is Senior Lecturer in the Department of Political Studies, University of Auckland. His publications include *China in the International System, 1918–1920: The Middle Kingdom at the Periphery* (1991), and *China in International Society since 1949: Alienation and Beyond* (1998).

Introduction

Yongjin Zhang and Rouben Azizian

This book brings together twelve research essays by leading Chinese and Russian scholars and explores political, economic, diplomatic and strategic responses of these two continental powers to the emergence of a group of independent states in Central Asia. It intends to provide a rare insight into the Chinese and the Russian perceptions of the evolving Central Asia conundrum.

The implosion of the former Soviet Union has left in its train five independent Central Asian republics: Kazakhstan, Kyrgyzstan, Tajikistan, Turkmenistan, and Uzbekistan. The emergence of these newly independent sovereign states in the former Soviet space is perhaps the most dramatic change in the geopolitical and geostrategic landscape of Eurasia in the post-Cold War period. Politically, economically, and strategically, Central Asia, erstwhile the '*terra incognita*', is fast becoming an important region in its own right in world politics, reviving its historic role of a cross-roads between Europe and Asia. What is more confounding to many is the fact that contrary to dire predictions and haunting fears, the sudden imperial withdrawal of the former Soviet Union from Central Asia in 1991 has not been followed by large-scale violence in the region (with perhaps the exception of Tajikistan) in spite of unrelenting ethnic and nationalist tensions unleashed by the abrupt Soviet imperial disengagement. In the last five years, a regional order in Central Asia has gradually emerged, while the five newly independent states are embarking on a turbulent search for their own national identity and state-building in the post-Cold War context.

The unusual, if not unprecedented, way in which Central Asian states obtained their independence – by virtue of the collapse of the Soviet Union, towards which their contribution was minimal – has, among other things, presented both China and Russia with a new and challenging geopolitical and geo-economic reality. Central Asia has become now a region of contention involving all states with Central Asian borders, including China and Russia. Almost by default, strategically, Central Asia has been made a buffer zone between China and Russia. Although the replay of a nineteenth-century 'Great Game' in Central Asia is unlikely,

China and Russia are now the two great powers most concerned with the region and are among the contending influences in the resurgence of Central Asia.

The interest and the stake of both China and Russia in the new Central Asia have dictated that both develop new thrusts of foreign policy towards this region. For Russia, Central Asia remains part of its 'near abroad', a natural sphere of influence in which Russia has strategic as well as political and economic interests. Politically, it has to contend with other influences, particularly those from the Muslim world. Strategically, Russia's total disengagement from Central Asia would expose the region to interests which may not necessarily be friendly to Russia. The new thrust of Russian foreign policy has also to deal with the economic dependence of Central Asian states on Russia, part of the Soviet economic legacy. In economic terms, the independence of Central Asian states is still more formal than real. Russia continues to provide subsidies to Central Asian economies in one way or another. Even Turkmenistan, the most reluctant Central Asian member of the Commonwealth of Independent States (CIS), needs more Russian assistance, partly because of its growing inability to collect payments for its gas exports. Last but certainly not least, the protection of millions of ethnic Russians and Russian-speaking populations in Central Asia, now minorities in the newly independent republics, weighs heavily on Russian foreign policy.

Central Asia also continues to be central to Russia foreign policy in the sense that Moscow's relations with Central Asia are one of the best indicators of its foreign policy intentions. Any dramatic change in Russian foreign policy towards either Zhirinovsky-style imperialism or Solzhenitsyn-style Slavic isolationism is likely to be tried in Central Asia first. Central Asia's heavy dependence on Russia makes it an easy target, both for the imperialists, who see direct control as a logical step, and the isolationists, who insist on relieving Russia from the 'burden' of Central Asian states.

Indeed, as argued in some chapters in this book, Russian policy towards Central Asia has already seen dramatic changes in the last few years and various schools of thought are contending for influence in the shaping of Russia's Central Asia policy today.[1] To silence criticisms from both the Communist and the nationalist oppositions that the present Russian government is abandoning the former Soviet republics to the West and to the Muslim countries, Boris Yeltsin, in the course of his 1996 presidential campaign, made a strong effort to develop contacts and co-operation with the former Soviet republics. Central Asia was one of the priority areas of that effort.

For China, the new geopolitical landscape in Central Asia is a mixed blessing. Three out of five successor states to the former Soviet Union in Central Asia, Kazakhstan, Kyrgyzstan and Tajikistan, border on China. Their independence has drastically reduced China's common borders with Russia, especially in Northwest China. It has also created a large buffer between China and Russia. Moreover, the independent states in Central Asia provide China's booming exports with a ready market. China's flourishing trade and economic cooperation with Central Asian states has made her a significant economic partner with Central Asia outside the CIS framework.

On the other hand, political instability and ethnic tensions in the newly independent Central Asian states threaten to spill over into China's Xinjiang Uighur Autonomous Region in the Northwest, arguably the most vulnerable to the influence of ethno-nationalism and radical religious movements such as Islamic fundamentalism. This vulnerability comes from a single fact of ethnic diversity in Xinjiang. Of Xinjiang's fifteen million residents, sixty per cent are Turkish Muslims with seven million Uighurs, one million Kazakhs, and one hundred forty thousand Kyrgyzs. They share religious beliefs, cultural values, and common heritage with their kin in Central Asia. However, any ethnic unrest and any separatist tendencies in Xinjiang are regarded as threatening to China's national security and territorial integrity, particularly when it is seen to have some input of outside influence. On top of that, China has to settle its territorial disputes with the new states. The challenge to China is that it has to come to grips with the dynamic changes in Central Asia and at the same time to develop a coherent foreign policy to deal with the region. It should be noted, however, as is clear from the Chinese contributions in this volume, that although Central Asia has become increasingly important in China's national security strategy and in the economic development of China's underdeveloped Northwest, it remains peripheral to Chinese foreign policy, which continues to be preoccupied with the Asia-Pacific region and with China's relations with the great powers.

China and Russia do share a common goal in their respective foreign policy approach to Central Asia, i.e. to secure and maintain the region's political and economic stability. Because of such foreign policy concerns and because of China and Russia's geographical proximity to Central Asia, the changing political situation, volatile economic transition, and unrelenting ethnic tensions in Central Asian states command considerable attention from China and Russia. Is it possible for Central Asian states to develop their nationhood in societies characterized by low ethnic awareness, tribalism and clanship? How can they develop their distinct statehood within artificial borders and with centuries of foreign domination? Is it inevitable that to sustain the viability of their statehood, Central Asian states have to bridge in an unprecendentedly short time the gap between the socio-economic basis of a pre-capitalist system and the requirements of the post-industrialist world? Is the current rise of nationalism a necessary component of modernization, or merely an expression against the century-old suppression of ethnic identity and nationalist consciousness in Central Asia? What are the prospects of Central Asia's transition to a market economy? What are the strategic implications of an independent Central Asia for China and Russia? These are among the questions addressed by the contributions in this volume, an effort by Chinese and Russian scholars to grasp the implications of the Central Asian conundrum for China and for Russia.

One topical question is raised but not answered in this volume. China's influence in Central Asia seems to have grown considerably in the last few years. Leaders of all five Central Asian states have visited Beijing, and all of them more than once. China's regulated economy, which is more compatible with the economies of the Central Asian states, its secular status and available financial means make it a more attractive model for pragmatic and authoritarian Central Asian regimes than, for example, Turkey, Iran and other neighbours. China also has a geographical advantage to exploit. China's offer of transit through its territory to the Pacific coast is invaluable in cutting down Central Asia's dependence on Russia and in promoting the integration of Central Asian economies with the world's most dynamic economies in the Asia-Pacific area. It also offers an attractive alternative, in the context of the continued difficulties for Central Asian states of gaining a southbound transit through war-torn Afghanistan.

Beijing's growing role, however, tends to reduce both the absolute and the relative influence that Russia wields in Central Asia. As China's influence increases in the post-Soviet space, particularly but not exclusively in Central Asia, is a new version of the 'Great Game' conceivable? Will it lead to an inevitable confrontation and clash between Beijing and Moscow? Is it possible that ethnic separatism and violence in Central Asia would bring China and Russia together in containing its spread to their territories? Or is it more likely that Beijing and Moscow would purposely cultivate ethnic tensions to undermine each other's position? These scenarios are possible, and they are possible at the same time. Contributions in this volume, so far as they have discussed the role of the resurgence of Central Asia in Sino-Russian relations, have largely discounted the possibility of serious confrontations and clashes between China and Russia over Central Asia in the short term. But what about in the medium and long term, when China becomes either stronger or weaker and when Russia goes fully democratic or starkly autocratic? How will the possible deterioration of Sino-Russian relations affect their Central Asian policies? Whatever the future scenarios may be, Central Asia remains a region of contention which could lead to growing tensions in relations between its two neighbouring giants with a history of mutual suspicion and fierce rivalry.

Given the topical nature of the Chinese and the Russian perspectives on Central Asia, it is surprising that the flourishing literature on Central Asia in English in the last few years has not given due attention to the implications of the emergence of Central Asia for the trilateral relationship between Central Asia, China and Russia. The existing literature tends to focus on domestic politics and ethnic conflicts in Central Asian states. Discussions of competition and rivalry among Central Asia's neighbouring states for prevailing influence in the region concentrate on examining in particular the policies of Turkey and Iran. They explore how and why Central Asian states forge relations with the region's southern tier and the Islamic world or look to the North, i.e. Turkey, for inspiration and for help.[2]

A particularly glaring gap therefore exists in the present literature on two accounts. First, China has been surprisingly ignored.[3] Suffice it here to give two examples. *Central Asia and Its Strategic Importance and Future Prospects*, edited by Hafeez Malik, and *The New Geopolitics of Central Asia and Its Borderlands*, edited by Ali Banuazizi and Myron Weiner, both published in 1994, have no meaningful discussions of China, either in the former's projection of the future strategic landscape of Central Asia or in the latter's section on 'Rethinking the Role of Great Powers'.[4] By the same token, questions concerning the trilateral relationship of China, Russia and Central Asia have not been addressed. Secondly, although a limited number of Russian academic works on Central Asia have appeared in numerous English-language journals and books, few Chinese contributions on Central Asia have been published in English. Still rarer is work on Central Asia that collects contributions from prominent scholars resident in China and Russia and addresses themes of common concerns.

This book is an attempt to bridge that gap. The essays in this volume are selected from a number of contributions from leading scholars of the Institute of Eastern European and Central Asian Studies, the Chinese Academy of Social Sciences and of various institutes of the Russian Academy of Sciences, including the Institute of Oriental Studies and the Centre for Central Asian Studies. Many authors in this volume are themselves involved in Central Asian policy-making in China and Russia.

We divide the twelve essays in this book into four parts.

Part I, *Political Challenges*, consists of three essays. They describe the arduous search by both China and Russia for a creditable response to the turbulent political transformations in Central Asia. The two Russian contributions investigate the uneasy evolution of Russia's Central Asian policy in the context of changing mutual perceptions between Russia and Central Asian states and of the latter's nation-building efforts. The Chinese contribution examines the new thrust of Chinese foreign policy towards the emergence of Central Asia and argues that a new relationship between China and Central Asia is in the making.

Part II, *The Ethnic Conundrum*, includes four essays. They explore the origins of diverse and complex ethnicity of Central Asia. The unique features of the ethnic tensions and ethnic conflicts in Central Asia and their implications for China and Russia are the central focus of the investigation. The growing ethnonationalism in Central Asia is examined against the background of centuries of Russian/Soviet colonization of the region and from the perspective of nation-building efforts by Central Asian states since their independence. The chapter on demographic dynamics in Central Asia and its surrounding countries makes a unique contribution to the discussions of the changing ethno-demographic landscape in Central Asia and its impact on ethnic conflicts in the region.

Part III, *Economic Agonies*, comprises three contributions. The importance of economic considerations in Chinese and Russian policies towards Central Asia is discussed. The question of a painful search by Central Asian states for their economic viability through opening and reform is addressed. A comparative study of China and Central Asia's transition to market economies highlights the social and economic dilemmas Central Asian states are faced with in their economic reforms.

Part IV, *Strategic and Security Issues*, is concerned with geopolitical and geostrategic changes in Central Asia and the responses of China and Russia to the new strategic and security contentions in the region. The Chinese contribution examines the emerging security questions in China's relations with Central Asia, while the Russian contribution explores broad strategic issues as Central Asian states struggle to be integrated into the world.

The division of this collection of essays into four parts is inevitably arbitrary. As, indeed, is clearly demonstrated in all contributions here, political challenges are closely related to strategic considerations; so is economic development to ethnic harmony. The purpose here is not to compartmentalize those areas of inquiry in our contributions, but to organize them into broad themes for the convenience of our readers and also to give some cohesion to this volume. There is no doubt that the essays in this book will inform our readers of the respective Chinese and Russian perspectives on Central Asia much more than what we have very briefly attempted to impart above.

Finally, a note about what is meant by 'Central Asia' in this study is due, although it may appear to have already been clarified by the brief discussion so far. As a geopolitical concept in contemporary international relations, 'Central Asia' remains to be clearly defined. As has been observed, it has been used to refer to 'the whole or any part of an area that extends from the Kipchak steppes of Central Russia to the Great Wall of China'.[5] 'Central Asia' is used rather restrictively in our discussions. It refers just to the five independent Central Asian republics in the post-Soviet space. This is the region of our concern.

As this book goes into print, three most recent developments further highlight the strategic importance of Central Asia to China and Russia. The NATO expansion into Central and Eastern Europe has prompted Russia to seek alternative military and strategic arrangements in areas vital to its security. The Central Asian states, unlike most other post-Soviet countries, have not shown visible interest in joining NATO. Some Central Asian leaders have even openly criticized the NATO expansion plans. On the other hand, the recent Taliban advance in neighbouring Afghanistan has alarmed the Central Asian elite, for fear of the potential spill-over of Islamic fundamentalism into Central Asia. Both events have served now as a powerful catalyst for renewed strategic co-operation between Russia and the Central Asian states. For China, the recent ethnic unrest in Xinjiang and terrorist attacks in both Xinjiang and Beijing accentuate the importance of Sino-Central Asian relations in maintaining security and political stability in the Northwest of China.

The editing of this volume has by no means been an easy task. All the original manuscripts of the Chinese contributions have had to be translated, and so have most Russian contributions before they were edited. Transglobal communication, though made much easier today by technology, still presents frequent hiccups for our correspondence with our contributors. From time to time, we have had to exercise our 'editorial power'. In such circumstances, it is very likely that some editorial errors have slipped through inadvertently. As editors, we are fully and solely responsible for that. They do not, however, dent or distort any interpretations and analyses presented by our contributors. In some cases, we have purposely preserved the Chinese and the Russian 'flavours' in our contributions where appropriate. It is our belief that they are helpful hints and tips for our grasp of the Chinese and the Russian policies towards Central Asia.

There is little doubt that the essays in this volume are valuable and timely elaborations of the respective perspectives of China and Russia, the two potentially dominant, yet contending powers in the region, on the evolving conundrum in Central Asia. As rarely available direct contributions from China and Russia, they are particularly helpful to our understanding of the Chinese and the Russian perceptions of the resurgence of Central Asia in regional as well as global politics.

NOTES

1. See Chapters 1 and 4 in this book. For further discussion of debate on Russia's Central Asian policy, see Zviagelskaia, I. D., *The Russian Policy Debate on Central Asia*, Royal Institute of International Affairs, London, 1995.
2. See in particular, Rashid, Ahmed, *The Resurgence of Central Asia: Islam or Nationalism?* Oxford University Press, Oxford, 1994; Naumkin, V., *Central Asia and Transcaucasia: Ethnicity and Conflict* Greenwood, 1994; Banuazizi, Ali and Weiner, Myron (eds.), *The New Geopolitics of Central Asia and Its Borderlands*, I. B. Tauris, London, 1994; Windrow, Gareth, *Turkey in Post-Soviet Central Asia*, Royal Institute of International Affairs, London 1994; Ehteshami, A., *From the Gulf to Central Asia: Players in the New Great Game*, University of Exeter Press, 1994; Haghayeghi, Mehrdad, *Islam and Politics in Central Asia*, Macmillan, Basingstoke, 1995, and Dannreuther, R., *Creating New States in Central Asia: The Strategic Implications of the Collapse of Soviet Power in Central Asia*, Adelphi Paper, No. 288, Brassey's (UK) Ltd., London, 1994.
3. The only exception is, perhaps, *The New Central Asia and Its Neighbours*, edited by Peter Ferdinand. There is a brief chapter on China contributed by Peter Ferdinand himself. See Ferdinand P. (ed.), *The New Central Asia and Its Neighbours*, Pinter, London, 1994; pp. 95–107 'The New Central Asia and China'.
4. See Malik, Hafeez (ed.), *Central Asia: Its Strategic Importance and Future Prospects*, Macmillan, Basingstoke, 1994; and Banuazizi, Ali and Weiner, Myron (eds), *The New Geopolitics of Central Asia and Its Borderlands*, pp. 233–72.
5. Ferdinand, P. (ed.), *The New Central Asia and Its Neighbours*, p. 1.

Part I
Political Challenges

1 Russia and Central Asia: Evolution of Mutual Perceptions, Policies, and Interdependence

Andrei Kortunov and Andrei Shoumikhin

I A CONCEPTUAL FRAMEWORK FOR RUSSIAN APPROACHES TO CENTRAL ASIA

Current political and academic discussions in Russia on Central Asian issues, including relations with individual Newly Independent States (NIS) of the region, reveal a wide variety of views, some of them of extreme polarity. The intensity and divergence of these discussions and views are reflective of the fact that in the opinion of many, Russian-Central Asian relations go beyond the realm of practical policies and acquire a high philosophic – even an existential – dimension. It appears that at stake is not just a set of geopolitical, economic, even military-strategic and other 'mundane' interests, but the very essence, the *raison d'être* of Russia as a state and society and particularly its civilizational quintessence, a choice between European and Asiatic modes of development and models of cultural orientation.

Basically, three most influential schools of thought may be identified in the above discussions. One of them may be called the 'Western school', which asserts that Russia's future should be intimately linked to the Western civilization whence the solution of the contemporary Russian problem is bound to be drawn. A second one, which may be defined as an 'Asiatic' or 'Oriental' school, expounds a totally different view and claims that Russia should recognize and reconfirm its roots in the Asiatic cultural stock and historic experience and opt for close ties with Asian countries – especially those closest to it in Central Asia – thereby abandoning a futile search for illusory linkages with the West. A third school of thought represents a blend of the ideas promulgated by the two mentioned above and emphasizes the uniqueness of the Russian geopolitical, historic and cultural position as a 'bridge' between Europe and Asia. According to its followers, Russia should take advantage of these peculiar qualities and enrich itself by establishing ties with both the West and the Orient. Furthermore, the 'Eurasian' line of thinking stresses the need to assert Russian values and not to subjugate them to anyone else's interests.

At the same time, proponents of the 'Eurasian' approach contend that Russia may perform exceptional functions both for Europe and for Asia, including Central Asia, as an intermediary between them in economic, political, military and other affairs. Naturally, within each school there exist factions and sub-factions. Occasionally there emerge interesting blends or hybrids of opinions that capitalize on the lines of reasoning developed by all three main schools of thought.

Interestingly, a similar divergence may be found in respective Central Asian societies, with the exception that Russia is not identified totally with the West but is singled out as a separate factor in an attempt to evaluate and to design policies and to establish 'vectors of orientation' in today's complex world.

In practice, Russia's Central Asian policy of the last few years has been put under the constant conflicting influence of the above-mentioned different conceptual paradigms as well as of various competing group interests. From this perspective, Russian policy towards Central Asia has become more versatile but also at the same time less predictable, compared to the 'good old Soviet times' when fewer basic factors were at work shaping its main parameters.

II RUSSIAN POLICY TOWARDS CENTRAL ASIA FROM MIKHAIL GORBACHEV TO BORIS YELTSIN: STAGES IN EVOLUTION

Unity in Favour of the Union

As the Soviet Union was close to its demise, the regional balance of power began to acquire important political meaning in the fight for succession within the hierarchy. Significantly, as is known, throughout his rule Mikhail Gorbachev could rely on the almost total support of a 'monolithic block' of Central Asian deputies in the Supreme Soviet of the USSR in his fight against internal opposition that since 1989 was progressively being identified with Boris Yeltsin. By the spring and summer of 1991, the Central Asian Republics turned into the most staunch supporters of Gorbachev's '9+1' proposal on assuring the survival of the USSR that would preserve powerful central authority while delegating more autonomy to other members of the new federate state.

Political elites of Central Asia were supporting Gorbachev and his plan for saving the Union by redistributing power within it for a number of important reasons. By the late 1970s and the early 1980s, these elites had acquired considerable autonomy from Moscow while preserving all the favourable advantages of an economic nature, such as redistribution of the Union budget in their favour through massive centralized subsidies.[1] In the highly regimented Soviet system, local Party leaders, represented by Central Asian nationals enjoying local pre-eminence by virtue of clan relations and access to financial and material resources as well as to means of propaganda and indoctrination, including mass media, could establish themselves as 'local lords', just as during the feudal times that had preceded the colonization of the region by Czars and commissars decades ago.

It should be noted in passing that to complete this analogy with the feudal past, there emerged a peculiar blend of official ideology in Central Asian republics that combined Communist cosmology with residual (to some, fairly adulterated) Islamic norms and notions, all of which worked in favour of local 'pseudo-Communist' elites by providing them with elements of both secular and quasi-religious authority to rule. Additionally, in each particular republic local chieftains were drawing heavily on the ethnic factor and the growing nationalistic attitudes and feelings of indigenous populations.

During the period *perestroika*, the autonomy of Central Asian republics, together with their ability to enjoy preferential treatment from 'the Centre', continued and was even raised to new levels. A salient example was the one and only serious attempt by Gorbachev to reverse the 'feudalization' of Central Asia by adopting in 1986 a Politburo decision to appoint a Russian as the First Secretary of the Kazakh Communist Party. The individual in question, a certain Kolbin, was resolutely rejected by Kazakh elites in favour of Nursultan Nazarbayev, who was both 'one of the people' and an influential representative of local clans. The nomination of Kolbin by Moscow provoked ethnic riots in Almaty which scared Gorbachev and his entourage to such an extent that, on top of revoking their decision, they actually stopped any further attempts to influence regional cadre policies anywhere in the country. As a result of this early controversy, Central Asian elites felt totally free to ignore the reformist zeal and verbalism coming out of Moscow and could concentrate on solidifying their positions while at the same time paying lip service to the 'unity of the country'.

For all practical purposes, had the Soviet Union been miraculously preserved, in terms of Moscow-Central Asian relations, it could have evolved into a perfect feudal-type state with a nominal 'sovereign' in the 'Centre' and powerful 'barons' in the periphery ruling their 'principalities' totally at their will.

Until the very end, regardless of the attempts by Moscow to cleanse the Politburo of Central Asian representatives and to fight criminality in Central Asia politics and economics, Central Asian elites supported Gorbachev, not for his own sake but because he was identified with lucrative benefits and sources of legitimacy for their own rule, such as support by the Army and the security apparatus. The fairly symbiotic relationship between Moscow (which could only loosely be identified with Russia and Russian interests under the Soviet regime) and Central Asian 'pseudo-Communist' elites was brought to an abrupt and painful end by the 'Belovezhskaya Pusha' agreements of late 1991.

Disdainful 'Democrats'

To Boris Yeltsin and his supporters, the Union had to be dismantled for exactly the same reasons that Central Asian and other parochial vested interests wanted it to be preserved and eternalized. Firstly, their personal political ambitions could be met only by the removal of the last General Secretary and the powerful political, security and military potential remaining at his command.

Secondly, they wanted to demolish the entire nomenclature system throughout the former Soviet Union, including established Central Asian elites, because they needed their own power base traditionally identified in Russia with the bureaucratic class.

Thirdly, in the early years Yeltsin and the numerous opposition groups that made him their champion and leader were seriously contemplating democratic political and sweeping economic reforms in Russia that to many seemed totally unrealistic while Russia still bore the heavy 'ballast' of backward, conservative and culturally 'alien' Central Asian societies.

Gradually Central Asian leaderships became fully aware of the significance and ramifications of the Belovezhskaya Pusha agreements. In the face of an imminent economic and political disaster, they tried to react by creating the so-called 'Turkestan Confederation'. Open confrontation between former Slavic and Muslim parts of the already defunct Soviet Union could be avoided only by energetic efforts at conciliation by such prominent leaders as Nursultan Nazarbayev, who helped negotiate Central Asian membership in the Commonwealth of Independent States (CIS).

However, further activities of the new Russian state are also illustrative. Radical economic reforms started without any consultations with Central Asian states; the exclusively pro-Western orientation of the Russian foreign policy, the creation of independent Russian Armed Forces, the introduction of national currency – all these demonstrated that at an earlier stage of Russian independence (at least until mid-1993), Central Asia was regarded as secondary and even tertiary to Russia's immediate and long-term interests. The quasi-isolationist course pursued during this period was often characterized by officially and unofficially expressed disdain and paternalism, bordering on racism, as far as the capability of Central Asian societies to modernize and assure their own democratic development was concerned.

Such notions gained special prevalence around late 1992 to early 1993, when Russia made particularly strong efforts to become integrated into Western economic and political structures. Evidently at that stage it was concluded in Moscow that Russia's ties with Central Asia might prevent it from being accepted by the West.[2]

Forced Reconceptualization

However, further events and ongoing intellectual debates on the state and fate of Russian internal and external policies demonstrated that the idealistic and fairly self-centred, even egotistical, positions of early Russian 'democrats'[3] did not reflect a stable national consensus on the principles and format of the Russian-Central Asian relations. In fact, as time went by the Russian foreign policy of Yeltsin, Gaidar, and Kozyrev, characterized by a heavy pro-Western accent and diminished interest toward Asiatic (Oriental) 'peripheries', was coming under heavy fire from various directions.

There emerged a rather peculiar coalition speaking in favour of restoring Russian-Central Asian 'special relations'. Firstly, it included influential industrial groups dependent on Central Asian raw materials and semi-finished products as well as on local markets for their own goods. Secondly, in an odd way some groupings within the remaining Communist factions could also be found in that coalition. Preserving ties with Central Asian NIS was for them one of the ways of restoring the Soviet legacy.

Thirdly, there were groups of Russian nationalists who considered Russian-Central Asian relations as a prerequisite for 'Eurasian unity'. In reality, for many of them 'unity' meant assertion of Russian imperial power over parts of the 'traditional Russian sphere of influence'. For others it was a sensible way of resolving the painful problem of Russian-speaking minorities in Muslim NIS. Fourthly, the antigovernment opposition on

Central Asian affairs was joined by parts of the Russian military-industrial complex that perceived the disintegration of the Soviet strategic space and depth, especially at the Southern flanks, as a direct threat to Russian security interests.[4]

Until October 1993 the epicentre of oppositional activities on issues related to Russian foreign policy, including its Central Asian component, happened to be in the then Russian Supreme Soviet. Critics of the Western 'slant' of this policy concentrated around the Parliament's Speaker Ruslan Khazbulatov, known for his special ethnic (Chechen) background and wide connections in the Muslim world. Support for the pro-Central Asian sympathizers would also come from the so-called 'power ministries', for example, the Ministry of Defence, the Interior and Counterintelligence.

Even more importantly, the 'reintegrationalist' approach to Central Asia got the upper hand in the new important government structure, the Russian National Security Council. That fact may be illustrated by the 'Main Aspects of the Concept of the Foreign Policy of the Russian Federation' adopted by the Council in April 1993.[5]

The 'Wisdom' of Presidential Policies

The bitter internal political conflict in Russia of October 1993 and the ensuing move towards the Presidential rule in the country ushered in a new stage in Russian foreign and Central Asian policies. It was evident that under the pressures of nationalists, epitomized by the resounding success of the Liberal Democratic Party of Vladimir Zhirinovsky at the December 1993 elections to the new Russian Parliament – the Federal Assembly – as well as in view of the failures of overly ambitious pro-Western policies, many key leaders of the Yeltsin regime, including Foreign Minister Andrei Kozyrev, began to change their rhetoric, if not their perceptions and devotions.[6]

In this connection a new noteworthy trend began to develop in early 1994, namely the integration of some opposition views and demands with regard to Central Asia into official pronouncements and positions among which the following were of special importance:

- Russia cannot 'leave' the Central Asian region without putting all of its southern 'underbelly' in jeopardy;
- Attempts to make its borders with Kazakhstan and other Central Asian republics secure and 'impregnable' will be extremely costly and largely counterproductive; therefore preservation of Russian control over CIS borders in Central Asia is a much more effective and desirable goal;

- The issue of the presence of Russian troops and bases in Central Asian republics should be resolved as a priority, since the latter should be looked upon as part and parcel of the overall infrastructure providing for Russian national security;
- Russia can ill afford the disruption of its economic ties with Central Asia, which could precipitate the collapse of numerous enterprises and whole branches of national economy dependent on the supply of Central Asian raw materials and parts;
- In the same way, Central Asian markets should be preserved for Russian exports, even if this implies extending preferential treatment to Central Asian partners;
- Russia should, in co-operation with Central Asian states, strive at creating free trade zones, mutual tariff, custom and currency regimes, joint capital and labour markets based on co-ordinated budgetary, taxation, crediting, production, and labour policies;
- Mindful of numerous ethnic, religious, territorial and other contradictions and rivalries in the region that also involve sizeable Russian minorities residing in Central Asian republics,[7] Russia should effectively involve itself in preventing, managing and resolving existing and future local conflicts, in particular by creating effective peace-keeping and peace-making mechanisms, taking advantage of Russian military capabilities and power;
- Russia should conduct its foreign policy in such a way as to prevent third parties from interfering in Central Asian affairs or taking unfair advantage of local difficulties, contradictions and weaknesses of socio-economic, political and ideological nature.[8]

It is evident that with some modifications these general perceptions created foundations for practical Russian policies towards Central Asia in 1994–1995.

However, before undertaking a more detailed analysis of these policies we propose to examine the factor of 'outside influences' that was acquiring progressive importance in the Russian assessments of its regional policies.

III SUSCEPTIBILITIES TO THE POLICIES OF OTHERS

As the Russian perspective on its relations with the West was changing, so was its approach to third-party involvement in Central Asian politics and economics. It was suddenly recognized that by 'abandoning' Central Asia and reducing its presence in the region, Russia left vacuums that began to be filled up by others, particularly Western countries, including Turkey as a NATO member, as well as China, Iran, Saudi Arabia, and Pakistan.

Turkey was recognized as a particularly alarming case because of its geographic, cultural, ethnic, and religious proximity to many former Soviet republics, its economic potential and its political backing by the US and other leading Western countries. Russian observers also clearly noted that the Turkish secular model of development could be highly attractive to the majority of Central Asian regimes that were looking for examples to follow, while at the same time remaining fairly concerned with the possibility of Islamic revival in general and the emergence of powerful fundamentalist oppositions inside their countries in particular. Furthermore, Turkish inroads into Central Asia that started almost as soon as appropriate NISs got their independence were progressively being viewed as a plot to create an artificial '*cordon sanitaire*' around Russia.[9]

Examples of growing Russian concerns abound. In May 1993 a quasi-official article by the Ministry for Foreign Economic Relations was published in the *Nezavisimaja Gazeta* that lashed out against the decision adopted by five Central Asian NIS to create the Central Asian Regional Council (presumably on the example of the Gulf Co-operation Council) that was intended to exclude the Russian Federation. V. Jurtayev and A. Shestakov, writing on behalf of the Ministry, asserted that Central Asian intraregional integration was hostile to Russian interests, undermined previous agreements on 'single CIS military-strategic space' and effectively neutralized the CIS Treaty on Collective Security. It was also claimed that these 'devious' integratory attempts were being orchestrated by Turkey and other Western powers and were intended to isolate Russia from the Islamic world, and particularly such important geo-strategic partners as Iran and Pakistan.[10] In a similar way, when in the summer of 1993 the majority of Central Asian NISs supported the Turkish idea for creating a custom and tariff union to involve Central Asia, the then First Deputy Prime Minister of Russia, A. Shokhin, declared that Central Asian regimes had only one choice to make, i.e. between integration with Turkey (alternatively with Turkey and Pakistan) or with Russia, Ukraine and Belarus. In the opinion of the influential Russian politician, Central Asia could not be involved in both communities.

Additionally, it may be noted that in line with mounting suspicions about third parties' intentions, an opinion began to form in Russian official circles that the West – and the US in particular – was 'objectively interested in preserving a relatively high degree of tensions in Central Asia',[11] since local instability could effectively enhance the Western role and influence in this and nearby areas all the way to the Persian Gulf region, while at the same time limiting Russian capabilities of making a positive impact on local politics.

Concurrently, Russia became more perceptive of what could be considered as 'positive' tendencies and moves in Central Asian NISs. Interestingly, as ideas of the 'Eurasian school of thought' began to take root in official Russian thinking, compatible ideas began to be felt in the Central Asian context, especially in Kazakhstan.[12] It was under such conditions that the proposal on creating a 'confederate union' between Kazakhstan and Russia was put forward at a congress of the Socialist Party of Kazakhstan (the legal heir to the Kazakh Communist Party) that took place on March 14, 1992.[13]

At a later stage some other Kazakh political groups, notably the People's Congress Party headed by O. Suleimenov, supported the idea of a Russia-Kazakhstan Confederation, although other such groupings of nationalistic orientation rejected the idea, fearful of the eventual 'degradation' of such a confederation into a federation and the re-establishment of total Russian control over Kazakh independence and sovereignty.[14] On the other hand, the official Kazakh plan on the creation of the Eurasian Union enunciated by President Nursultan Nazarbayev may have been to a certain extent influenced by concepts of the 'Eurasian school of thought', though its implications were quite different from those expounded by Russian 'Eurasianists', who were primarily concerned with Russian and not Central Asian interests.

IV PECULIARITIES OF PRACTICAL RUSSIAN POLICIES

Russian policy towards Central Asia has developed along three intertwined lines: political, military and economic. Political exchanges have dealt with most general issues of bilaterial and multilateral affairs: the future of the CIS, problems of borders, and local conflicts, the status of minorities and foreign nationals. Dialogues within the political ambit have borne a fairly formal character and as a rule have been called upon to minimize or even conceal differences. Admittedly, the greatest progress in developing contacts of this nature and achieving practical results out of them was registered in Russia-Kazakhstan relations. By mid-1995 the two countries had come closely together on such key issues as customs control and co-ordination of foreign policies.

Whereas economic interaction is the most considered and in many respects the most vitally important area for the interests of Russia and its

Central Asian counterparts, military relations is an even more involved area. Under current conditions, it includes military-political co-operation, addressing the resolution of issues related to the presence of Russian troops, installations and property as well as the conduct of joint peace-keeping operations. In view of their salience, the following analysis concentrates primarily on the military and economic aspects of Russian practical policies towards Central Asia.

V MILITARY-STRATEGIC ASPECTS

In a most general sense, Russia's military relations with its Central Asian neighbours are to be regulated by the Treaty on Collective Security signed in Tashkent on May 15, 1992.[15] The Treaty sets out the obligation of non-use of force or threat of force in relations between its members. They should also resolve their differences by peaceful means, abstain from entering into blocks hostile to each other, conduct consultations on security matters, and co-ordinate their defence polices. For that purpose, the Council on Collective Security (CCS) was created. However, five years after it was put into effect, the Treaty is nowhere near implementation. From this perspective it has met with the same fate as almost two hundred other treaties and agreements concluded within the ambit of the CIS.[16]

Understandably, one of the immediate Russian concerns after the dissolution of the USSR was preserving for itself as much former Soviet property left in the territories of other NISs as was possible. Negotiations on installations such as the Baikanur launching facility and bases for Russian troops, as well as the presence of these troops in Central Asian republics, began at an early stage of independence of former Soviet republics. Some of them concluded to establish general frameworks and payments for the use of appropriate installations. Though the financial burden for Russia that was thus being created (for Baikanur alone Russia is supposed to pay one billion US dollars in rentals) is substantial, in many cases there is simply no other choice for the Russians.

Economic and political pressures associated with the Russian military presence in Central Asia may work both ways: either to lead to eventual Russian withdrawal from appropriate republics or to push Russia towards more aggressive policies aimed at securing additional benefits and alleviating perceived hardships created by the receiving nations.

In contrast to the subdividing of former Soviet property, the area of peace-keeping proved to be more productive in terms of military-political and military-operational co-operation between Russia and Central Asian states. Because of its social, ethnic and demographic complexity, the Central Asian region experiences numerous tensions and is prone to various conflict situations. Russia has been and will be involved in these conflicts as well as in attempts at their resolution for various reasons: geopolitical, economic, as well as cultural.

Early attempts at regulating joint Russian-Central Asian activities in conflict management, including peacekeeping, date back to March 1992 when a CIS decision was adopted on creating military observer groups and collective peacekeeping forces. Originally, the creation of 'classical' peacekeeping forces was envisaged – small contingents monitoring agreements, facilitating disarmament, and contributing to peaceful negotiations. These forces were not supposed to undertake combat missions, and they also had to be 'impartial' to all sides in a particular conflict. Their mandate could become effective only upon the termination of actual hostilities. Evidently their functions were modelled on the example of traditional UN peacekeeping operations that were themselves becoming more and more ineffective and obsolete.[17]

The stark realities of Central Asian politics and the growing intensity of local contradictions and conflicts demonstrated the insufficiency of limited or 'reactive' efforts at peacekeeping, and progressively demanded the direct use of counterforce in achieving important goals of maintaining and safeguarding regional peace. Events in Tajikistan were the most important test of the desire of local powers as well as Russia to apply such counterforce and, in a general sense, to devise new tactics of peacekeeping that implied the fairly wide use of military force.

At an earlier stage in the Tajik conflict,[18] Moscow tried to avoid direct involvement and concentrated on guaranteeing the republic's outside borders. The Russian motorized division No. 201 deployed in the republic had particular trouble in staying 'neutral', since it had many Tajik conscripts within its ranks. However, that task was performed with relative success because of the superior skills demonstrated by the division's commanding officer, General Ashurov, and the fact that at the initial stages the 'democratic Islamic' opposition was contained and defeated with the help of Uzbek troops.[19]

Until late 1992 the Russian troops could limit their role to protecting strategic installations in the Tajik territory, i.e. the Kurgan Tube chemical works, the Nurek hydro-electric station and the Dushanbe railroad and airport. Shortly afterwards Moscow adopted a decision to support the Rakhmonov government,[20] and gradually replaced Uzbekistan in performing important power projection, both on the Tajik-Afghan border and inside Tajikistan.

It is noteworthy that it was under the impact of the Tajik war that in September 1992 a new CIS agreement on collective peacekeeping forces was adopted which modified the latter's mandate to include the functions of 'collective defence'. To support that decision, the Joint Command of CIS Peacekeeping Forces was created. Further events in the Tajik civil war led to the escalation of direct Russian military involvement. However, one thing was especially important: the majority of Central Asian elites were by and large prepared to accept Russia's role as an intermediary and a direct 'legitimate' participant in the process of conflict resolution, if not a guarantor of regional political settlements. Interestingly, oppositions in Central Asian states recognized Russia in such a role as well. When the Tajik opposition managed to gain power for a brief period in 1992 it immediately appealed to Moscow for armed interference for purposes of stopping the local conflagration.[21]

From that perspective, Central Asia is a unique region, compared to all other areas outside Russia in the former USSR. The situation there is significantly different from that in the Trans-Caucasus, where (at least until the autumn of 1993) the conflicting parties tended to appeal for help to the UN, CSCE and NATO, but not to Russia. The explanation for this phenomenon is to be found not in personal devotions or biases but in stark geopolitical facts.

Firstly, Central Asian states find themselves in the least favourable geostrategic situation compared to other NISs. They are surrounded by militarily powerful neighbours, the majority of which have totalitarian, authoritarian and/or theocratic regimes. Therefore, even though today Central Asian republics are not being directly threatened by these neighbours, they still need Russia as a counterbalance to potential external challenges.

Secondly, Central Asian NISs experience serious handicaps in their military structure. In particular, they lack experienced officer corps composed of their own nationals. Furthermore, unlike Ukraine and Belarus, they could not acquire sizeable parts of former Soviet military arsenals. Kazakhstan may be an exception. However, it is still unable to operate numerous bases and sophisticated installations such as the Baikanur launching centre on its own, while much of its military production potential is situated in the Russian-dominated northern areas.

Thirdly, Central Asian republics lack even limited experience in managing and resolving local conflicts. In the majority of cases they need outside support to preserve internal stability, which is also often identified with the stability and survival of ruling regimes which tend to be either authoritarian or semi-authoritarian.

The Russian experience of involvement in Central Asian conflict resolution demonstrates that in the future the need for direct intervention may actually grow. By any estimate, the conflict potential of the region is unprecedented. So far, Central Asia has yet to become one of the key regions of Western or international responsibility. Russia is the only outside power that may be summoned to do the badly needed 'dirty work' of disengagement and appeasement of warring factions. At the same time, it is evident that efforts required for fulfilling peacekeeping missions go well beyond what others, including the US, were able to come up with in compatible situations in other regions, including Cambodia, Haiti, Somalia, Bosnia (with the only recent possible exception of the Gulf War). Therefore, it appears that by and large Russia is faced with a 'no win' situation in the military-political area in Central Asia. Wherever a serious regional conflict erupts, Russia is almost unavoidably drawn into it for reasons such as geographical proximity, former 'Imperial' involvement, the need to protect Russian populations, the remaining presence of Russian troops in Central Asian republics, and internal pressures exerted by the segments of the Russian political sector that insist on 'activist' Russian foreign policies and demand that Russia 'shows its colours' in any situation of CIS tensions.

However, once direct Russian involvement becomes a reality, it creates unbearable psycho-political and economic burdens. The obvious reasons are: the internal divisiveness of Russian politics that prevents 'monolithic support' of foreign policy actions enjoyed by previous Communist regimes; the lack of financial resources for large-scale and protracted military efforts (the Chechen war seems to be an exception; however, even though its approximate cost has not been calculated nor tentatively appraised in terms of recovery); and an inability to muster real CIS and international support on the analogy of what the US could accomplish in situations of the Gulf War type.

The Russian population inside the Federation remains wary of their regime's military involvement outside and inside Russia's borders. The bitter experience of Afghanistan, accentuated by the tragedy of 'restoring constitutionality' in the Chechen republic, contribute overwhelmingly to such a sensation, while Russian attempts to police the Tajik-Afghan border as if it was the Federation's border, and to keep a particular regime in power in Tajikistan, remain ill-understood and fairly unpopular in the Russian mind.

In view of all these and other peculiarities, Russia will be well advised to continue to refine multilateral mechanisms within the CIS that may assist it in the performance of onerous duties of conflict resolution in Central Asia. Additionally, it may try to attract greater international attention (from the

UN, CSCE, NATO, and the US, for example) to the mounting Central Asian problems so as to be able to muster additional support for its peace-keeping activities in the region, in case its own and other CIS efforts turn out to be insufficient.

VI RUSSIA'S ECONOMIC ROLE

As we mentioned before, the eagerness with which Boris Yeltsin and his supporters agreed to the dissolution of the Soviet Union was in large measure predicated on the conviction that Russia 'did not need to continue carrying the burden' of subsidized 'alien' republics such as those in Central Asia. Characteristically, not a single Central Asian leader was invited to Belovezhskaya Pusha where the decision on dissolution was made. However, it was not long before it became patently clear that Russia could ill afford to sever all economic ties with Central Asia. Even after the commencement of radical economic reforms in Russia, local economies in Central Asia remained important partners for Russian industries.

In 1992 alone, Russia provided 68 per cent of Kazakhstan's imports, 58 per cent of those of Uzbekistan, 51 per cent of Kyrgyzstan and 48 per cent of Tajikistan and Turkmenistan respectively. At the same time Russia absorbed 61 per cent of Uzbekistan's exports, 54 per cent of those of Turkmenistan, 53 per cent of Kazakhstan and 39 per cent of Kyrgyzstan.[22]

Confronted with the ineffectiveness of some radical reforms at an earlier stage, the Yeltsin government moved, as of the beginning of 1993, to aggressive and protectionist foreign economic policies that created serious difficulties for Central Asian NISs. Particularly damaging were Russian steps towards establishing world price levels for its oil and gas exports and the 'squeezing out' of Central Asian states from the so-called 'rouble zone'. The monetary reform undertaken by Russia led to 150 to 300 per cent increases in consumer good prices in these states over the period of a few days. Local financial institutions were brought to the verge of bankruptcy, while economic activities came to a virtual halt.[23] Adding insult to injury, Russia put forward certain conditions for admitting Central Asian states into the 'new rouble zone' and providing them with new currency notes that actually prevented them from conducting independent economic, budgetary and financial policies.[24] Under the circumstances, Kazakhstan, Uzbekistan, Turkmenistan and Tajikistan had to accept the conditions for temporary inclusion into the 'rouble zone of the new type'. However they all decided to move rapidly towards introducing their own national currencies.

For the sake of fairness, it should be mentioned that at least some of the Central Asian republics contributed to the collapse of the 'rouble zone' in 1992 by extending gigantic rouble credits to their enterprises, undermining the efforts of the Russian Federation to combat inflation.

In a political and psychological sense, some Central Asian leaders exacerbated their own problems by accusing Russia of economic imperialism and colonialism and announcing their readiness to move to other arrangements in foreign trade and co-operation. Evidently they were counting primarily on other Islamic countries, particularly Turkey. High hopes were also raised in connection with the idea to create a regional common market by expanding the Organization of Economic Co-operation (OEC).[25]

Indeed, in 1992 Turkey seemed to have started to invest massively in the solution of Central Asian problems. That year alone it provided as least US$1 billion worth of credits to Central Asian states and began a number of impressive business projects, primarily in transportation and communications. On top of that, 10,000 students were invited to attend Turkish schools and universities.[26]

However, by late 1993 it became evident that neither Turkey nor Pakistan nor Iran had the colossal resources needed for the reconstruction of Central Asian economies. Further disappointments were caused by failures in acquiring financial support from Japan, the US, the European Community, the countries of the Gulf and others. At the same time, international economic and financial institutions were setting up conditions for loans that were even more severe than those imposed by Russia. The positions of the West proved to be particularly undesirable because of the linkages established between extension of loans and credits and the necessity to introduce democratic changes into local political structures and regimes.[27]

As a consequence of rush decisions amounting to 'shock therapy', considerable economic destabilization occurred, not only in Russia but in all of Central Asian NISs, during 1992–1993. Central Asian states were particularly unprepared for the model of development that demolished traditional patterns and failed to compensate for galloping inflation, monetary crises and social deprivation. It is not surprising that under these conditions many dormant ethnic and other conflicts began to enter virulent stages. Nostalgia for the 'good old Soviet times' became more acute, as did the political polarization of local societies.

It may be concluded that to a considerable extent Russia and the insensitive policies of its regime may be held responsible for the considerable deterioration of the Central Asian situation during that period, and the expansion of regional potential for conflictual behaviour.

IN LIEU OF CONCLUSION: STABILITY IN CENTRAL ASIA

In any discussion of stability or instability in all the former Soviet republics, an important clarification should be introduced. Given the circumstances that accompanied the dissolution of the USSR and the historically insignificant time period that was allowed for nation-building in all NISs, it is obvious that their 'stability' should be understood in a rather narrow sense of the word, more like the preservation of a tentative and fragile status quo than anything else.

This is especially pertinent in view of several additional factors. Firstly, many of the NISs including those in Central Asia, may hardly be considered states in the classical sense. They lack such important attributes of statehood as control over borders, independent monetary and financial systems and monopoly on the use of armed forces within their territories.

Secondly, the legitimacy of the regimes established in these countries as the result of sovereignization is often less than clear-cut and is usually challenged by powerful internal, and in some cases external, opposition.

Thirdly, these newly independent entities have so far been unable to make conclusive choices as to their ways of development in the socio-economic and political sense. It is not at all clear whether in the future they will be affected by reintegratory tendencies and again lose part or all of their sovereignty.

In this connection, external factors – for example, influences by outside powers: Russia in particular, but also Turkey, China, and Iran – may acquire considerable importance. Admittedly, though, it is much easier to destabilize the situation in Central Asian NISs than to increase their internal stability and the legitimacy of the existing regimes.

In view of the numerous actual and potential difficulties associated with Central Asia, the Russian political leadership is beginning to pay more and more attention to the notion of 'stability' as it applies to that region. At the same time, it appears that the term has numerous, sometimes conflicting connotations which reflect the contradictory nature both of Russian foreign policy in general and of its attitudes towards the Central Asian region in particular. What then is stability in Central Asia?

Firstly, such stability is seen as the absence of major regional conflicts that may pose threats to the Russian hinterland, its borders and interests. The intense controversy in Tajikistan is a clear indication of such threats unavoidably leading to direct Russian military involvement that may become extremely costly in economic and political sense.

Secondly, stability in the region is looked upon through the socio-economic prism and implies the relative effectiveness of local economies and the capability of Central Asian regimes to resolve the complicated social issues confronting their nations. Meeting these conditions will mean that Russia will not have to provide for local peoples the way it did under the Soviet form of 'fraternal help' redistributing scarce resources in favour of 'the most needy and underprivileged'. Moreover, the socio-economic stability of Central Asian NISs may form the basis for extensive co-operation between them and the Russian Federation, especially if they all develop according to free enterprise and open market matrices.

Thirdly, Central Asian stability is understood in terms of the benign evolution of ethnic and religious relations that involve the Russian minority in Central Asian states. For various reasons (the prominence of ethnic issues in internal Russian politics, the heavy burden of caring for immigrant and refugee populations, for example), concerns for the Russian population outside the Russian borders (and especially in the non-Christian or Islamic environment) have been steadily mounting for the last few years. It will not be a surprise if this issue assumes a predominant place in future Russian internal and external policies.

Fourthly, the ecological and demographic situations in Central Asia are becoming ever more crucial for evaluating the region's stability and chances for orderly development. Man-made catastrophes such as the depletion of the Aral Sea and unrestrained birth rates may eventually turn some areas of Central Asia into epicentres of disaster not unlike those in other less developed parts of the Third World.

Fifthly, there is a horde of less visible problems that nonetheless have a direct bearing on regional stability and therefore on Russian interests: the production and trafficking of narcotic substances; the illegal trade in arms; the disruption of communication infrastructures; violations of human rights; the spread of corruption and criminality; the expansion of fundamentalist ideologies and resort to violence by specific groups, including those pursuing clericalist policies.

Evaluating the relative stability of Central Asian NISs leads to another crucial question: *what should Russia do (or not do) to enhance the quality of local politics, economics, and social conditions?* In this connection – and in view of the fairly limited resources available to it at this stage – the Russian leadership is faced with a bitter choice: either to allocate a huge share of these resources to stabilizing neighbouring states or to concentrate entirely on internal Russian difficulties, forgoing expensive foreign policy obligations, including those in the military-political sphere. Basically, it is a choice between external activism and isolationism; a combination of both is hardly possible, because opinions and positions within the body politic on the conduct of internal and external policies of the Russian

Federation are extremely controversial and often mutually exclusive. This polarity on issues of substance is reflected in the formulation of Russian strategy towards Central Asia and in the functioning of appropriate mechanisms of foreign policy decision-making.

It is clear that the interests of various institutions, political groups and economic structures contradict each other on issues of Russian–Central Asian relations. It is no less evident that there are no effective ways and means of a constitutional, political, administrative or other nature that may help negotiation between the differing interests and assist in bringing about a coherent and consistent national policy based on consensus.

Therefore we are bound to arrive at a more general and final conclusion: that Russian Central Asian policy will be characterized by contradictions and inconsistencies, at least for a considerable period in the near future unless and until the traumatic hurdle of mutual separation albeit alienation can somehow be surmounted by all the former Soviet republics.

NOTES

1. According to IMF data even in 1991, 44% of Tajikistan's budget, 42% of the Uzbek budget, 34% of that of Kyrgyzstan, 23% of Kazakhstan's and 22% of Turkmenistan's were subsidized from Moscow. See Marnie, Shelia and Witlock, Erik, *Central Asia and Economic Integration*, RFE/RL Research Report, Vol. 2, No. 14, April 1993, p. 34.
2. Mac-Farlane, Neil S., 'Russian Conception of Europe', *Post-Soviet Affairs*, Vol. 10, No. 3, July–September 1994, pp. 241–44.
3. The terms 'democracy', 'democrats', 'democratic' have acquired special meanings in post-Communist Russia, sometimes devoid of the 'classical' elements making up Western definitions of these notions. To be 'democratic' often means to be anti-Soviet, pro-reformist or even anarchistic and apolitical. Many of those, who, like Yeltsin himself, would opt for forceful, and even violent, military solutions of the country's problems, would still call themselves 'democrats'.
4. In 1991–1993, a vigorous discussion was started in Russian intellectual, academic and political circles on these broad issues, which was reflected in numerous publications. See for example, Narochnitskaya, Natalia, 'Osoznat' svoyu missiyu', *Nash Sovremennik*, No. 2, 1993; Ambartsumov, Evgeni, 'Interesy Rossii ne znayut granits', *Megapolis Express*, May 6, 1992. A certain culmination was reached at the Foreign Ministry Conference on 'The Transfiguration of Russia' that demonstrated a deep divergence of opinions on Russian Central Asian policies as reported in *Mezhdunarodnaya Zhizn*, No. 3–4, 1992.

5. In particular, the document called for the establishment of 'positive relations' with the 'near abroad' nations for the purposes of overcoming destabilizing disintegratory processes in the territory of the former USSR. Achievement of the Russian military and economic interests, including the preservation of its great power status, was declared to be the essence of Russian foreign policy, while actions undermining integration processes within the CIS were identified as presenting the worst threats and challenges to Russian national security. See *Izvestia*, 16 April 1993.
6. In November–December 1993, while campaigning for his own election to the State Douma, A. Kozyrev startled everyone by making a number of anti-Western statements. Further along the way the Russian Foreign Minister, considered to be the prime architect of the rapprochement with the West under Yeltsin, was making one dramatic reversal of position after another. In the spring of 1995, for example, he was on record as claiming that Russia should defend the rights of Russians living in other NISs 'with all the means available to it', which was interpreted by many as a thinly veiled threat aimed primarily at Central Asian countries where ethnic Russians and the Russian-speaking population were subjected to progressive pressures and discrimination.
7. The problem of Russians in Central Asia and other NISs has numerous parameters in Russia. It has not only emotional, cultural and political but also direct economic implications and consequences. Already today, according to the UN High Commissioner for Refugees, Russia is receiving more refugees and immigrants than any other country in the world. The deterioration of Russian–Central Asian relations or internal disturbances in Central Asian NISs may lead to an exodus of hundreds of thousands, if not millions, of Russians and other Russian-speaking minorities into the Russian Federation that may in turn exacerbate the economic and social situation in some regions of the country to the extreme.
8. For the discussion of these and other views intended to rationalize close Russian-Central Asian interaction, see Poznyakov, Eduard, 'Sovremennyie geopolititcheskie izmeneniya i ikh vliyanie na bezopasnost i stabilnost v mire', *Voennaya mysl*, No. 1, 1993; Pleshakov, Konstantin, 'Missiya Rossii Tretya Epokha', *Mezhdunarodnaya zhizn*, No. 1, 1993; Migranyan, Andranik, 'Podlinie I mnimie orientiry vo vneshnei politike', *Rossiskaya Gazeta*, 4 August 1991; and Stankevich, Sergei, 'Fenomen Derzhavy', *Rossiskaya Gazeta*, 23 June 1992.
9. Such views began to be shared by the Russian Foreign Ministry. To exemplify, the draft 'Concept of Russian Foreign Policy' elaborated by the FM in late 1992 specifically mentioned that Turkey and a number of other close neighbours of the former USSR tried to take advantage of the demise of the Soviet empire in order to create a loose union of states that would be based on principles of ethnic and religious affinity and would serve to undermine the Russian security and economic interests. According to the text of the 'Concept', Russia 'intends to actively oppose any attempts at increasing military-political presence undertaken by third countries adjacent to Russia'. See 'Kontseptsiya vneshnei politiki Rossiskoi Federatsii', *Diplomatitcheskii Vestnik*, January 1993, Spetsialnyi vypusk, p. 8.
10. See *Nezavisimaya Gazeta*, 13 May 1993.

11. In a way similar to what could be allegedly observed in the Middle East ever since the creation of the state of Israel.
12. See Evstafyev, Dimitri, 'Rossiya, islamskii mir i Blizhnii. Vostok' (geostregitcheskii obsor). *Assotsiatsiya voenno-politicheskikh i voenno-istoritcheskikh issledovanii*, Moscow, 1992, p. 17.
13. A resolution of the Congress stated that SPK 'sees the future of Kazakhstan within the CIS entirely through confederate arrangements'. In May 1993, the joint declaration of the Political Executive Committees of the socialist Parties of both Russia and Kazakhstan emphasized that the CIS should eventually evolve towards 'the conclusion of a confederate Union treaty between former republics of the USSR', *Sovety Kazakhstana*, 26 August 1993.
14. *Argumenty I Fakty*, 26 June 1993.
15. The Treaty was signed by four Central Asian states with the exception of Turkmenistan, which concluded a bilateral agreement on military matters with Russia in June 1992 that is in many respects similar to the letter and spirit of the above treaty.
16. For CIS agreements concluded but not implemented, see Sheeky, Ann, *Seven States Sign Charter Strengthening CIS*, RFE/RF Research Reports, Vol. 2, No. 9, 26 February 1993, p. 10; Crow, Suzanne, *Russia Promotes the CIS as an International Organization*, RFE/RL Research Reports, Vol. 3, No. 11, 18 March 1994, p. 33; and Hague, Elizabeth, *The CIS: An Unpredictable Future*, RFE/RF Research Reports, Vol. 3, No. 1, January 1994, p. 9.
17. By the early 1990s, these 'traditional' UN peacekeeping operations were being singled out for intense criticism. Many politicians and specialists began to insist that the new 'multilateral international peacekeeping operations for the second generation 'should be introduced' implying more resolute and direct use of military force. See Mackinlay, John and Chopra, Jarat, 'Second General Multilateral Operations', *Washington Quarterly*, Vol. 15, No. 3, Summer 1992, pp. 113–32; and Boutros-Ghali, Boutros, *Report on the Work of the Organization from the Forty-Seventh to the Forty-Eighth Session of the General Assembly*, New York, September 1993, p. 2
18. The civil war in Tajikistan came as the result of political, ethnic and regional divisiveness. It was rooted in the power struggle between the opposition using democratic and Islamic slogans against the conservative neo-Communist regime. As the result of this struggle, the unity of the Tajik ethnic group was destroyed, leading to a clash between Northern and Southern ethnic groups. The opposition was concentrated in the Garm and the Nagorno-Badakhshansk autonomous districts. Local military operations led to a considerable loss of lives and triggered massive flight of the population to other NISs and into neighbouring Afghanistan. The socio-economic life of the country was all but paralysed, while the ability of the Rakhmonov government was severely handicapped. Under these circumstances political vacuums were created that contributed to the exacerbation and extension of warfare and outside involvements.
19. Dubnov, Aleander, 'Katastrofa v Tadjikistane o kotoroi v Rossii nichego ne znayut', *Novoye Vremya*, No. 4, 1993.

20. Yusin, Mikhail, 'Rossiya delayet stavku na novoye tadjikskoye rukovodstvo', *Izvestia*, 14 April 1993.
21. 'Civil War in Tajikistan', *Central Asian Monitor*, No. 5, 1992, p. 8; 'Events in Tajikistan', *Central Asian Monitor*, No. 6, 1992, pp. 2–4.
22. A number of Russian industrial giants, e.g. Magnitogorsk and Chelyabinsk metallurgical plants, KAMAZ, VAZ and others, depend almost entirely or to a very large degree on imports from Central Asia. Light industry is being affected in a similarly dramatic way.
23. See Michalopoulos, Constantine and Tarr, David, (ed), *Trade in the Newly Independent States*, Washington, 1994, pp. 229–235; and Whitlock, Erik, *The CIS Economies: Divergent and Troubled Paths*, RFE/RL Research Reports, Vol. 3, No. 1, 7 January 1994, p. 9
24. In particular, these conditions included Central Asian obligations to co-ordinate its banking, crediting, customs and taxation rules and regulations with Moscow and to bring them in line with the Russian norms and law.
25. OEC was created in 1985 to include Iran, Pakistan and Turkey. In November 1992 it was joined by Azerbaijan, Afghanistan and all five Central Asian states. From the geographic and demographic point of view, the organization may indeed become another European Economic Community with a territory of 7.2 million square kilometres and a population of 300 million.
26. *The Economist*, 26 December 1992–8 January 1993.
27. In the Western view, only Kyrgyzstan merited the title of a democratic state in all of Central Asia. Other countries were accused of antidemocratic practices and human rights violations. See *Implementation of the Helsinki Accords: Human Rights and Democratization in the Newly Independent Republics*, U.S. Congress, Commission on Security and Co-operation in Europe, Washington, January 1993, pp. 170–204.

2 China and Central Asia: Towards a New Relationship

Guangcheng Xing

In the last decade of the twentieth century, revolutionary changes have taken place in the international system. The collapse of the former Soviet Union can be said to be the most revolutionary change of all, which has posed a daunting question of practical significance to politicians and diplomats the world over: what important impact would the collapse of the Soviet Union exert on the rapidly changing world?

For China, the collapse of the Soviet Union presents only moderate problems for Sino-Russian relations. These relations are to a large extent a continuation of Sino-Soviet relations, which were fully normalized in 1989 and are not replete with uncertainties. Besides, China has since 1949 dealt with the ups and downs in its relations with the Soviet Union and has learned lessons and accumulated experiences. It shows therefore sufficient confidence in dealing with Russia after the collapse of the Soviet Union. The problem lies very much in how to conduct and develop bilateral relations with the fifteen new sovereign states which declared their independence during the implosion of the former Soviet Union.

Naturally, from the very start China wished to establish a new relationship with the five newly independent states in Central Asia and showed great interest in nurturing this relationship in the region. Several years have passed since the independence of these Central Asian states. What is the general situation of Sino-Central Asian relations? How should we evaluate the evolution of the new relationship between China and Central Asia? I would argue that China and the Central Asian states have established an entirely new relationship in the last few years. This new relationship, based on equality, friendship, mutual trust and sincere co-operation, has been developed to establish good neighbourhood relations and to make progress in common economic prosperity for both China and the Central Asian states. High-level state and government visits by Chinese and Central Asian leaders in the last few years stand as a testimony of this developing new relationship.[1]

I. PRINCIPLES IN SINO-CENTRAL ASIAN RELATIONS

While radical political changes were taking place in the former Soviet Union in the early 1990s, China adhered to its principle of 'non-interference in the internal affairs of other countries'. As the former Soviet republics declared their independence one after another, the Soviet Union collapsed. Later the Commonwealth of Independent States (CIS) was inaugurated. China quickly recognized the new sovereign states in Central Asia in accordance with its principle of 'respecting the choice made by peoples in other countries'.[2] The Chinese government also promptly sent a delegation headed by Li Lanqing, then Minister of Foreign Trade and Economic Co-operation, to visit the newly independent states in Central Asia.[3]

The question remains: what principles should be adopted in developing Sino-Central Asian relations? As in the case of China's relations with other states, the five principles of peaceful coexistence are the basis on which China intended to develop its relations with Central Asian states. These five principles – mutual respect of sovereignty and territorial integrity, mutual non-aggression, non-interference in each other's affairs, equality and mutual benefit and peaceful coexistence – have been the guiding principles for China in developing and in handling its foreign relations in the last forty years. They should be the general principles in Sino-Central Asian relations. That is why, when the Soviet Union collapsed, the Chinese government did not behave like some Western governments which clearly manifested their big-power chauvinism and hegemonism in making indiscreet remarks on and even interfering in the internal affairs of the newly independent states of former Soviet republics, including Central Asian states.

While taking the five principles of peaceful coexistence as general principles, the Chinese government also took steps to specify some particular principles which are specifically applicable to China's relations with countries of the CIS. In July 1994, Chinese Foreign Minister Qian Qichen elaborated these principles as follows: 1. Respect the choices made by peoples in those countries, and respect and understand foreign and domestic policies made by those countries in accordance with their own circumstances and international environment; never interfere in their internal affairs; 2. Maintain that differences in social systems, ideologies and development models should not stand in the way of resolving problems in bilateral relations; 3. Adhere to the principle of equality and mutual benefit in conducting trade and economic co-operation in accordance with norms of international economic exchanges and strive for common economic development and prosperity; 4. Sincerely hope for domestic stability of all

CIS states and for peaceful solution of all conflicts among CIS states so as to realize the regional political stability of the former Soviet Union. He also stated that the development of China's relations with the CIS states was not directed against any third country. These principles are concrete expressions of the application of five general principles of peaceful co-existence to bilateral relations between China and CIS states, including the five Central Asian states.[4]

Central Asian republics as newly independent sovereign entities are China's new neighbouring states. As such, China attaches great importance to developing Sino-Central Asian relations. In April 1994, during his visit to Central Asian states, the Chinese Premier Li Peng put forward four principles in developing China's relations with Central Asian states: 1. maintaining good neighbourly relations and peaceful coexistence; 2. promoting mutually beneficial co-operation and seeking common economic prosperity; 3. respecting the choices made by Central Asian peoples and never interfering in their internal affairs; and 4. respecting other countries' independence and sovereignty and contributing to regional stability.[5]

To elaborate these principles further, 'maintaining good neighbourly relations and peaceful coexistence' means that China wants to establish a normal and friendly relations with its Central Asian neighbours.

It goes without saying that good neighbourly relations are important in relations between states. Strained relations between neighbouring states not only have negative impact on domestic policies and economic development of the states concerned; they also affect the regional political and economic stability. That is why it is important that the principle of 'good neighbourhood' should be adhered to in relations between neighbouring states. Three of the five newly independent Central Asian states share common borders with China. Kazakhstan, Tajikistan and Kyrgyzstan are new neighbours of China's Northwest. China has long land frontiers with these three states, totalling more than 3000 km. It is possible for China to establish entirely new relations with these three neighbouring states because there is no historical baggage in their bilateral relations. As the Central Asian states are newly independent, there are no long-standing problems in Sino-Central Asian international relations.

The tragic and unpleasant history of Sino-Russian and Sino-Soviet relations is the result of the imperial expansion of Czarist Russia and the big-power chauvinism of the former Soviet Union and has nothing to do with the peoples of Central Asia. In the nineteenth century, Imperial Russia grabbed large areas of Chinese territory. In the 1960s, the former Soviet Union engineered a large-scale armed rebellion in the Northwest of China.

These historical events caused serious harm to the dignity and feelings of the Chinese people and left indelible scars in Sino-Russian and Sino-Soviet relations. Central Asian states, it should be argued, have in fact suffered from the same imperial expansion of Czarist Russia and from Soviet domination. Now that the Central Asian states have become independent, common historical experience could facilitate the establishment of entirely new and friendly neighbourhood relations between China and the Central Asian states. Such relations can contribute to the common prosperity and stability of China's Northwest and Central Asia and constitute a precondition for the rapid economic development of the inner Asia region.

'Promoting mutually beneficial co-operation and seeking common prosperity' means that with good friendly neighbourhood relations, China and Central Asian states can and should conduct mutually beneficial economic exchanges and economic co-operation in a joint effort to achieve rapid economic development.

Central Asian economies are going through a period of systemic transformation accompanied by economic difficulties and economic crises. The Chinese economic reforms are also in a critical period. Under these circumstances, mutually beneficial economic co-operation can help economic reforms in both China and Central Asia. In expanding its trade and economic relations with Central Asia, China could also alleviate severe economic difficulties in Central Asian states. Such trade and economic co-operation should have no other conditions attached and should be conducted in accordance with the commonly accepted norms and rules in international trade and economic relations. For China, a Central Asia which is capable of overcoming its economic difficulties and getting out of its economic crises has a better chance of achieving economic prosperity and political stability. China can benefit greatly from its stable and prosperous neighbouring states. Only when Central Asian states are politically stable and economically prosperous can Sino-Central Asian economic co-operation be conducted effectively and smoothly. Such economic co-operation can and will speed up economic development in the Northwest of China. It can therefore be argued that *to a large extent the stability and prosperity of Northwest China is closely bound up with the stability and prosperity of Central Asia.* It is, rightly, because of this consideration that China advocates and promotes active trade and economic co-operation between China and Central Asian states for common economic prosperity.

'Respecting the choice made by Central Asian peoples and never interfering in their internal affairs' is a reflection of China's full respect of its new 'neighbours'.

The independence of Central Asian states was achieved under very special historical circumstances. The collapse of the former Soviet Union was an implosion. The independence of all fifteen former Soviet republics had different dynamics and followed diverse momentum. As far as Central Asian states are concerned, it could be argued that they were not fully prepared when they rushed to declare their independence. Although they declared themselves as fully independent sovereign states, they had all been pursuing a strategy to be sovereign states within the framework of a federation or confederation. When the CIS was inaugurated by the three Slavic states of the former Soviet Union, Central Asian states were not initially included. They eventually joined the CIS as founding members, largely because they found it was impossible for them to be completely independent of any political framework predetermined by the Soviet past. China firmly believes that how the CIS states choose to be independent and how independent is entirely up to the peoples in those states to decide. In fact, that indicates that peoples in those countries now have control of the destiny of their own countries, which used to be determined from Moscow. By the same token, the way in which Central Asian states choose to achieve their independence proves that peoples in Central Asian states have seized the historical opportunity to decide the destiny of their own countries.

Central Asian states have also been faced with the difficult task of choosing their economic development models and their political and social systems. China shows particular respect for the choices of Central Asian peoples in this aspect. China does not concern itself with what systems and what models Central Asian states choose to adopt. One of the most important principles in China's international relations is to delink interstate relations from ideology in developing friendly relations with countries that have different social systems. This is, of course, also applicable to Sino-Central Asian relations. At the same time, China is aware that there is a wide variety of systems and models from which Central Asian governments and peoples can choose. To take one example: there are various opposed political systems such as Eastern vs Western, secular vs religious, democratic vs authoritarian, and decentralized vs centralized. Central Asian states have also been faced with very difficult choices because all political forces and states in the world have been trying to influence the choices of Central Asian peoples so that they will follow the courses desired by the forces and states concerned. China also realizes that in economic development terms, some Central Asian states have expressed interest in the 'China model', some in the 'Turkey model', and still others in the 'Korea model'. China has no intention of forcing any Central Asian states to follow the example of China and adopt the 'China model' in their economic development. After more than fifteen years of economic reform and opening up the Chinese economy has made outstanding achievements which have attracted worldwide attention. The rapid growth of the Chinese economy has been, however, achieved under very special internal and external circumstances for China. China will never 'export' its economic development model. It is, of course, a completely different matter if some Central Asian states are willing to learn from the Chinese experience in economic reform so that they may draw lessons from that experience. China is willing to exchange reform experience and lessons with Central Asian states so that they can learn from each other and avoid unnecessary mistakes and setbacks in their reforms and economic development.

'Respecting other countries' independence and sovereignty and contributing to regional stability' means that China respects the sovereignty of Central Asian states, and recognizes their status as equal members of the international community and as subjects in international law. That underlines China's commitment to the principle of equality in developing Sino-Central Asian bilateral relations. China is a great power regionally. However, China never presents itself as a bully in the region wantonly abusing the sovereignty of other states. China believes that regional stability must be built on the basis of mutual respect of sovereignty. Without such a basis, regional stability would not be possible to realize. That is why China fully supports every effort by Central Asian states to enhance their roles in world politics and in the global economy. China, for example, has supported the applications of Central Asian states for membership of the United Nations and many other international organizations.

The evolution of China's relations with Central Asia in the last few years has demonstrated that with the guidance of the five principles of peaceful coexistence and of the four principles in Sino-Central Asian relations, China's political and economic relations with Central Asian states have developed smoothly and successfully. There have been frequent high-level state and government visits between China and Central Asian states. A large number of inter-governmental agreements have been signed between China and Central Asian states. Political relations are well co-ordinated. Economic co-operation, particularly in trade, has seen rapid and impressive development. Cultural and scientific exchanges are increasingly frequent.

II. CHANGES IN GEOPOLITICS AND GEOECONOMICS

The rapid rise of Central Asian states from the ruins of the Soviet empire has fundamentally transformed the geopolitics and geoeconomics of Eurasia.

Central Asia is located close to the region where Europe meets Asia. From ancient times, it has been an area of special strategic importance contested by different powers. The opening in 1991 of the second Eurasian transcontinental railway that goes right through Central Asia makes Central Asia an important transport corridor connecting East with West.

Central Asia, on the other hand, is where various cultures, religions and traditions meet and impact on each other. In terms of culture, the Muslim, Slavonic, Chinese, Indian and Persian cultures all interact with and penetrate each other in Central Asia. In terms of ideology, Communism, Islamic fundamentalism and the Western liberalism clash with each other. Since the independence of the Central Asian states, various ethnonationalisms such as Pan-Turkism, Great Kazakhism, Great Uzbekism and Great Tajikism have all become increasingly active in various Central Asian states. All considered, Central Asia has become one of the areas in the post-Cold War world where serious contentions and clashes between different cultures, traditions and ideologies have been unfolding.

Another feature of Central Asia is the complex ethnicity of peoples living in the region. More than one hundred different ethnic groups inhabit Central Asia. The main nationalities in the region are Uzbeks, Kazaks, Turkmens, Kyrgyzs and Tajiks. In Soviet times, a large community of Russians were moved to Central Asia. In addition, there are Ukrainians, Belarussians and Germans in the region. For example, whereas 46 per cent of the population of Kazakhstan consists of Kazakhs, 41 per cent are Russian. Ethnic harmony and ethnic conflicts have constantly accompanied the evolution of politics in Central Asia. Since independence, ethnic rivalries and tensions among ethnic groups have haunted the political stability of the region.

On top of this, Central Asia is rich in natural resources of strategic importance. It has rich resources of uranium, for example, which is indispensable in the production of nuclear weapons. It is also rich in such mineral resources as petroleum, natural gas and gold. It produces high-quality cotton. Geo-economically, therefore, Central Asia is strategically important just as it is geopolitically.

It is for the above reasons that, upon the independence of five Central Asian states, Central Asia as a region became an interesting area of contention in world politics and attracted a lot of attention in international diplomacy. Global and regional powers were all trying to establish themselves in Central Asia.

From the Chinese perspective, the strategic importance of Central Asia is also seen in the uncertainties of regional political and economic development and in the potential of the region for the future. It should be argued that *the independence of Central Asian states was an important signpost that the world was going beyond the Cold War. By the same token, it will exert great impact on the development of post-Cold War international political and economic systems.*[6]

It should also be realized that because Central Asian states have achieved their independence for only a short period of time and generally lack experience in dealing with relations between nations as independent sovereign states, these states are easily susceptible to outside influences in conducting their international relations.

Following the independence of the Central Asian states, Turkey and Iran have manifested great enthusiasm in the region. Both welcomed the advent of independence of these states and, at the same time, tried to exert influence on them, politically, economically, culturally and religiously. Turkey took advantage of its common heritage with the Central Asian states and tried to establish a great Turkic sphere of influence through economic penetration. Iran, on the other hand, is geographically and culturally well positioned to exert influence in Central Asia. It has taken a number of diplomatic initiatives towards Central Asian states in an attempt to put these states under the influence of Islam. It also intends to create a great Middle East–Central Asia Islamic sphere of influence. It should be noted that Turkey and Iran have also been competing with each other in Central Asia for their respective spheres of influence while at the same time co-operating in Central Asian affairs. It was following a proposal made by both Turkey and Iran that all five newly independent Central Asian states participated in the Economic Co-operation Organization (ECO).[7]

Western countries, particularly the United States, are loath to see Iran expand its influence in Central Asia. In the global strategy of the United States, Central Asia is of special strategic interest. Firstly, Central Asia is becoming increasingly important in the national security considerations of the United States. It is of vital importance that the US should take firm action to stop the spread of the influence of Islamic fundamentalism into newly independent Central Asian states. For the United States, if the influence of Islamic fundamentalism prevails in Central Asia, the strategic interests of the United States (and of the West as a whole) in the Middle East and in Central Asia will be faced with a serious and malign challenge. It will also constitute a great threat to the security system of the West. Central Asia has rich resources of uranium and has the capacity to produce weapon-grade uranium for the production of nuclear weapons. More disquieting, Kazakhstan was for a time in precarious control of some operational nuclear weapons.[8] If Islamic fundamentalism controls Central

Asia, it is possible that from Central Asia to the Middle East and to North Africa, a large region of 'Islamic storms' will be instituted. That should explain why the United States and other Western countries have largely supported Turkey's policies towards, and political presence in, Central Asia. In the view of Western countries, Turkey is a secular state and market economy. Equally important, it is a NATO member. The expansion of Turkey's influence in Central Asia could serve as a shield to stop the penetration of Islamic fundamentalism into the region. Secondly, because of the strategic location of Central Asia, domination by the United States of the region could ensure that the regional strategic milieu is always in favour of the strategic interests of the United States and its Western allies. Such domination could influence Russia to the north, contain Iran and Afghanistan in the south, balance China in the east and command the Caucasus in the west. Thirdly, Central Asia has great economic potential. The United States and other Western countries have no intention of giving up this lucrative market.[9]

It is therefore only natural that Central Asia should have become a hot spot for international diplomacy in the last few years. This is partly determined by the strategic importance of the region itself, and partly because, in the first few years of their independence, Central Asian states had been groping for an international and diplomatic strategy in global and regional affairs. They seem to have now identified their position in world politics and in the global economy.

China follows closely geopolitical and geo-economic changes in Central Asia. In considering its strategy for developing Sino-Central Asian relations, China has paid particular attention to the 'Russian factor'. Historical circumstances and contemporary political and economic conditions have determined that Central Asian states have to be closely related to Russia. To a large extent, the presence of the 'Russian factor' plays a role in regional stability. The recent situation in Tajikistan is a testimony to this. It is, of course, difficult to rule out the possibility that Russia may use this factor to attempt to control Central Asian states. The Russian Foreign Ministry has repeatedly stated that all regions of CIS are of vital importance to Russian interests, a simple fact that Russia will never lose sight of.

Although there are various political and economic conflicts between Central Asian states and other CIS members, the historical close economic interdependence established almost by default makes it impossible for Central Asian states to break away from the CIS, particularly from Russia. In terms of the military, Central Asian states have just started to organize their respective independent armed forces. In fact, it is mostly the armed forces of the CIS – predominantly Russian – that patrol and defend the outer borders of Central Asian states. This simple fact also explains why it is extremely difficult for Central Asian states to break away completely from Russia. In fact, all Central Asian states have made relations with Russia their foreign policy priority and view these links as the foundation of their foreign relations.

China clearly realizes that whatever function the 'Russian factor' plays in Central Asia is important to China's relations with Central Asian states. However, this is principally the business of Russia and the Central Asian states. China respects the choices made by the Central Asian states as long as the Russian armed forces stationed in Central Asia do not constitute a military threat to China. The Chinese government also clearly realizes that although China is of some importance to the international relations of Central Asian states, it does not occupy the most important place in the international strategy of these states. History has predetermined this condition.

It could be argued, therefore, that China is not competitive with any other countries for influence in Central Asia, even with radical changes unfolding in the regional geopolitics and geo-economics. China will not participate in any such competition because she does not seek any special interest in the region. As Chinese Premier Li Peng emphatically pointed out when elaborating China's policies towards Central Asia during his tour of the region in April 1994, 'China seeks no sphere of either economic or political influence in Central Asia'.[10] China opposes any policies and activities that are aimed at or likely to bring about regional political instability and the destruction of economic prosperity. China firmly believes that the real independence of Central Asian states depends on the full support and understanding of the international community.

III. CHINA'S POLICY CONSIDERATIONS

As argued above, China will not enter into any competition with other countries for a sphere of influence in Central Asia because China does not seek any special interest in the region. Nevertheless, the emergence of independent sovereign states in Central Asia has radically changed geopolitical and geo-economic situations in the region adjacent to China's Northwest. China has to face this new reality. The changing geopolitical and geo-economic situation in Central Asia has thus entailed a number of new policy considerations for China. Before the independence of the Central Asian states, China had to deal with only one country, the Soviet Union. Now China has to deal with a number of independent sovereign states on its periphery in the Northwest. Since the Central Asian republics are now independent sovereign states, different and sometime divergent foreign policies are made and pursued to serve their respective national interests. It is therefore imperative for China to have a comprehensive strategy and flexible policies towards Central Asia in order to meet the regional challenges. What then are the major policy considerations entailed on China by the independence of Central Asian states?

In the first place, the independence of the Central Asian republics of the former Soviet Union has brought radical changes in the geopolitical relations between China and Russia. Just like Mongolia, the Central Asian states have now become a strategic buffer zone between two great powers: China and Russia. The independence of Central Asian states has substantially reduced the common borders between China and Russia in the West. The new geopolitical reality is that Sino-Russian borders are now mostly located in China's Northeast, not its Northwest. What are the implications of this change?

It has often been argued in recent years by Chinese scholars and officials alike that the international environment on China's peripheries in the early 1990s is the best since the establishment of the PRC in 1949.[11] That includes the security environment of China's Northeast and Northwest. In the past, Czarist Russia and the Soviet Union often presented a great military threat to China's national security from both the Northeast and the Northwest. That threat seriously constrained China's choice of domestic policies and development strategy. Following the collapse of the Soviet Union, Russia has shown great interest in developing friendly relations with China. Sino-Russian border areas have been unprecedentedly peaceful. That situation is desirable for China, which is now bent on its economic reforms and on the realization of its four modernizations. Even if in the future – in an extremely unlikely scenario – the extreme nationalists in Russia control the Russian government, Central Asia will serve as a buffer to compromise the possibility of direct conflict between China and Russia in China's Northwest.

It must be admitted that the collapse of the former Soviet Union has also brought some strategic uncertainties to the area – for example, concerning nuclear weapons in the region. There remain also such problems as the Russian military presence and territorial disputes and border negotiations. In the last few years, some strategic problems and uncertainties have been resolved. Kazakhstan has handed over all the nuclear weapons stationed on its territory to Russia.[12] It has been decided that Sino-Central Asian borders are to be defended and patrolled by CIS armed forces. Territorial disputes between China and Kazakhstan have been largely solved.[13] Negotiations on border disputes between China and other Central Asian states are an ongoing process in Sino-Central Asian relations.[14]

There is now a favourable security environment in China's Northwest conducive to the opening and economic reforms in the region. In the long term, Central Asian states are unlikely to constitute any military threat to China as long as they follow international norms and standards in conducting their international relations. Of course, China will never resort to the use of force in its relations with Central Asia.

Secondly, the independence of Central Asian states provides China with a historical opportunity. That is simply because Central Asia has now become a great market and a region with huge potential for economic co-operation. The emergence of such a market along China's northwestern frontier is most propitious as the strategy of the comprehensive opening of China has just started to develop the Northwest of China. Indeed, as argued in the chapter by Qingjian Liu in this book, in the past few years China has taken this historical opportunity to quickly establish close economic relations with Central Asian states and to conduct trade and economic co-operation widely, on the basis of equality and mutual benefit. Economic development in China and in Central Asian states in the last few years has greatly contributed to the region's economic prosperity.

China and Central Asia have a long history and tradition of economic co-operation. The 'Silk Road' is a historical testimony of traditional economic and cultural exchanges between China and Central Asia. The 'Silk Road' also testifies to the great contributions China and Central Asia have made to the development of world civilizations. The 'Silk Road', which has now been revived at the dawn of the 21st century, is likely to exert greater impact on Central Asia. In the past, China's policies towards its northwestern frontiers could be summarized in one word: 'defence'. Now the main thrust of Chinese policies is 'opening'.

In the economic structure of the former Soviet Union, the Central Asian republics had a dual role to play: as a production basis for resources-based raw materials and as the market for consumer goods. Consequently, mining industry, agriculture and animal husbandry in these republics are comparatively well developed, whereas processing industries are extremely primitive. There are few new industries such as electronics and telecommunication. The collapse of the Soviet Union seriously affected the traditional economic linkages between Central Asia and Russia, and between Central Asia and Ukraine and other CIS states. While the Central Asian states are no longer willing to sell their resources to Russia at discount price, Russia is reluctant to provide Central Asian states with subsidized consumer goods, many of which Russia itself is acutely short of. As CIS states have yet to establish, mutual trust among themselves, Central Asian states have to look for economic partners beyond the framework of the CIS. China becomes a natural choice for the Central Asian states. Both the geographical proximity and the complementarity of Chinese and Central Asian economies make it so. This opens up an unprecedented opportunity for China to enter the Central Asian markets.

In fact, the Chinese government had already taken initiatives to map out its strategy to open up the Northwest to Central Asia. As early as June 1992, the provincial leadership of five provinces and autonomous regions of China's Northwest–Xinjiang, Gansu, Ningxia, Qinghai and Shaanxi – was summoned to Beijing for discussions on China's strategy of economic reforms and opening in the Northwest. Chinese Premier Li Peng urged the provincial leadership to take the historical opportunity to expand trade and economic and technical co-operation with China's neighbouring states, particularly the Central Asian states. He stated that Northwest China was now presented with a huge market across the borders. As the Chinese economy and Central Asian economies were essentially complementary, the prospect for the growth of trade and other economic exchanges and technical co-operation between Northwest China and Central Asia was particularly promising. Northwest China should take full advantage of its own economic strength and cultivate the whole Chinese economy in developing its economic relations with Central Asia; the expansion of trade between China and its neighbouring states in the Northwest could serve as a boost to the economic development of the region.[15] Shortly after this meeting, the Xinjiang Uighur Autonomous Region submitted its strategy to open itself up to Central Asia. With unprecedented speed in its decision making, Beijing approved the Xinjiang strategy within a week of the submission. Soon after, the State Council made a decision to grant Xinjiang eight preferential policies to speed up its opening to the international economy.[16]

Thirdly, after the collapse of the Soviet Union, what the Chinese government was most concerned about was the possible negative impact that extreme ethnonationalism and Islamic fundamentalism in Central Asia could exert on China. It could be argued that of all the newly independent states emerging from the collapse of the Soviet Union and residing now in the framework of the CIS, only the Central Asian states, which constituted a new geopolitical reality, could politically impact on China directly in a negative way. Why? Northwest China is heavily populated by China's national minorities. There are ethnic groups that straddle the borders between China and the Central Asian republics: some of the same ethnic group reside in China, while others live in Central Asia. For example, about one million Kazakhs live in China's Xinjiang Autonomous Region. Whereas Xinjiang has around seven million Uighurs, across the border in Central Asia, 400,000 Uighurs live in the five Central Asian states. More significantly, ethnic unrests involving the Uighurs and other ethnic minorities in Xinjiang have been recently reported.

At the time when ethnic nationalism seems to be gaining worldwide ascendancy, ethno-nationalism in Central Asia has also tried to infiltrate into China. For example, the 'Inter-Republic Uighur Association' has already frequently engaged in all sorts of activities in Kazakhstan. The United National Revolutionary Front for Eastern Turkestan is also active in Kazakhstan, openly advocating the independence of Xinjiang. It is small wonder that during the Chinese Premier Li Peng's visit to Central Asia in April 1994, assurances were repeatedly sought by the Chinese government from the governments of Central Asian states that they should unite to fight against ethnic separatism.[17] In September 1995, a joint statement was issued by the Kazakhstani President Nazarbayev and the Chinese President Jiang Zemin in Beijing, emphasizing that China and Kazakhstan 'oppose national separatism in any form, and will allow no organizations or forces to engage in such separatist activities against the other side'.[18] The Chinese government's concern over a possible spill-over of ethno-nationalism from across the borders reflects its concern for the long-term stability of China's Northwest.

A fourth issue, closely connected with the problem of ethno-nationalism, is China's concern over the spread of Islamic fundamentalism and Pan-Turkism. Both Islamic fundamentalism and Pan-Turkism stand in the way of the democratization of Central Asian states and present obstacles to the transformation of Central Asian economies into market economies. Furthermore, if Islamic fundamentalism or Pan-Turkism prevails in Central Asian states, it would jeopardize regional stability and the bilateral relations between Central Asian states and their neighbours. At present, Islamic fundamentalism and Pan-Turkism have gained some momentum in Central Asia. To safeguard the political stability and economic prosperity in Central Asia, the Central Asian states have been trying to contain the influence of both Islamic fundamentalism and Pan-Turkism. China, Russia and Western states share the same concern about the spread of Islamic fundamentalism in Central Asia. China, Russia and Iran have similar interests in checking the influence of Pan-Turkism in the region. China therefore supports and co-operates with the Central Asian states in their efforts to oppose Islamic fundamentalism and Pan-Turkism.

IV. PROBLEMS AND PROSPECTS

Generally speaking, Sino-Central Asian relations have developed smoothly since the independence of the Central Asian states. Prospects are promising. There are, however, some problems that need to be dealt with.

One of these problems is presented by territorial disputes – a particularly thorny problem in relations between states, and even more so in post-Cold War international relations. China has border disputes with all three neighbouring states in Central Asia, namely Kazakhstan, Kyrgyzstan, and Tajikistan. This is a legacy bestowed by history. The solution of this problem is possible only if both China and the Central Asian states make common efforts towards a compromise.

It should be noted that the collapse of the Soviet Union has had a dual effect on the solution of China's territorial disputes in Central Asia. On the one hand, there is a negative effect. In the past, China had to negotiate with only one state, the Soviet Union. Territorial disputes in the Northeast of China and those in the Northwest of China could be negotiated as 'one deal'. Settlement could be reached, for example, with compensation made for loss in the Northwest with gains in the Northeast. That gave China some room to manoeuvre. The situation has changed radically now. China has to settle with three new states with different demands. Negotiations are difficult and time-consuming. On the other hand, there is also a positive effect. As the three Central Asian states are newly independent sovereign nations, there is no historical baggage in bilateral relations between China and those states. Therefore, both China and the Central Asian states can lay the blame for territorial disputes in the region on the shoulders of Czarist Russia and of the former Soviet Union. That could facilitate the solution of the border disputes. The Chinese government also realizes that the successful solution of border disputes with the three newly independent Central Asian states will contribute to the transparency of the borders in the region and thus to the regional peace and stability desired by both China and Central Asian states.

Another problem is in trade relations. Most Sino-Central Asian trade is still conducted through barter. This method has many limitations where the expanding trade relations between China and Central Asia are concerned, and has caused a lot of problems. For example, a large quantity of consumer goods of inferior quality have been exported from China to Central Asia in barter trade in the last few years. That has seriously damaged the reputation of Chinese-produced consumer goods in Central Asia. By the same token, it has troubled Sino-Central Asian trade relations. This primitive form of trade has now become an impediment to the further development of Sino-Central Asian trade and to the full exploitation of potential in bilateral economic co-operation.

There is also the problem of the operation of the second Eurasian transcontinental railway. Only joint efforts by China and the Central Asian states can ensure the smooth operation of this railway and its unimpeded passage in Asia. This is an important area of economic co-operation between China and Central Asia. This railway is particularly important for both China and Central Asia because all five Central Asian states are located in the hinterland of the Asian land mass. None of them is even close to a seaport. The Eurasian transcontinental railway, which goes right through Central Asia and connects China's Northwest with East China, makes seaports along China's East coast easily accessible to Central Asian states. Such access can help Central Asian states to initiate and sustain close economic contacts with Japan, Korea, Hong Kong, Taiwan, Singapore and other Southeast Asian states. Indeed, the significance of the second Eurasian 'landbridge', as many Chinese call it, is to connect Central Asia to the Pacific rim, thus facilitating the economic development of the Central Asian states. By promoting closer economic co-operation and trade exchanges between Central Asia and other parts of Asia, it plays an important role in 'returning Central Asian states to Asia'.

Last, but certainly not least, Central Asian states must prepare themselves to return to Asia. For historical reasons, the Central Asian states have closer economic and political relations with Russia, the CIS states and Eastern Europe. The economic interdependence between their economies is like flesh and blood. Such an economic interdependence is bound to influence the choices made by Central Asian states in their foreign policy and economic development strategy. It is predetermined by historical circumstances that Central Asian states should have given priority in international relations to their relations with the CIS states, and particularly with Russia.

In the long term, however, in pursuing rapid economic development, the Central Asian states should form closer economic relations with the Asian economies, at the same time maintaining and expanding their relations with the CIS states. In other words, Central Asia must 'enter' into Asia. In the last few years, economic practice in the Central Asian states has demonstrated their reluctance to assert a return to Asia and their lack of understanding of Asian economies. It may also be true that following their independence the Central Asian states are not fully prepared to return to Asia, especially psychologically. It is, however, in the best interests of the Central Asian states that they should march out of the Asian hinterland to capitalize on the dynamics of the Asian economies. Asia is now the fastest-growing economic region in the world. The Asia-Pacific Economic Co-operation (APEC) is putting new impetus into the development of the Pacific-rim economies. With the rise of the Northeast Asian economies, even Russia has adopted a strategy to develop links with this dynamic region. China can assist Central Asian states in participating in the political, economic and cultural affairs of Asia. It is in this direction that the new Sino-Central Asian relationship developed in the last few years can be further strengthened.

NOTES

1. Before the Chinese Premier Li Peng made his return state visit to Central Asian states in April 1994, the heads of states or of the governments of five Central Asian states had visited China since their independence in late 1991. For example, in 1992 alone, the Premier of Kazakhstan, the Presidents of Kyrgyzstan and Uzbekistan all visited China. See Tian Zengpei (ed.), *Gaige Kaifang Yilai de Zhongguo Waijiao* (China's Diplomacy since Its Reform and Opening), pp. 317–20.
2. *Renmin Ribao*, (People's Daily), 28 December 1991.
3. *Renmin Ribao*, 29 December 1991.
4. *Renmin Ribao*, 4 July 1994.
5. *Renmin Ribao*, 19 April 1994. For more details, see 'China's Basic Policy Towards Central Asia', *Beijing Review*, Vol. 37, No. 18, 1994, pp. 18–9.
6. For further elaboration of this point, see Guangcheng Xing, *Jueqi de Zhongya* (The Rise of Central Asia), Sanlian Press, Hong Kong, 1993, p. 5.
7. The ECO is a regional organization in Western and Central Asia. It has at present ten members: Turkey, Iran, Pakistan, Afghanistan, Uzbekistan, Turkmenistan, Azerbaijan, Kazakhstan, Kyrgyzstan, and Tajikistan. All of them are Muslim countries. The founding members were Turkey, Iran, Pakistan and Afghanistan when they established Regional Economic Cooperation (REC) in 1970. After the Iranian Revolution in 1979, REC became defunct. It was renamed and revived in 1985. All other six members joined the newly named ECO in 1993.
8. Nuclear warheads were not completely removed from Kazakhstan until June 1995.
9. For an earlier discussion of China's concern about political changes in Central Asia, see Zhang Xiaodong, 'Central Asia on the Rise', *Beijing Review*, 3–9 Aug. 1992, pp. 12–3.
10. *Renmin Ribao*, 27 April 1994.
11. Tian Zengpei (ed.), *Gaige Kaifang Yilai de Zhongguo Waijiao* (China's Diplomacy since Its Reform and Opening), pp. 18–20.
12. The Kazakhstan government announced in June 1995 that Kazakhstan had removed all nuclear warheads from its territory.
13. The Sino-Kazakhstani agreement on border demarcation was signed in April 1994 during the Chinese Premier Li Peng's visit to Almaty. The Kazakhstan government ratified the treaty in June 1995.
14. By April 1995, fifteen rounds of border talks had been conducted between the working group of the border negotiations delegation of the Chinese govern-

ment and the working group of the joint delegation of the governments of Russia, Kazakhstan, Kyrgyzstan and Tajikistan. *Renmin Ribao*, 14 April 1995.

15. *Renmin Ribao*, 8 June 1992. See also *Beijing Review*, Vol. 35, No. 25, 1992, pp. 4–5.
16. *Renmin Ribao* (Overseas edition), 6 July 1992.
17. See reports on Premier Li Peng's visit to Central Asia in *Renmin Ribao*, 18 April to 30 April 1994. See also *Nanhua Zaobao* (South China Morning Post), 28 April 1994.
18. *Xinhua News Agency*, 12 September 1995. Earlier in February, *Lien Ho Pao* (United Daily) in Hong Kong reported that at the request of the Chinese government, Kazakhstan banned activities by the Xinjiang independence movement in Kazakhstan. *Lien Ho Pao*, 27 February 1995.

3 Ethnopolitical Issues and the Emergence of Nation-States in Central Asia

Algis Prazauskas

GENERAL APPROACH

Unlike the colonial empires in the first half of the present century, the Soviet Union collapsed so abruptly that all its constituent parts found themselves more or less unprepared for independent existence. Even bureaucracy, the most developed element of state machinery, was in most cases inadequate to perform all the functions required in the independent state. In every republic, except Russia, it had virtually no experience in defence matters, external relations and foreign trade. None of the newly independent states were able to establish effective control over their borders and in a number of cases (Georgia, Moldova, Azerbaijan, to some extent also Russia) even parts of their territory. Economically, all the non-Russian republics were closely tied to Russia, which was the principal supplier of oil, gas and most industrial equipment and the chief importer of raw materials, industrial and agricultural goods from these republics. From virtually any point of view, the former Soviet republics in 1991, particularly the southern ones, were far less ready for independence than most of the former colonies in Asia in Africa, which Robert Jackson called quasi-states,[1] because they are perpetuated by international law and external aid but could scarcely survive without such external support. As Fred Riggs writes about post-imperial regions, 'In some of these states, small groups of ambitious elites have been able to defeat their rivals and seize control by means of violence and authoritarian methods. In other cases, continuing competition among such groups and their inability to establish or implement relevant public policies has led to anarchy, a generalized condition of lawlessness and disorder in which everyone suffers'.[2] This generalization basically is applicable to the post-Soviet states in the Caucasus and Central Asia.

Among the political options for the newly independent states, the choice between the models of a nation-state and a plural society is the most crucial issue. The difference between the two, although not defined legally and often ignored in political studies, is of crucial importance. In a nation-state a single ethnic community is both politically and demographically prevalent, and ethnic minorities, if any, are bound to accept the culture and language of the majority as normative. In this sense, even such a heterogeneous nation as the United States is a nation-state, not to mention Great Britain, France, or New Zealand. In those countries where ethnic heterogeneity is politically institutionalized, the culture and language of any particular group are not accepted as normative. Typical examples among many such countries are Switzerland, Belgium, India, Pakistan, Indonesia and Singapore.

The crucial factor which determines the choice between the two models is ethno-demographic situation, i.e. the proportion of particular ethnic groups among the total population and their territorial distribution. If the minorities constitute a small fraction of the population, they are more likely to accept the normative function of the culture and language of the dominant majority, provided that minorities are not compactly settled in within their ethnic homelands and/or do not form a majority in the cities. However, there are a number of less important social, cultural, historical and political variables which affect the choice between the two models.

With few exceptions (Armenia for instance, after the Azeri exodus), all the post-Soviet states have a number of features, characteristic of plural societies in the sense of the term as used by Furnivall, Cooper and M. G. Smith. Except for relatively small sections engaged in modern sectors of economy, there was very little social interaction between diverse ethnic communities. Ethnic cleavage between almost exclusively urban Russian Diasporas in the non-Russian republics and largely rural indigenous populations (except for the Baltic republics, Ukraine and Byelorussia) remained as deep as ever, and the trend toward sociocultural integration was increasingly neutralized owing to the persistence of negative stereotypes and the growth of ethnic nationalism among titular nationalities of the Union republics.

Nevertheless, even before the dissolution of the USSR both Communist and non-Communist (in the Baltics, Georgia and Armenia) regimes in the Soviet republics opted for the model of a nation-state by proclaiming the languages of titular nationalities as official ('state') languages and directly or indirectly curtailing the privileges and rights of ethnic minorities. The constitutions adopted by the republics after the dissolution of the Soviet Union reiterated this option, in many cases stressing that the proclamation of independence expressed the will of the titular majority for self-determination and consolidation of the independent nation-state.

Two sets of issues need to be examined in this connection. The first is why the regimes of the newly independent states opted for the nation-state model without any serious discussion about the multi-ethnic alternative of the Swiss, Belgian, or Indian type. The second issue is the feasibility of this option in the ethno-demographic, ethnopolitical and sociocultural context of each particular state.

The motives for the preference of the nation-state model, although rejected outright by minority leaders and many liberal (not to mention Communist) social scientists, are fairly evident for any non-partisan observer familiar with the situation in the non-Russian republics. Soviet nationalities had virtually no experience of genuine ethnopolitical pluralism and national equality. Despite all the propaganda about the multinational Soviet state and the 'blossoming of nations', the Soviet Union in many ways looked like a Russian state. Although the official concept of the 'Soviet people' deprived Russians of much of their cultural heritage and tended to dilute their ethnic identity, the Russian nation was to serve as the integrating core of the 'Soviet people'. In sociocultural terms, the words 'Russian' and 'Soviet' overlapped and in many cases were synonymous. Most important, the Russian language was obligatory nation-wide, while the languages of the non-Russian nationalities were increasingly relegated to the background within the respective republics and were generally regarded as non-existent beyond their borders. In urban areas of Ukraine, Byelorussia, Kazakhstan, and Kyrgyzstan, vernacular-medium schools almost disappeared, and only Russian was used in government offices and the modern industrial sector. Almost all of the accessible global culture was also supplied in Russian transcription.

Actually, the Russian language and major elements of Russian culture had become normative all over the country, while the languages and cultures of non-Russian groups were increasingly ousted to the periphery of public life and survived mostly in rural areas. This process was very uneven in different parts of the country, and in some regions, notably the Baltic republics, Georgia and Armenia, the competition between indigenous and Russian languages and cultures for normative status was going on. However, these regions formed only a small part of the country and did not interfere effectively with the prevailing trend of Russian acculturation of minorities. Actually, sociocultural integration in the USSR was perceived by non-Russian minorities in terms of Russification and assimilation, and evoked negative reaction, particularly among the indigenous intellectual elites.

Similar processes are common in many countries and cannot be regarded as exclusively positive or negative. Modernization in most nations, including independent ones, has among its features the spread of major languages, serving the purposes of global or, at least, regional communications, and the loss of many traditional ethnic features. From a technocratic and functional point of view, the process of homogenization can be, and often is, viewed as progressive. The opposite view is that assimilation means the disappearance of particular cultures, and the replacement of cultural diversity by uniformity is likely to have highly negative consequences for the whole of mankind. Technocratic and cultural approaches are, in fact, two incompatible philosophies of ethnocultural evolution, reflecting the on-going process of integration and differentiation.

However, in the short-term perspective, psychological factors are of crucial importance. The group undergoing assimilation has to renounce its language and certain elements of culture because it is conditioned by various means to regard them as inferior and/or there is a strong motive (e.g. in the form of social rewards and various benefits) for assimilation. This policy was fairly effective in a number of regions of the Soviet Union, particularly in urban areas, but simultaneously it produced a characteristic minority complex and evoked strong negative reactions among a section of non-Russian intellectuals. Another important factor is the collective historical memory of an ethnic group, particularly memories of past relations with the dominant majority: even intensive indoctrination, starting at the preschool level, can succeed only as long as it does not try to impose totally unacceptable ideas, especially about relatively recent events, remembered by the elder generation. The Bolshevik regime had re-annexed the non-Russian peripheries mostly by force and, since those events took place relatively recently (1918–1921) and were followed by mass repression, deportations and even (in Ukraine, Kazakhstan, and Kyrgyzstan) unprecedented famine, the historical memory of non-Russian groups generally carried a heavy negative load and was a major obstacle for the formation of the 'Soviet people'. Despite all official protestations to the contrary, the elites of the titular nationalities generally remained suspicious of 'Moscow', and this suspicion came into the open during political liberalization in the late 1980s and especially after the proclamation of independence in 1991.

To sum up, the nationalities policy of the Soviet regime, particularly its strategic aim of moulding diverse nationalities into the single 'Soviet people', produced a survival syndrome among virtually all non-Russian groups. The choice of the nation-state model was actually conditioned by this syndrome.[3]

CENTRAL ASIA: NATIONS IN THE MAKING

Much as in the former colonies of the Western powers, the emergence of states in Central Asia precedes the formation of ethno-nations as fairly homogeneous sociocultural and sociopolitical formations of a modern type. Numerous factors combine to make the titular nationalities of the Central Asian states look amorphous compared to modern European nations. A low percentage of urban population (22 per cent to 38 per cent), limited social and territorial mobility of the population, and undeveloped communications systems combine to conserve traditional sub-ethnic divisions and identities among the titular nationalities. In Turkmenistan, the most important social units are tribes, among whom the Teke and Yomuds are the largest, followed by Ersaris, Salyrs, Saryks and Chowdurs. The Kazakhs are divided into three large segments, called Senior, Medium, and Junior zhuzes. There are leftovers of the tribal division of Kyrgyzs, each tribe belonging to either 'right wing' (Ong) or 'left wing' (Sol). Among Uzbeks and Tajiks, who have been settled agricultural communities for a longer period, the principal cleavages are among territorial (e.g. Kulyabans, Hissarians, Khujanndias in Tajikistan) and, in some cases, religious groups (e.g. Ismailite Pamyrians are not perceived even as Muslims by other Tajiks).

Another feature, by far more conspicuous in Central Asia than in other post-Soviet republics, is the contrast between the core areas (which, owing to favourable climatic conditions and their location along the traditional routes of the caravan trade, have been more advanced and developed) and the neighbouring desert or mountainous periphery. The difference between 'core' and 'periphery' in Central Asian states is by far more obvious than in the western post-Soviet republics, not to mention developed countries, and forms a significant sociocultural cleavage.

To a large extent this intra-ethnic segmentation reflects the fact that during the long history of the region there was no trend towards the emergence of polities coinciding with ethnic boundaries. Retrospectively, 'national' histories of the present states were written after the creation of the respective republics in 1924, and there were attempts to identify different ancient and medieval states with particular modern nations. The Uzbek-Tajik debate about the ethnic affinities of the earliest population of the region and particular states is the best example of these efforts.[4] However, the fact remains that it was the territorial reorganization of 1924 which created the prototypes of nation-states in the region, and the subsequent period was too short to make the idea of ethno-nation-statehood part of mass consciousness.

Finally, during the Soviet period a new cleavage emerged between the urban intellectuals, educated mostly in Russian-medium schools and universities, and the rural population, speaking only their native language and preserving much of their traditional culture and institutions. In the cities of

Kazakhstan and Kyrgyzstan by the late 1980s very few vernacular-medium schools survived; only Russian was used as the medium of instruction in colleges and universities (except for the local-language speciality). The number of books published in local languages was far from sufficient, and the library collections contained mostly books in Russian.[5] The net result of these trends was twofold: first, a very large number of indigenous intellectuals, particularly engineers, doctors and economists had a poor knowledge of their native tongues; second, the languages of the titular nationalities were increasingly incapable of serving all the needs of modern society, especially in the areas of science and technology, where only the Russian language was used. Thus the linguistic situation was not conducive to the formation of nation-states, and the constitutional act which proclaimed the vernaculars as the only 'state languages' in the republics tended to deepen the existing linguistic cleavages rather than expand the functions of the local languages.[6]

The cultural fragmentation of the Central Asian nations means that so far no national cultures capable of performing normative functions for the civil society have emerged. For the rural population the prevailing majority of which are five titular nationalities of the region, the idea of national culture, be it Kazakh, Tajik, or Uzbek, does not have much meaning. What they actually know is the local folk culture, in many cases markedly different from the emerging national culture. The situation is further complicated by the losses caused by the process of de-Sovietization, since much of what was created during the Soviet period and forms a large block of modern culture still has become unacceptable for ideological and political reasons, while the cultural legacy of the distant past, however rich it may be – especially in the case of Tajiks and Uzbeks – is inadequate to satisfy the needs of the modernizing society. As for the global culture, it is known to the peoples of Central Asia, (especially those who do not have old urbanistic traditions, Kazakhs, Kyrgyzs, and Turkmens, for example) mostly in its Russian transcription, especially because for decades – even officially – the Russian language had a virtual monopoly of serving as the only 'window into world culture'. Reorientation towards the mass culture of modern Turkey or Iran is also problematic due to sociopolitical and sociocultural differences, which became reinforced after the annexation of the region by the Russian Empire. Besides, as the experience of many countries shows, the cultural 'import' often tends to slow down, rather than contribute to, the development of national cultures.

Thus, the national cultures of the Central Asian nations are not quite adequate to perform normative functions and this circumstance presents a serious obstacle to the formation of nation-states. The cultural elites of

Central Asia seem to recognize the problem and are looking for ways to solve it. Some leaders, especially those from the Islamic Revival Party (outlawed in all Central Asian states) propose to use Islam and its rich cultural heritage as a version of national culture. However, Islam in predominantly Muslim areas cannot serve the purposes of cultural differentiation, crucial for the emergence of nation-states, and, more importantly, the Islamic revival can prove risky for the ruling ex-Communist elites. Finally, since Islam is the religion of all titular nationalities of the region, it can serve to promote pan-Islamic solidarity and Muslim identity rather than the consolidation of ethno-nation-states.[7]

Cases where local cultural differences tend to be more important than the emerging national culture and the nation lacks minimal homogeneity form a major obstacle to the formation of nation-states and nurture particularistic trends in the area of politics. Such situations are fairly common in history, and actually the majority of modern ethno-nations are consolidated after the emergence of the respective states. Generally, as the consolidation of the nation-state proceeds and national institutions and cross-cutting social and ideological cleavages develop, ethno-regionalism, although never eliminated completely, ceases to serve as a platform for political mobilization. However, the Central Asian states have a long way to go before they reach that stage. Most observers and analysts agree that sub-ethnic divisions are the principal reason for the ongoing civil war in Tajikistan, and remain one of the principal lines of the power-struggle in other states of the region.[8]

Another important issue in the nation-building process is the consensus over national interests. The fragmentation of Central Asian nationalities along different lines is a major obstacle to achieving this type of consensus. Actually, the nationalist elites of the region have so far had no opportunity to discuss the contents and priorities of their national interests. The political liberalization of 1987–1991 did not, unlike in the Baltic and Transcaucasian republics, affect the basic features of the system and generally did not provide for mass political mobilization. The symptoms of 'national revival' also could be hardly noticed, and hardly went beyond the publication of some epics, forbidden by the Soviet censorship, and modest attempts to revise the official Soviet interpretation of the consequences of annexation of Central Asia by Russia.

Finally, the Central Asian republics did not experience even the short period of national solidarity which swept the republics of the western region and popularized nationalist aspirations, interests and symbols. Birlik in Uzbekistan, Alash in Kazakhstan, the Democratic Movement of Kyrgyzstan and other associations which appeared in the late 1980s actually were political clubs for youth and intellectuals and did not have anything like grassroots organizations or mass support. For this reason the idea of the nation-state did not catch the imagination of the people and was not perceived as the principal item among national interests. Unlike in the western Soviet republics, the population of Central Asia was not much preoccupied with the issue of ethnic survival and did not cherish the idea of independence: over 90 per cent of positive replies about the preservation of the 'renewed Union' during the March 1991 referendum cannot be explained exclusively by the specific features of the political culture and electoral behaviour of the population, unfamiliar with democratic norms and practices of western democracy.[9]

MINORITIES ISSUE

Another set of issues complicating the evolution of Central Asian republics as nation-states is presented by the ethno-demographic situation.

At the beginning of the modern period of history there were no ethnically homogeneous states in the region comparable, for instance, with the late medieval states of Western Europe. As in many other regions of the world, the trend towards the emergence of such states was hardly present and the existing states were generally multi-ethnic. The Bukhara emirate and the Khiva, Kokand and Tashkent Khanates, not to mention the earlier states, were multi-ethnic formations, and hence the political and ethnic identities of the population did not coincide. As a result, the indigenous population of Central Asia did not associate the state with ethnicity, and it was not by chance that claims for autonomy, which gained some popularity after the Russian revolutions of 1917, were framed exclusively in pan-Turkic or pan-Islamic terms, which in fact stressed the unity of the region. This traditional attitude could certainly facilitate the creation of a single multi-ethnic state in the region. It was after the creation of the Soviet republics along ethnic lines in 1924 that intellectual elites, educated sections of the population, and those groups who became ethnic minorities (e.g. Tajiks in Uzbekistan, Uzbeks in Tajikistan) became increasingly aware of the relationship between ethnicity and state.

The presence of large minorities, often settled in compact areas and in some cases making up to one-third of the population (Uzbeks in Tajikistan, Russians in Kazakhstan) is the most serious obstacle to the success of the nation-state model in several republics of the region and forms a potential source of grave conflict, both within and between particular states. In the process of the formation of nation-states, the interests of dominating majorities and ethnic minorities clash in all important areas – economic, cultural, political, as well as territorial – and can easily lead to the outburst of ethnic conflicts of the respective types.

Socio-economic causes – in the case of Central Asia, principally the fierce competition over the most valuable resources, particularly land, water, and housing – have been examined in numerous reports and are well-known. However, up till the late 1980s no serious attempts were made to examine the ethno-social stratification of the region.

The most characteristic feature of the ethno-social situation in Central Asia is the contrast between the overwhelmingly rural autochthonous population and urban Russian-speaking groups (ethnic Russians, Ukrainians, Tatars and some other groups). In three republics of the region 94 per cent to 97 per cent of ethnic Russians were settled in urban areas, and only in Kazakhstan and Kyrgyzstan was the proportion lower (77 per cent and 70 per cent respectively) owing to agricultural migration since the beginning of the century. The Russian-speaking groups are engaged almost exclusively in skilled jobs in industry, transport and construction, as well as the engineering, medical, and teaching professions. However, in the spheres of culture and administration the share of non-indigenous groups has decreased dramatically during the last few years. The latter development, which broadly corresponds to the general process of indigenization of post-colonial societies, is interpreted as discrimination and emergence of 'ethnocracies', and causes discontent among ethnic Russians. However, generally the existing division of labour and ethno-social stratification does not make competition for jobs the principal source of discord between the European and indigenous populations. Rather, on the contrary, the repatriation of ethnic Russians will inevitably lead to the close-down of many industries, as has already happened in Tajikistan, and this prospect causes problems for the administration of the Central Asian states, especially in Kazakhstan and Kyrgyzstan.[10] The situation is likely to change if in the course of economic reform, industries (and land in Kazakhstan and Kyrgyzstan) are transferred to private owners, and most of the industrial sector passes into the hands of ethnic Russians. The fear that the emerging class of 'Russian capitalists' will dominate the economy of the newly independent states is obviously one explanation for the conservative economic policies of the Central Asian regimes.

At present, the most likely source of ethno-social conflicts is the problem of land in ethnically mixed areas, especially in the Fergana valley. Violent conflicts of this kind occurred in the late 1980s, and the issues which caused them either have not been resolved or have been managed in a way which set a bad precedent: the Meskhi Turks, after mass riots and killings in Uzbekistan in 1989, have been simply resettled in Russia. Still, ethno-social conflicts, as a rule, are local affairs and can be resolved if the economic situation improves.

In a long-term perspective, ethno-territorial conflicts, generally preceded by the formation of separatist and irredentist movements, pose a greater threat for the states of the region. The territorial reorganizations of 1924–1936 had as one of their consequences the partition of the Fergana valley, which since ancient times has been the geopolitical, cultural, and economic core of the whole region. In the process, some three-quarters of the Tajik ethnic area, including the principal cultural centres of Samarkand and Bukhara, was transferred to Uzbekistan. The ethno-demographic balance in Kazakhstan changed significantly after the Semipalatinsk and Akmolinsk oblasts (regions), with their predominantly Russian population, were attached to Kazakhstan in 1922. After numerous reorganizations, the political map of the region has turned into a jigsaw puzzle: on the territory of Kyrgyzstan there are three enclaves belonging to Uzbekistan, and two more forming part of Tajikistan; the communication lines between the southern and northern regions of Tajikistan, Turkmenistan and Kyrgyzstan cross the territory of Uzbekistan, while the railway between Khoresm and Bukhara is for the most part located on the territory of Turkmenistan.

Since during the Soviet period the boundaries between republics had basically administrative importance, the population of many peripheral regions gravitated rather towards the regional industrial centres in the neighbouring republic than towards the far-off capital of their own 'state'. In those fairly numerous cases where such a periphery is inhabited by ethnic minorities, there is a potential threat of separatist or irredentist movements, unless the regime exercises a quasi-totalitarian control over the situation. Since all present international frontiers and boundaries of ethnic areas differ widely, any territorial conflict can produce a domino effect and explode the situation in the region. This is the principal reason why the presidents of all these republics stress that the existing borders should be inviolable and suppress any groups which insist on the revision of the political map of the region.[11] Except for cases of civil war (as in Tajikistan) or the specific case of Kazakhstan, the present regimes in Uzbekistan, Kyrgyzstan and Turkmenistan can feel fairly sure about their territorial integrity. But the problem of integration of compactly settled ethnic minorities remains a serious challenge to their nation-building strategies.

In Central Asia, as in all cases of nation-building, a major issue is the historical memory of the majorities and minorities. Historical memory as a set of ethnic stereotypes, self-images and popular ideas about past ethnic relations has its own inertia and changes rather slowly under the impact of indoctrination and socio-political developments.

The historical memory of both the autochthonous and non-indigenous communities of Central Asia contains a significant block of ideas, myths and images which adversely affect inter-ethnic relations in the region and the process of national integration. In each republic there are historical cleavages along different lines: between traditionally sedentary and nomadic groups, between core and periphery, between the peoples with strong Islamic traditions (Tajiks, Uzbeks) and less Islamized ones (Kazakhs, Kyrgyzs), between Persian-speaking and Turkic groups, and so on. The debates concerning the 'original' rights of some group to its present territory, the ethnic aspects of ancient and medieval states, the ethnic affinities of great personalities of the past and conflicting claims to cultural heritage are common, and (as the experience of other multi-ethnic countries shows) can be easily moved from academic journals into the mass media and become an extra cause of inter-ethnic animosities.

However, at present the principal issue of historical memory in the region is the cleavage between the titular nationalities and the Russian population. Soviet historiography since World War II invariably stressed the progressive consequences of allegedly peaceful and voluntary incorporation of the region into the Russian Empire, viz., the introduction of more advanced cultivation and technology, the creation of prerequisites for the transition from a feudal system to capitalism, the development of communications, the introduction of law and order and, curiously, the opportunity to take part in the revolutionary struggle of the Russian proletariat.[12] Due to the absence of special studies, it is difficult to judge how far this propagandistic version of history affected the historical memory of the present generation of the peoples of Central Asia. However, indirect evidence, casual observations and some latest publications show that the impact was not very strong. Except for the northern regions of modern Kazakhstan, the annexation was anything but voluntary, and took place relatively recently in the middle of the 19th century.[13] Although the annexation stimulated the economic development of the region and put an end to internal warfare, the colonial modernization of Central Asia was still very slow and superficial and in any case its impact was humble compared to, for instance, the consequences of British rule in neighbouring India.[14]

Despite prevailing opinions to the contrary, contacts between the indigenous groups and the European population in Central Asia did not produce much of mutual accommodation. The earlier Slav peasants who settled in Turkestan before World War I adopted some of the local techniques, mainly irrigation practice, but hardly anything more. The adaptation was basically one-way traffic and meant in practice the Russian acculturation, especially the adoption of the Russian language and some urban life habits of the Russians, of the natives. Social, religious, civilizational and racial differences combined to prevent genuine sociocultural integration and the emergence of civil society. The differences rather increased during the Soviet period with the massive settlement of skilled Russian workers and technical personnel as industries developed in larger cities. The ethno-social stratification pattern tended to reinforce the idea of the 'civilizing mission' and the superiority of Russians over the indigenous population.[15] The dissolution of the USSR and the reduction of the Russian Diaspora to the status of a minority could neither change the traditional attitudes, nor make the European population welcome the idea of the nation-state.

Historical memory and culture define to a large extent the external orientation of particular ethnic groups. In the case of ethnic Russians, they tend to identify with Russia, rather than the newly independent states, as their homeland. According to some researchers, 'psychologically Russians at present hardly identify themselves as citizens of the new states' and, unlike in the Ukraine, Belarus, or the Baltic states, most of them – especially those who have a chance to settle in Russia and the younger population – intend to leave the region.[16] However, the differences between Russian settlers in particular republics need to be noted: very few Russians remained in Tajikistan owing to the ongoing civil war, while repatriation from predominantly Russian regions of northern Kazakhstan has been so far relatively insignificant.

On their part, the local history-writing and mass media lay stress on the negative consequences of the incorporation, aggressive and oppressive policies of the Russian empire in the region. This is especially the case in Kazakhstan, which became part of Russia several centuries earlier than the rest of Central Asia and was an area of intensive colonization by Russian settlers.[17] To the consternation of many Russians, almost all towns founded by Russian settlers in Kazakhstan, including Petropavlovsk, have been given new Kazakh names, the streets have been renamed, and the symbolically important monument to Yermak, the conqueror of Siberia, has been demolished.[18]

Thus, there is a wide sociocultural and psychological gap between the indigenous titular nationalities and ethnic Russians. The Kazakh social scientists A. Akhmedjanov and A. Sultangaliyeva write about the differences: 'While sharing a number of common features, they [Kazakhs and Russians in this case] have different social and demographic structures, religion and political culture. These differences of their evolution, reinforced by the topological cleavage of the two ethno-systems, are shaped originally by civilizational divergence'.[19]

It is this difference which makes the success of national integration and the emergence of civil society as a principal feature of the nation-state highly problematic. So far there is no precedent of an integrated society comprising an Asian Muslim majority and a European minority, and it is unlikely that Central Asia can be an exception. Actually the dilemma for ethnic Russians in Central Asia is either to leave for Russia, or to mobilize themselves politically and strive for the political institutionalization of ethnic heterogeneity. Both choices are difficult. Repatriation is complicated because most of the Central Asian Russians were born in the region or have lived there for decades, and cannot easily find a place for themselves in Russia, especially under the present conditions of economic crisis and rising unemployment. On the other hand, the authoritarian regimes of the Central Asian states (with certain reservations concerning Kyrgyzstan) hardly permit voicing any collective claims.

The situation in particular republics is very different. In Uzbekistan and Turkmenistan any political movements and organizations which do not profess loyalty to the regime are actually outlawed, and the Uzbek authorities on several occasions have taken action against participants in the human rights movement even beyond the borders of the republic. With the civil war going on in Tajikistan, the majority of Russians have fled the republic. Several hundred thousand Russians, mostly young people, have moved to Russia from the remaining republics, too. As a consequence, repatriation increases the rate of demographic change in favour of the titular nationalities and in this sense facilitates the formation of nation-states in the region.

THE CASE OF KAZAKHSTAN

One major exception is Kazakhstan. Although the Kazakh demographers predict that in some two decades the Kazakh share will reach two-thirds of the total population, at present the two major ethnic communities are about equal.[20] Unlike other republics, where Russians are settled dispersedly in industrial centres and large cities, in Kazakhstan they are heavily concentrated and form a majority in northern regions of the country and the capital, Almaty. There are several more important circumstances that make the case of Kazakhstan particularly complicated and create a potentially explosive situation.

Geographically closer to Russia, the area came under Russian influence several centuries ago, or much earlier than the predecessors of other modern Central Asian states. Actually, the northern part, the homeland of the Junior zhuz, accepted Russian suzerainty after the devastating Dzungar invasions in the early 18th century. In the course of Russian expansion to the south a number of Russian forts were built: Guryev (1640), Semipalatinsk (1718), Ust-Kamenogorsk (1720), Orenburg (1745), and Verny (modern Almaty, 1854). All these forts were manned mostly by troops of the Siberian and Semirechye Cossack formations, and the whole border was transformed into fortified 'lines'. The Kazakh tribes, (called Kyrgyzs until as late as the 1920s), were predominantly nomadic; the vast grazing grounds they owned were declared state property by the Czarist government and distributed among Cossacks and (since the late 19th century) among peasant settlers from the European part of the empire following the official policies of colonization.

Hence, it is natural that a large section of Russians, who have lived there for several generations, regard the steppes of northern Kazakhstan as their homeland, while Kazakhs interpret the growth of Russian settlements and the alienation of lands in their favour as colonization in its worst form. Despite the Russian acculturation of a section of Kazakhs, the relations between the two communities grew increasingly strained under the Czarist regime. The uprising of 1916, initially caused by the enlistment of Kazakhs to help the war effort, led to violent conflicts and was ruthlessly suppressed by the government troops and Cossacks.

During the Soviet period, in the course of collectivization, mass famine and migration of Kazakhs to China reduced their number by half, and only in the 1960s, despite the high fertility rate, did the number of Kazakhs reach the level of 1926. Of the titular nationalities of the Union republics, including Belarus, who had been badly decimated during World War II, the Kazakhs suffered the heaviest loss of the population. During the last few decades the Kazakhs were still a small minority in the cities, including Almaty, and the process of linguistic assimilation was in full swing, as only some 40 per cent of Kazakhs could speak their mother tongue fluently. Many intellectuals were increasingly worried also by the damage caused by nuclear explosions at the Semipalatinsk testing grounds. Gorbachev's decision to replace Dinmukhamed Kunayev, the First Secretary of the Communist Party of Kazakhstan since 1960, by a Russian, Gennady Kolbin, in December 1986 led to the first open outburst of discontent which became a regular feature of the Soviet Union in the late 1980s.

Thus culture, language, historical memory, and social structure combine to draw a sharp line between the industrial, urbanized and Russian-populated North and the predominantly rural Kazakh regions of the South. Unlike in other republics of the region, the Russians are in a position to challenge the regime and its strategy of building a Kazakh nation-state. What they lack is an umbrella political organization. In Kazakhstan, the danger of ethno-political polarization is one of the major reasons for the regime to curb the proliferation and activities of political, especially nationalist, movements and organizations.[21]

Some of them have been denied official recognition, others are under permanent surveillance and pressure, especially if they raise demands for the unification of northern regions of Kazakhstan with Russia, much in line with the idea of Solzhenitsyn,[22] or the creation of an autonomous Russian republic within Kazakhstan. The major Russian organizations are the Congress of Russian Communities, and the Lad Movement, based mostly in northern regions. Neither of them raises separatist claims, and both concentrate their efforts on achieving decentralization, recognition of the official status of the Russian language and dual citizenship for Russian-speaking groups.

Among formal institutions, the City Soviet of Ust-Kamenogorsk has become the main centre of resistance to the nation-building strategies of the regime. In 1990 it demanded amendments of the Languages Act and changes in the Declaration of Sovereignty of Kazakhstan, proclaiming that if these demands were rejected, the region would insist on territorial autonomy on the basis of the existing law of the USSR.[23] However, acceptance even of the latter moderate demands would bury the idea of the Kazakh nation-state and adoption of the Belgian or Canadian model. Even before the dissolution of the USSR, the government of Kazakhstan clearly showed its preference for the nation-state model by adopting the Languages Act, which proclaimed in September 1989 Kazakh as the state language and accorded Russian a legally obscure status of 'language of inter-ethnic communications'.[24] At the same time President Nazarbayev attempted to play down the trend of Kazakhization and tried to strike some balance between incompatible ethno-political claims. It was not accidental that Kazakhstan was the last among the Soviet republics to declare independence: while almost all proclaimed immediately after the failure of the August 1991 coup, Kazakhstan adopted a similar act on December 16, a week after the dissolution of the USSR was sealed by the leaders of Russia, Ukraine and Belarus.

At present, it is the Cossack Movement which is regarded by the government as potentially the most dangerous force threatening the unity of Kazakhstan. The joint meeting of the Cossacks of Siberia and Kazakhstan, held in Omsk in early 1994, proclaimed the merger of the two Cossack unions into a Siberian Cossack Force. The Cossack organizations are not recognized officially, and their leaders have been arrested on numerous occasions, especially after Cossack demonstrations in several northern cities and Almaty in November 1994, when they demanded that Kazakhstan join Russia.[25]

Despite efforts of the regime and moderate Russian organizations, the process of ethno-political polarization is going on. Many Russians either do not feel secure, or have serious doubts about their future life in the republic. Many are leaving for Russia. According to the available data, the number of persons who left Kazakhstan increased from 23,600 in 1988 to 306,000 in 1991 and over 400,000 in 1994 (however, these figures include a large share of Volga Germans, deported to Kazakhstan in 1941), and according to the opinion poll by the Hiller Institute, 44.7 per cent of non-Kazakhs would prefer to emigrate.[26] It can be expected that in a few years Kazakhs will constitute an absolute majority of the population, and the trend of ethnic homogenization is likely to grow.

The establishment is looking for different ways to ensure both the territorial integrity of Kazakhstan and the success of its strategies of building a nation-state. President Nazarbayev, speaking at the General Assembly in October 1992, insisted that the rights of ethnic minorities should be clearly defined because, owing to the absence of clear criteria, their right to self-determination is used to challenge the territorial integrity of the existing states. Similarly, his proposal, later approved by the Supreme Soviet, to shift the capital to Akmola in the north of the republic is largely intended to thwart the separatist aspirations of the northern periphery. Another tactic of the regime is to contain as far as possible the growth of militant nationalism, both Russian and Kazakh. This can be achieved only if Kazakhstan manages to maintain close relations with both Russia and its Central Asian neighbours, so that both Russian and Kazakh sections of the population can be convinced that their external orientation is taken into account and the process of ethno-political polarization is slowed down. Along with economic calculations, this is a major reason why President Nursultan Nazarbayev supported the consolidation of the CIS into some kind of a confederation and later proposed the idea of a Eurasian Union with supranational legislative and executive bodies, a proposal which did not find much positive response outside Kazakhstan and was not supported even by some high-ranking Kazakh officials. The ethno-demographic situation and ethno-political situation considered, it seems that only a regime of an authoritarian type able to impose compromise solutions and contain the growth of incompatible ethno-regional claims can avoid the threat of ethnic war in the republic.

CONCLUSIONS

1. As in all post-Soviet republics, since 1989–90 the regimes in Central Asia have opted for the model of nation-states wherein the language and

culture of the titular ethno-nation perform normative functions for all groups. However, this strategy, modelled after relatively homogeneous old nation-states and being a reaction to the Soviet policy of nation-building, does not take into account the ethno-demographic structure of, and the ethno-political situation in the newly independent states of the region.

2. One major obstacle to the consolidation of nation-states in the region is the sub-ethnic fragmentation of the titular nationalities, composed generally of diverse ethno-regional segments with a strong sense of identity, and inadequate development of ethno-national languages and cultures to meet all the requirements of the modern society. As in the post-colonial societies of other countries in Asia and Africa, the modern sectors, including government offices, university-level education, industries and much urban activity, have been shaped under the strong influence of the 'imperial' culture and used a foreign (Russian in this case) language as the principal means of communication in modern spheres of social life. Except for Uzbekistan, the indigenous cultural infrastructure is not sufficiently developed to replace the Russian language and urban culture in their normative capacity.

3. Urban ethnic minorities, generally unfamiliar with local languages, traditions and history, are not psychologically ready to accept the shift of cultural norms and perceive the nation-building strategies of the present regimes in terms of discrimination, violation of human rights, and emergence of 'ethnocracies'. This is particularly so in the case of numerous Russian Diasporas, which cannot accept the nation-state policies due to the deep civilizational cleavage, traditional attitudes, the proximity of Russia and the lack of adequate social rewards.

4. The relatively high share of non-titular minorities, their territorial distribution, and the existing pattern of ethnic stratification do not favour the emergence of national unity and perception of common national interests. On the contrary, virtually from any point of view ethnic cleavages tend to reinforce each other and provide grounds for the political mobilization of minorities on the platform of ethnic nationalism. Under the conditions of political liberalization this leads inevitably to the emergence of demands for autonomy, revision of the present state boundaries and separatism, which together contribute to destabilizing the political situation in the whole region.

5. Hence, regimes of the authoritarian type remain the only effective instrument to prevent ethno-political polarization and instability in the region. Along with the absence of democratic traditions and institutions and in the context of the current economic crisis, there seems to be no viable alternative to the authoritarian system of government. Extension of

the president's term up to 2000, however undemocratic from the Western point of view, may actually be the only way to ensure stability in the region and to exercise sufficient control over the ethno-political situation to avoid violent inter-ethnic clashes while the new nation-states are in the making.

NOTES

1. Jackson, Robert H., *Quasi-States: Sovereignty, International Relations, and the Third World*, Cambridge University Press, Cambridge, 1990.
2. Riggs, Fred W., 'Ethno-national Rebellions and Viable Constitutionalism' [unpublished paper, 1994], p. 9.
3. While presenting the draft constitution to the Supreme Soviet of the republic, President Nursultan Nazarbayev of Kazakhstan stressed: 'The departure point of the draft is the idea, unknown in our constitutional practice, of the construction of nation-statehood alongside civil society. In the strategy of development of Kazakhstan I start from the presumption that the nation cannot exist without statehood. In its turn, the disappearance of the nation deprives the existence of the state of any meaning'. See *Kazakhstanskaya pravda*, 2 June 1992
4. Thus, Tajik scholars, including the academician Bobojan Gafurov (1908–1977), who, as the head of the Institute of Oriental Studies in Moscow, held the highest official position in Oriental Studies, spared no effort to prove that the original inhabitants of Central Asia were of Iranian stock. The Uzbek historians, on the contrary, tried to prove the Turkic affinities of the earliest population of the region.
5. In all Central Asian republics, unlike those of the Baltic and Transcaucasian regions, more books were published in Russian than in the languages of the titular nationalities. The respective figures for 1989 are 1261 in Russian and 597 in Kazak for Kazakhstan, 1157 in Russian and 929 in Uzbek for Uzbekistan and as low as 288 in Russian and 363 in Turkmen for Turkmenistan. See *Pechat' v SSSR v 1989 godu*, Moscow: Finansy i statistika, 1990, pp. 144–147. The library collections in vernaculars were from 20 per cent in Kazakhstan to 44 per cent in Uzbekistan. See *Narodnoye obrazovaniye i kul'tura v SSSR, Statisticheskyi sbornik*, Finansy i statistika, Moscow, 1989, p. 274.
6. The linguistic situation was and remains different in particular republics. In Kazakhstan, where according to sociological research about 40 per cent of Kazakhs hardly speak their native language, even the draft constitution was written and published in Russian. The Uzbek and Tajik languages, which had a much longer literary tradition and were more widely used in the modern sector, were more developed to perform the function of official languages.
7. Obviously it is for this reason that President Islam Karimov of Uzbekistan has given up his earlier promises to make Uzbekistan an Islamic state.

8. Vasilyeva, O., *Central Asia: One Year after the Coup*, Gorbachev Foundation, Moscow, 1993 (in Russian), and Kaiser, R. J., 'Ethnic Demography and Interstate Relations in Central Asia', in R. Szporluk (ed.), *National Identity and Ethnicity in Russia and the New States of Eurasia*, M. E. Sharpe, London, 1994, pp. 230–265.
9. The favourable replies varied from 94.6 per cent in Kyrgyzstan to 97.9 per cent in Turkmenistan, compared to 71.3 per cent in the Russian Federation and 82.7 per cent in Belarus. See *Izvestia*, 27 March 1991.
10. The Presidents of Kazakhstan, Kyrgyzstan and Uzbekistan have declared on numerous occasions that they are against the departure of Russians from their republics.
11. The Presidents of Uzbekistan and Kazakhstan, the two largest states of the region, are the most vocal protagonists of the status quo because in the case of any revision of boundaries they have most to lose – since if the principle of ethnic self-determination is applied, they are likely to lose huge tracts of territory to Russia and Tajikistan respectively.
12. It is claimed, for example, 'The accession of non-Russian peoples to the Russian state had a progressive historical importance for their fate. The peoples of the backward periphery of Russia found themselves in a powerful country and established contacts with the peoples who had reached a higher stage of socio-economic and cultural development ... The most important consequence of the annexation to Russia was the involvement of the peripheral peoples in the active struggle, headed in the 19th century by the Russian proletariat, the most revolutionary in the world, against Tsarist autocracy, social and national yoke.' See *Modern Ethnic Processes in the USSR*, Nauka, Moscow, 1977, p. 37.
13. Already in 1991 the anniversaries of annexation and particular battles between the Russian troops and local forces were marked by mass meetings and condemnations of the Russian invasions.
14. Suffice it to mention here that not a single modern college or university was opened, and the vernacular press appeared only after the revolution of 1905, while in India education and the local press developed rapidly.
15. A Russian member of the Supreme Soviet of Kazakhstan admitted that 'we have preserved our great-power and imperial haughtiness, the feeling of superiority and big-brother attitudes, and it will take 40 years more before it disappears.' See *Kazakhstanskaya pravda*, 9 June 1992.
16. Brusina, O., *Russians in Central Asia and Kazakhstan: A National Minority with the Past of the 'Big Brother'*, Institute of Oriental Studies, Institute of Russian History and 'Turan' Agency, Moscow, 1993, p. 317.
17. Moyseyev, V., 'Modern Historiography of Kazakhstan'. See *Nezavisimaya gazeta*, 20 April 1992.
18. *Izvestia*, 26 January 1994.
19. See *Eurasian Space: Potential for Integration and Its Realisation*, Almaty, 1994, p. 103.
20. In 1926, there were 3,717,100 Kazaks, 57 per cent of the total population of the republic, besides 1,280,100 Russians (19.8 per cent), and 861,000 Ukrainians (13.2 per cent). In 1959 the number of Kazaks was 2,787,000

(30 per cent), Russians 3,972 (42.7 per cent), and Ukrainians 761,000 (8.2 per cent).

21. The Supreme Court in November 1992 refused to renew the registration of 'Yedinstvo' (Unity), which practically banned the organization. 'Yedinstvo' was founded in 1990 and raised the demand that the Russian language be granted equal status with the Kazakh.
22. In his widely-publicised essay, Solzhenitsyn stressed the fact that the Kazakhs were concentrated in the southern regions of the republic, and 'in case they want to secede with that area, so God help them'. See Solzhenitsyn, A., 'How Should We Reconstruct Russia?', *Patriot*, Moscow, 1991, p. 6 (in Russian).
23. *Izvestia*, 28 September, 1990.
24. *Kazakhstanskaya pravda*, 28 September 1989.
25. Following the arrests in November 1994, the leaders of the Semirechye Cossacks circulated an appeal to the 'international community', the government of Russia, Russian Cossack forces and political associations and parties of the former Soviet Union to denounce the policies of the establishment towards the Cossacks. See 'The Statement of the Atamans Board of the Semirechye Cossacks'.
26. *Nezavisimaya gazeta*, 31 March 1994.

Part II
The Ethnic Conundrum

4 Ethnic Harmony and Conflicts in Central Asia: Origins and Policies

Gengchen Liu

In ethnic terms, Central Asia constitutes a maze. Both during Czarist times and under Soviet rule, Central Asia was full of sharp ethnic contradictions. Frequent ethnic conflicts and struggles of ethnic minorities first against Russian and then Soviet domination, were an essential part of the history of Central Asia. Since the Central Asian republics declared their independence at the end of 1991, ethnic harmony has been seen as the most fundamental condition for political stability in all five newly independent multi-ethnic Central Asian states. In the last few years, governments of the Central Asian states have all wrestled with problems of ethnic conflicts and ethnic harmony. Policies of various Central Asian states towards ethnic minorities have also attracted worldwide attention, including the attention of one of Central Asia's neighbouring states, China.

This essay looks first at the origins of the ethnic conundrum and ethnic conflicts in Central Asia. It then examines various policies developed by Central Asian states after their independence in handling ethnic relations.

ETHNIC GROUPS IN CENTRAL ASIA: PAST AND PRESENT

The starting point for understanding the Central Asian maze of ethnicity is to observe and analyse the characteristics of Central Asian ethnic groups today. At the risk of oversimplification, what ethnically characterizes the Central Asian states of Kazakhstan, Kyrgyzstan, Tajikistan, Turkmenistan, and Uzbekistan can be summarized as the following:

1. The Composition of Ethnic Groups in All Five Newly Independent Central Asian States is Highly Complicated

All five Central Asian states are multi-ethnic. The number of ethnic groups in any given Central Asian state ranges from several dozen to more than one hundred. Kazakhstan, for example, boasts more than one hundred different ethnic groups. The dominant ethnic groups in Central Asia are the Kazakhs, the Uzbeks, the Kyrgyzs, the Tajiks and the Turkmens. However, the Russians account for a large proportion of the population. In four out of five Central Asian republics, the Russians are effectively the second largest ethnic group. In Kazakhstan, whereas the Kazakhs account for 39.7 per cent of the population, the Russians are closely behind at 37.8 per cent.[1] In Kyrgyzstan, the population consists of more than eighty ethnic groups. The relative percentage of the Kyrgyzs and the Russians is respectively 52.4 per cent and 21.5 per cent. Of all the ethnic groups in Uzbekistan, the Uzbeks form 71.4 per cent. The Russians, at 8.3 per cent are still the second largest ethnic group there. In Turkmenistan, there are 72 per cent of Turkmens and 9.5 per cent of Russian. Only in Tajikistan are the Russians, accounting for 7.6 per cent of the population in 1991, the third largest ethnic group behind the Tajiks and the Uzbeks.

The complicated composition of ethnic groups in the Central Asian population, and, in particular, the high percentage of Russians in Central Asia, are a direct result of the Czarist and the Soviet policies towards ethnic minorities and towards Russian migration to Central Asia.

From 1860 to 1880, Imperial Russia systematically annexed Central Asia with force. After that, not only did Russian merchants swarm into Central Asia but there was also organized migration of Russians into the region. In Northern Kazakhstan, a large number of Russian settlements were set up in the late 19th century. By 1911, more than 1.5 million Russian peasant settlers had found their way into the Kazakh steppes. At the beginning of the twentieth century, the Imperial Russian government started a land reform in Russia, the purpose of which was to foster the interests of rich peasants. A large number of peasants in Russia were forced to sell their land and leave their homes. Some of them wandered into Central Asia. From 1906 to 1910, around 2.5 million Russian peasants moved to Central Asia and other remote areas of Imperial Russia.[2]

After the October Revolution in 1917, political, economic and cultural developments in Central Asia compelled the attention of the Soviet government. In order to eliminate the existing inequality among nationalities in the Soviet Union, the Soviet government decided that it was imperative to help Central Asia develop its economy. In the 1920s, the Soviet government allocated considerable capital to Central Asia for economic construction, and relocated some Russian manufacturing plants to Central Asia. A large number of skilled workers, engineers, technicians, technical experts, teachers and doctors were also dispatched to work in Central Asia at the same time. For example, in the first five-year plan period from 1929 to 1932, more than twenty-five thousand technicians and technical experts were dispatched to Turkmenistan alone.

During the Second World War, more than three hundred large-scale Soviet manufacturing plants were moved lock, stock and barrel to Central Asia. With them came a large number of Russians. At the same time, the German invasion of the Soviet Union forced a large number of Russian residents out of the German-occupied areas in the West of the Soviet Union. Some of them fled into Central Asia. Within two years, from July 1941 to July 1943, more than half a million Russian residents either fled or were evacuated from the western front and other regions and were settled down in Kazakhstan alone.[3] Between the summer and autumn of 1941, Kyrgyzstan also helped 139,000 Russian residents fleeing from the German invasion to settle down in its region. On top of that, from 1941 to 1944, the Soviet government accused the Crimean Tartars and ten other small ethnic groups of 'treason' and 'collusion with the Nazis' and relocated all of these ethnic groups – a total of more than five million people – in Central Asia and Siberia.

In the early 1950s, the Soviet government started a programme of large-scale reclamation of land in Kazakhstan, the so-called Virgin Lands Scheme. For that purpose, the Soviet government mobilized a large number of young volunteers to go to the reclamation area. In the first few years of the Virgin Lands Scheme, about one million people came to work in the Kazakhstan reclamation area. Migration into Central Asia from other parts of the Soviet Union continued unabated after the 1950s. It was reported that from 1959 to 1970, two million people from various parts of the Soviet Union migrated to Central Asia. Of this total, about one million Russians migrated to Kazakhstan.

To summarize briefly, in the last 140 years, both in the Imperial Russian and in Soviet times, streams of migrants have been pushed into Central Asia from various parts of the Russian empire and the former Soviet Union. These migrants have lived and multiplied in the region. The Russians, Belarussians, and Ukrainians comprise a sizeable Slavic population in Central Asia. This most important factor redefines the ethnic frontiers of the population in the region.

2. Religion Further Complicates the Ethnic Frontiers

The ethnic circumstances in Central Asia are further made intricate by religion. Although Islam is dominant in the region, other religions also have considerable followings, largely because of the ethnic mix in Central Asia. The five titular nationalities – the Kazakhs, the Uzbeks, the Kyrgyzs, the Turkmens and the Tajiks, as well as the Tartars and the Uighurs – are Muslims. Among the Muslims, however, there is sectarian strife. The confrontation between revolutionary Muslim elements and Islamic fundamentalism is a good example of this conflict. Of the minor religions in the region, Orthodox Christianity has many adherents among the Russians, the Belarussians and the Ukrainians. Christianity finds many disciples among the Germans and Buddhism among the Koreans. In Kazakhstan, for example, in addition to 60 per cent of Muslims, there are the Orthodox, the Protestants, the Catholics and the Buddhists. Potentially, religion is a divisive issue in the relationship between ethnic groups.[4]

The importance of religion in the development of relationships between ethnic groups in the region is underlined by the rising influence of Islam in the political, economic and social life of the newly independent states of Central Asia in recent years. Take Tajikistan and Uzbekistan as examples. In 1989, Tajikistan had only 70 mosques. In 1992, less than one year after its declared independence, a phenomenal growth to 2870 was reported.[5] In 1989, Uzbekistan had around 300 mosques. By 1993, it had more than 5000. Most of the mosques were built with financial assistance from Saudi Arabia, Iran, Pakistan and Afghanistan.[6] It is interesting to note that in both Tajikistan and Uzbekistan, where the influence of Islam increased rapidly, Islamic fundamentalism has also taken root. In particular, in Tajikistan the Islamic Revival Party (IRP) is the major component of the opposition to the existing government.

3. The History of Central Asia is Characterized by Ethnic Tensions and Frequent Ethnic Revolts

Before the declared independence of the Central Asian republics in 1991, Central Asia had been a place where ethnic conflicts and struggles of ethnic minorities against Russian domination had been unfolding. This is true both for Czarist Russia and for Soviet times.

From the beginning of the 18th century to the 1870s, Imperial Russia resorted to brutal force and systematically conquered Central Asia. With the arrival of the Russians as conquerors came the actual colonization of Central Asia. It has often been argued by Soviet and Russian scholars that Russian colonization and the Soviet system brought advanced civilization, science and technology to Central Asia and helped develop the economy and culture in the region. While there may be some truth in this argument, it cannot be denied that Russian colonization and the Soviet domination of Central Asia did make Central Asia virtually a 'prison for minority ethnic groups'.

Already in Czarist Russia, there had been ethnic revolts against Russian political oppression, economic exploitation, and cultural enslavery in Central Asia. In the second half of the 19th century, the Kazakhs, for example, had waged constant revolts against the Russian colonization.[7] In 1875 there was a large-scale revolt against the Russian colonial authorities in Uzbekistan. The Turkmen tribes also put up strong and bloody resistance against Russian rule.

The First World War accentuated the ethnic tensions in Central Asia. As part of the Russian empire, Central Asia shared the burden and the toll of Russia's participation in the war. On the other hand, the war significantly weakened the Czar's control of Central Asia, which was far from the war front. Ethnic tensions quickly exploded into a full-scale uprising against the Czarist rule. In July 1916, anti-Russian rebellion started in the Fergana Valley in Uzbekistan against the Czar's conscription orders. This was followed by major anti-Russian revolts by the Kazakhs and the Kyrgyzs in Kazakhstan. The Central Asian uprisings were not completely crushed by the Czar until February 1917. It was estimated that 150,000 people were killed in the uprisings.

In Soviet times, there were no large-scale ethnic uprisings as had been seen in Czarist Russia. However, ethnic tensions persisted and took on new dimensions. Stalin's mapmakers divided Central Asia into what are the presently known republics in the 1920s and did not take into consideration the ethnic frontiers of the time. Stalin's purges in the 1930s did not spare the nationalist leaders of Central Asia, who joined the Bolsheviks in Lenin's time. Indeed, Stalin used the purge to get rid of those leaders he believed to be nationalistic. Stalin also used Central Asia as an ethnic dumping ground. As discussed before, some minority groups were forcibly relocated *in toto* in Central Asia. On top of that, Northern Kazakhstan continued to see streams of Russians settling in the region to relieve the population pressure in Russia. As the Soviet government relocated and built large-scale manufacturing plants in the Central Asian republics, a large number of Russians came to take residence in urban centres and take up the best jobs in the area.

Khrushchev's policy of giving limited economic planning autonomy to the Soviet republics and of promoting local cadres in the late 1950s and the early 1960s had only a very limited effect in Central Asia. Brezhnev reversed Khrushchev's policy and recentralized economic decision-making. The continued efforts to make a 'Soviet man' did not alleviate the tensions between the Russians and other ethnic groups, but aggravated the resentment of ethnic minorities against the Russification of their culture and their political and economic life.

At the end of April 1969, ethnic rioting between the Russians and the Uzbeks broke out in Tashkent, the capital of Uzbekistan, during a football game. Fifteen Russians were killed in the riot. This was followed by a large-scale demonstration by the Uzbeks, demanding that 'Russians get out of Uzbekistan'. The Soviet government used the army to break up the demonstration and 150 people were arrested. In December of the same year, the second secretary of the Central Committee of the Turkmenistan Communist Party (TCP), a Russian, was forced to resign because of the strong resentment of Turkmens against alleged Russian chauvinism in his policies.

This resentment against the Russification of Central Asia also found expression in the teaching of Russian in Central Asian republics. One report by the Uzbek government and the Central Committee of the Uzbek Communist Party (UCP) on 18 May 1965 revealed that many teachers and lecturers in the schools and the higher educational institutions 'refused to carry out' the government decision to improve the teaching of the Russian language, and were reluctant to teach students to speak and write proper Russian. On 28 January 1973, the Soviet Kyrgyz Newspaper reported that a prominent Kyrgyz scholar had voiced the criticism that the Kyrgyz language had too many 'foreign terms' [i.e. Russian terms]. He openly advocated that the Kyrgyz language 'must make some fundamental improvement' and the Kyrgyz people must 'struggle to keep the integrity of their language'.

Protests against the Soviet government under Khrushchev and Brezhnev to change at will the borders of the Central Asian republics to 'strengthen production specialization' were also voiced strongly. In 1972, for example, in Kyrgyzstan, a Krygyz professor strongly argued in the newspaper that 'any changes of the already strictly demarcated borders between the republics enforced against the peoples involved should be regarded as annexation and aggression. It is the rape of the principle of national self-determination'.[8]

In the Gorbachev period, with the onset of *perestroika*, ethnic tensions in Central Asia, especially in the two larger republics of Kazakhstan and Uzbekistan, threatened to explode. There were increasing protests against Russian domination and frequent incidents of ethnic conflicts. In December 1986, Moscow charged Kunayev, an ethnic Kazakh, with corruption, and replaced him with Kolbin, an ethnic Russian, as the First Secretary of the Kazakh Community Party. The Kunayev-Kolbin change caused strong resentment among the Kazakhs and sparked off the so-called 'Almaty Incident'. Thousands of people took to the street and demonstrated, shouting 'Russians go back to Russia!', 'Kolbin go back to Russia!', 'Kazakhstan for the Kazakhs'. In the two-day unrest, thirty people were killed and hundreds were wounded. In 1989, there were more protests from Central Asian republics. The Kyrgyz leaders complained that only a small percentage of their republic's skilled workers were local people and the Kazakh leaders claimed that the use of Kazakhstan as the testing ground for nuclear weapons was destroying the economy and the environment of the region. On the other hand, ethnic riots became more frequent. In mid-June 1989, ethnic fighting broke out between the Kazakhs and the Cossacks in Kazakhstan. Three were killed and many were injured. Also in late May and early June of 1989, a riot flared up in Kussvi and Tashlak of Fergana between the Uzbeks and the Meskhetian Turks who had been forcibly relocated to Central Asia during the Second World War. The riot quickly spread to the whole of the Fergana Valley; about one hundred people were killed and thousands were injured. In mid-July 1989, in Isfara in Tajikstan, ethnic conflict broke out between the Tajiks and the Kyrgyzs over their disputes over land and water. Thousands were involved. In June 1990, there was a bloody conflict between the Kyrgyzs and the Uzbeks in Osh in Kyrgyzstan in fighting over a piece of land for building houses. Forty people were killed and more than two hundred were wounded in the ethnic violence. In the Gorbachev period, the Crimeans and the Tartars in Central Asia also staged frequent petitions, demonstrations and gatherings, demanding self-rule and return to their homeland. The largest such gatherings were attended by several thousand people.

4. The Presence of a Large Proportion of the Russian Population Remains a Major Problem in Ethnic Relations in Central Asian States

Boris Yeltsin's decision to dissolve the Soviet Union left thousands of Russians in the lurch in Central Asia. With the declared independence of the Central Asian republics, the Russians suddenly found themselves a minority in the multi-ethnic new states of Central Asia. According to the 1990 statistics, there were at the time 9.7 million Russians in the Central Asian republics. In Soviet times, the Russians in Central Asia usually enjoyed many privileges: they occupied important positions in the government and had better jobs in enterprises. The break-up of the former Soviet Union and the independence of the Central Asian republics changed the political and social settings for the Russians in Central Asia. The titular nationalities in Central Asia began to assert themselves and the Russians, now a minority, began to lose the privileges they had previously enjoyed politically, socially and economically. Many Russians felt that they were suddenly reduced to the status of second-class citizens. The legacy of ethnic tensions in the Soviet times, combined with the present plight of the Russians in Central Asia, forms the undercurrent of ethnic confrontation in Central Asian states.

The confrontations between the Russians and the major ethnic groups in Central Asian states have been most clearly visible in Kazakhstan, where 70 per cent of the Russians in Central Asia live. There were reports of ethnic riots between the Russians and the Kazaks. The Russians also found it necessary to set up their own organizations to safeguard their interests. In Kazakhstan, members of the United Movement for Ethnic Harmony are mostly Russians. They are mainly opposed to the 'Kazakhization' of Kazakhstan. They have also demanded that the Russian language should have equal status with the Kazakh language. Largely as a result of ethnic confrontations and ethnic tensions, a large number of Russians have left the Central Asian states, although many of them could not hope to have the same standard of living in Russia as they had enjoyed in Central Asia. According to statistics provided by the media of Kazakhstan in 1992 more than 175,000 Russians left Kazakhstan and again in 1993, another 170,000 Russians opted to migrate out of Kazakhstan. It has been openly admitted that such a large-scale emigration of Russians from Kazakhstan has a lot to do with 'ethnic tensions and relations' in Kazakhstan.[9]

The Russians have also left other Central Asian republics. In 1992 alone, more than 70 per cent of the Russian population in Tajikistan left for other CIS states because of the civil war and ethnic tensions. Uzbekistan, Kyrgyzstan and Turkmenistan also saw large-scale emigration of their Russian population in 1992. Because most of these Russians are engineers, skilled workers and teachers, their leaving Central Asia not only exacerbated tensions and confrontations between ethnic groups but also deprived Central Asian states of the expertise most needed for economic and cultural development after independence.

ETHNIC POLICIES OF NEW CENTRAL ASIAN STATES

The highly complicated ethnic composition and the potential for ethnic strife in Central Asia were very much on the mind of leaders of the Central Asian states at and after independence. These leaders clearly realized that political and social stability and the efforts at nation-building of their newly independent states depended on whether they could properly handle the Soviet legacy of inter-ethnic conflict and deal effectively with new problems in relationships between ethnic groups. Since their independence, all five Central Asian states have taken various measures to implement their ethnic policies to strive for ethnic harmony. The following aspects are the main thrusts of their policies.

Firstly, all leaders in Central Asian states attach great importance to ethnic unity and harmony in their nation-building efforts. Kazakhstan's

President Nazarbayev, for example, has repeatedly emphasized on various occasions that ethnic harmony is vital for Kazakhstan's political, economic and social development as an independent state. He claimed in 1993 that 'the major asset of the Republic is harmony and stability. Only by common efforts can we keep and strengthen this asset'. He also warned that 'whoever tries to stir up discord and disharmony between the Kazakhs and the Russians will be the common enemy of the two nationalities'.[10] In his 1995 New Year message, Nazarbayev asserted that it was an indisputable achievement of his government that harmony among various ethnic groups and political stability were maintained throughout Kazakhstan in 1994. Kazakhstan has initiated tough laws to punish those who are believed to have stirred up inter-ethnic enmities.

In Kyrgyzstan, President Akayev and his government stressed that the unity of all nationalities was of the first importance in the nation-building efforts of Kyrgyzstan. Without ethnic harmony, it would be impossible for the country to make any progress in social and economic development. On 12 November 1994, Akayev pointed out strongly that the policy of prime importance for his government was to 'strengthen the ethnic harmony', because without that, 'our democratic reforms would not advance a single step'.[11] Akayev's government therefore maintained that every ethnic group constituted an integral part of the whole of the people of the Kyrgyz Republic. In Uzbekistan, President Karimov's government has also frequently called for reconciliations among ethnic groups. Even in Turkmenistan, which has enjoyed relative political stability, President Niyazov has emphasized the importance of ethnic harmony and unity in support of the efforts by his government in nation-building.

Secondly, some republics have established special institutions in their endeavour to build and sustain the harmony between ethnic groups. Kazakhstan and Kyrgyzstan are two good examples. Kazakhstan's President Nazarbayev proposed, for example, that a national congress of national unity and ethnic harmony be convened every two years to discuss questions and concerns in ethnic relations. On 14 December 1994, a national congress of all nationalities of Kazakhstan was convened in Almaty. The Congress called for the unity of all nationalities in Kazakhstan. The Congress also adopted President Nazarbayev's proposition. On 15 December 1994, the 'National Congress of Unity and Harmony of All Nationalities of Kazakhstan' was established. Representatives to the Congress were from various walks of life, from all nationalities, and from a number of religious organizations. It professed to be an unofficial and non-political organization. The Committees attached to the Congress include the Committee for Ethnic Harmony and the Committee for Religious Co-operation. The proclaimed aim of the

Congress was to strive for ethnic harmony and equality of all nationalities in Kazakhstan in social, economic and political affairs. In March 1995, Nazarbayev indicated that Kazakhstan would initiate programmes to encourage its citizens to learn and master two or more languages spoken in the Republic.[12]

In Kyrgyzstan, under the leadership of President Akayev, a policy for ethnic harmony was made part of the government's drive for the political stability of the republic. For that purpose, more than forty cultural centres of nationalities were opened. There were also a number of associations aimed at protecting the interests of different ethnic groups in Kyrgyzstan. Most important, perhaps, are two organizations: the Committee for Citizen's Amity and Ethnic Harmony of Kyrgyzstan and the Social and Political Consultation Committee of the Kyrgyzstan Republic, which is directly under the President. The main functions of these bodies are to listen to and to consider the concerns of all nationalities, to co-ordinate the interests of ethnic groups and to help the government solve problems in ethnic relations.

Thirdly, all Central Asian republics have made provision in their new constitutions for the protection of ethnic groups. In the new constitutions of all five Central Asian republics, it is stipulated that citizens are equal before the law. No one should be discriminated against because of his/her birth, sex, race, nationality, language, religion, or political beliefs. The new constitutions also provide the basic protection of universal human rights. Some Central Asian states – for example, Kyrgyzstan – have also promulgated by-laws to protect the interests of minorities in those countries.

Fourthly, the governments of all Central Asian states have taken strict measures to limit the development of extreme nationalist organizations. The rise of extreme nationalism and related organizations spread quickly after the independence of five Central Asian republics. This is perceived as detrimental to national unity and ethnic harmony in Central Asia by the Central Asian governments. In the last few years, restricting the growth of these organizations has been part of the policies adopted by Central Asian governments for encouraging the unity of nationalities. In the Constitution of Kyrgyzstan, it is clearly stipulated that 'any actions to preach and to stir up hostility between different nationalities are deemed an infringement of the Constitution.'[13]

Central Asian governments have also prohibited some extreme nationalist organizations from registration, thus denying the legalization of their activities. The Alash in Kazakhstan, for example, was established in 1990. It is, however, still not yet permitted to be registered by the Ministry of Justice of the Kazakhstan government at the time of writing, as it is an extreme nationalist organization. It openly advocates that the Kazakhs are the 'masters' of Kazakhstan and that only the Kazakh language should be the national language in Kazakhstan. It puts Pan-Turkism, Islam and democracy together as its political platform and promotes the restoration of the Turkish and the Islamic traditions in Central Asia. It also calls for the establishment of a 'Greater Turkestan' encompassing the area from Istanbul to Vladivostok. It is opposed to the participation of Russians in the politics and the government of Kazakhstan and advocates restricting the use of the Russian language and severing relations with Russia.

Fifthly, all Central Asian states are resolutely opposed to Islamic fundamentalism. Religion plays an important role in political, economic and social life in Central Asia. After independence, the revival of Islam and other religions in Central Asia has gathered momentum. While all constitutions of the Central Asian states have provisions to guarantee the freedom of religious beliefs of their own peoples, they also stipulate that Central Asian states are to be 'democratic and secular states'. Religions and religious activities must be separated from state affairs. No political parties based solely on religious beliefs should be allowed to be established. Religious organizations should not pursue political goals and should not interfere with state affairs.

Islamic fundamentalism promotes a completely different principle in state-building. It advocates the establishment of a state which integrates religion with politics. It promotes the revival of all Islamic traditions. For these reasons, Islamic fundamentalism has been seen as the most dangerous threat to the secular status of all Central Asian states. The Islamic Revival Party (IRP) in Uzbekistan, for example, strongly advocates the establishment of an Islamic republic in Uzbekistan, and demands that the Koran be the guide in national politics and the daily life of the people. For that reason, the IRP has been prohibited from registration by the government and in effect has been outlawed. President Rakhamonov has also outlawed the Islamic Revival Party in Tajikistan.

Islamic fundamentalism is also seen by Central Asian leaders as undermining relations between ethnic groups and the political stability of the region. Kazakhstan's President Nazarbayev has promised many times that he will take all necessary steps to 'stop Islamic fundamentalism from rising' in Kazakhstan. He has also said that Kazakhstan has a special responsibility in directing the Central Asian states away from subjection to the influence of Islamic fundamentalism and of Iran. President Akayev of the Kyrgyz Republic has stated that he would do everything he can to stop Islamic fundamentalism from harming the interests of Kyrgyzstan. Niyazov, President of Turkmenistan, has said that he did 'not trust and would take every step to oppose the spread of Islamic fundamentalism' in his country. The Prime Minister of Uzbekistan has pointed out that Islamic fundamentalism is 'incompatible with' the national development in Uzbekistan and its spread should be 'held back'.

Sixthly, Central Asian states have taken steps to improve the relations among themselves and with Russia. This is also part of their effort to strengthen ethnic harmony and political stability. A good example of this is their collective approach to the question of common borders.[14]

The present borders of Central Asian states were largely decided by Stalin in the 1920s to the 1930s and modified by Moscow later with little respect to the ethnic frontiers and economic and social realities of Central Asia. Many ethnic groups live across the borders of these newly independent states. Because of this, the ethnic policies of any one state always have effects beyond its own borders. By the same token, bilateral relations between two states also impinge on ethnic harmony.

The declaration of independence of the Central Asian republics turned overnight the existing borders of these former Soviet republics into borders between independent sovereign states. Border disputes among Central Asian states became a thorny issue in bilateral relations and had implications for regional stability. To maintain stability in Central Asia, a *status quo* policy was strongly advocated by Central Asian leaders. Immediately after the dissolution of the former Soviet Union, Akayev, President of Kyrgyzstan, proposed that an agreement be signed among the Central Asian states on 'maintaining the existing borders and the status quo of the use of land'. Speaking at a press conference in the UN headquarters in May 1992, Nazarbayev of Kazakhstan also maintained that the existing borders between all states of the Commonwealth of Independent States (CIS) should be maintained as a status quo. He emphasized that the inalterability of existing borders was 'the basis of stability' in Central Asia. In February 1995, the three leaders of Kazakhstan, Kyrgyzstan and Uzbekistan reiterated in an agreement that none of them would try to change the status quo of the border demarcation.[15] This status quo policy seems in the last few years to have avoided any serious territorial disputes between Central Asian states. That has helped to foster ethnic harmony in Central Asia, particularly the harmony of ethnic groups which straddle the borders of Central Asian states.

The question of the civil war in Tajikistan is another example of Central Asian states taking a collective approach to regional issues of common concern. After the outbreak of civil war in Tajikistan, the spread of the war across national borders was a major concern for other Central Asian governments. Central Asian leaders have frequently met among themselves and with the Russian leaders in an active effort to seek resolutions. They supported the Russian proposal to establish a peacekeeping force in Tajikistan, and some Central Asian states, notably Kazakhstan and Kyrgyzstan, have participated in the peacekeeping operations.

Relations with Moscow have always been at the top of the foreign policy agenda of all five Central Asian states. There are obvious political and economic reasons. Friendly relations with Moscow are also helpful in promoting ethnic harmony between the Russians and the main ethnic groups in all five Central Asian states. To alleviate the tensions between the Russians and other main nationalities in Central Asia, both the Turkmenistan and the Tajikistan governments have implemented a policy to allow and to recognize dual citizenship for the Russian residents in the two states. That is to say, the Russians can have the nationality of their resident country as well as Russian nationality. In Kyrgyzstan and in Kazakhstan, although pressure from Russia for the two states to recognize dual citizenship of Russian residents in the two countries was resolutely resisted by the two governments, there were also some compromises. In Kyrgyzstan, Bishkek Slav University was established with financial assistance from Russia in accordance with the Kyrgyzstan-Russian Treaty of Friendship and Mutual Assistance of June 1992. The purpose of setting up this university was to alleviate severe problems for the Russian-speaking population to enter higher education institutions in Kyrgyzstan using Russian as the teaching medium after the disintegration of the former Soviet Union. In June 1994, President Akayev issued a decree giving the Russian language the status of an official language in regions where Russians were a majority.[16] In March 1994, at a meeting in Moscow between Yeltsin and Nazarbayev, it was agreed that Russian residents in Kazakhstan and Kazakhs living in the Russian Federation should be allowed to migrate freely to Russia/Kazakhstan. They should automatically obtain the nationality of the country they migrate to.[17]

MAJOR PROBLEMS IN INTER-ETHNIC RELATIONS IN CENTRAL ASIA

While the series of policies implemented by the Central Asian governments to strive for ethnic harmony and political stability (discussed above) have helped stabilize the political situation and mitigate the tensions between ethnic groups, serious problems still exist in inter-ethnic relations in Central Asia. In April 1993, Nazarbayev acknowledged that problems in the relations between the Kazaks and other ethnic groups were 'far from being resolved'.[18] Current inter-ethnic discontent and tensions in Central

Asia are indeed still intense. Three major problems challenge inter-ethnic harmony in Central Asia today.

First, there is the rise of ethno-nationalism in Central Asia. The five titular nationalities – the Kazakhs, the Uzbeks, the Kyrgyzs, the Tajiks and the Turkmens – had once been subjected to the oppression and enslavement of Czarist Russia and lived in an abyss of misery. Soviet policies to promote political and economic development in Central Asia did change the social status and political position of these nationalities. Yet Soviet domination was still overwhelmingly oppressive in nature for these peoples. Soviet nationality policies deprived them of opportunities to advance their cultures and their national identities. With the dissolution of the former Soviet Union and the independence of the Central Asian states, these five main nationalities became the titular nationalities in their respective independent sovereign states. It is perhaps understandable that long-suppressed anti-Russian feelings should have developed in a short period of time into an assertive ethno-nationalism. Excessive assertion of such ethno-nationalism is, however, not conducive to ethnic harmony. It is particularly detrimental to ethnic unity between these ethnic groups and the Russians.

The imposing revival of national culture after the independence of Central Asian states could be seen as an expression of an assertive ethno-nationalism. In Kazakhstan, for example, the spelling of the capital Almaty has been changed from the Russian to the Kazak form. The name of the capital of Kyrgyzstan has also been replaced by a more historical name, Bishkek. The Constitutions of the newly independent Central Asian states all stipulate that the language of the titular nationality is the national language of the respective states. The linguistic transition in Kyrgyzstan sets its timetable for a complete transfer to Kyrgyz by 1997. In September and October 1992, a world conference of Kazakhs and a world conference of Turkmens were convened respectively in Almaty and Ashkhabad to promote the revival of the Kazakh and the Turkmen national cultures in the process of de-Sovietization and de-Russification of Central Asia.

Ethno-nationalism has more telling expressions. There are conscious policies to ensure the dominance of the titular nationalities in the governments of their respective states. In the constitutions of all five Central Asian states, there is a provision that only those citizens who are proficient in the national language can be elected president. The constitution of Turkmenistan even clearly stipulates that only a Turkmen can be elected the Turkmenistan president. At present, the presidents of five Central Asian states are all from their respective titular nationality. In February 1995, of the 78 parlimantarians elected in the first two rounds of elections in Kyrgyzstan, about 90 per cent were Kyrgyz, whereas only six per cent were Russian, although just 52.4 per cent of the total population were Kyrgyz, while the Russians accounted for 20.9 per cent of the total population. In Kazakhstan, the president, the vice-president, the prime minister, the first deputy prime-minister and ministers of national defence, of foreign affairs and of finance, are all Kazakhs, although the Russian population is almost as large as the Kazakh population. In Uzbekistan, President Karimov issued directives to keep Russians out of the important positions of government. Fluency in the national languages of the states concerned has now become a requirement in seeking government jobs in Central Asian states.

The Kazakhstan government has also adopted a policy to welcome Kazakh residents in other countries 'back to the homeland'. It is estimated that there are more than 3.5 million Kazakhs living outside Kazakhstan in 30-odd countries world-wide. In 1992 alone, more than sixty thousand Kazakhs migrated from Mongolia and other CIS states and resettled in Kazakhstan with Kazakhstan government help and subsidies. Such policies certainly have serious ramifications for inter-ethnic relations. Excessive assertion of ethno-nationalism of the titular nationality is at odds with the goal of ethnic harmony.

Second, tensions and conflicts between ethnic groups are exacerbated by the stark disparity in their social and economic conditions. For historical reasons, ethnic groups tend to concentrate in one region of a given Central Asian republic. In both Tajikistan and Kyrgyzstan, there is a clear divide between the North and the South. For example, in Tajikistan, the two economically underdeveloped and impoverished regions, Ghorghan Tepeh in the South and Gorno-Badakhshan in the Southeast, are mostly inhabited by Tajiks. In contrast, in the more industrialized Leninabad in the North, where the living standard is much higher and the economy is more developed, there are a large number of Uzbeks. Most Tajik leaders in Soviet times were from the North. In the Tajik civil war, Ghorghan Tepeh and Gorno-Badakhshan became the base for the rebels of the IRP, whereas Leninabad and Kulyab in the North supported the government. The roots of the Tajik civil war lie as much in socioeconomic conditions as in ethnic tensions.

In Kyrgyzstan, too, there is a clear economic disparity between the North and the South. Whereas the Slavic population is relatively concentrated in the economically more developed North, the economically less developed South is mostly inhabited by Kyrgyzs and Uzbeks. With the transition to a market economy in the last few years, such economic disparity has been further increased rather than bridged. The coincidence of economic disparity with ethnic frontiers complicates inter-ethnic relations in Central Asia, to say the least. By the same token, the development of national economies and the more even distribution of wealth in Central Asian states must be incorporated in their policy for ethnic harmony.

Third, problems in inter-ethnic relationships in Central Asia are compounded by factors and elements beyond Central Asia. The Tajik civil war can be taken as a prime example. Several months after the declared independence of Tajikistan in September 1991, Tajikistan was plunged into a civil war. With the help of Russia and other Central Asian states, the Tajik government forces were able to deal a fatal blow to the IRP and other armed opposition groups in early 1993. In 1994, both sides negotiated agreements for a ceasefire, for the repatriation of refugees, and for the exchange of prisoners of war. However, it is difficult to see how peace and stability can return to Tajikistan. This is not only because the government and the opposition hold fundamentally different views about what political system, secular or Islamic, Tajikistan should adopt; more importantly, perhaps, it is also because of the Tajiks residing in countries beyond the borders of Tajikistan, particularly in Afghanistan. Tajikistan shares long land frontiers of more than 1000 km with Afghanistan; more than three million Tajiks live on the Afghan side of the borders. In March 1993, after the military defeat of the Tajik rebels, some of them fled into Afghanistan and established government-in-exite there. The rebels have many sympathizers among the Afghan Tajiks who support the cause of the rebels. The Afghan government (Mujheddin) also sympathizes with the rebels. The main component of the opposition, the IRP, is an organization of Islamic fundamentalism, as is the (Tajik) Jihad in Afghanistan. They share the same goal of establishing an Islamic state in a number of cross-border attacks into Tajikistan. The Tajik civil war is far from over. The involvement of the Russian military in the Tajik civil war and in guarding the Tajikistan-Afghanistan borders has resulted in killings of Tajik rebels by Russian soldiers and of Russian soldiers by Tajik rebels. That situation has further complicated inter-ethnic relations in Tajikistan.

ETHNIC QUESTIONS IN CENTRAL ASIA AND IMPACT ON CHINA

Three out of five Central Asian states are China's neighbours. Kazakhstan, Kyrgyzstan, and Tajikistan share a common border of more than 3300 km with China. A number of ethnic groups reside across borders in China's Xinjiang Uighur Autonomous Region and Central Asian states. According to Chinese statistics, about 600,000 ethnic Chinese are now living in

Central Asia, whereas in Xinjiang there are more than one million Kazakhs, 140,000 Kyrgyzs, 33,000 Tajiks and 14,500 Uzbeks.[19] Because of geography, religion and ethnicity, ethnic groups across the borders in China and Central Asia have maintained a traditional friendship and have always kept up frequent contacts.

In the last few years since the disintegration of the former Soviet Union, the independence of the Central Asian states and ensuing ethnic conundrum in Central Asia have made some impact on the political, economic and social development of China's Northwest – in particular, China's Xinjiang Uighur Autonomous Region. There are two aspects of such impact, positive and negative. The positive impact can be seen, for example, in the following:

1. The independence of Central Asian states largely eliminated the military threat to China's Northwest from the former Soviet Union. In the last few years, the Chinese delegation and the joint delegation of Kazakhstan, Kyrgyzstan, Tajikistan and Russia have conducted many rounds of talks on border disarmaments and military confidence building. Border demarcation talks with both Kazakhstan and Russia have made impressive progress. Such an environment is conducive to the economic development and modernization of Xinjiang, thus promoting political stability and ethnic harmony.

2. With the independence of the Central Asian states, a large market has emerged to China's Northwest, a market with rich mineral and human resources. It has opened new opportunities for the opening of China's Northwest and in particular, for economic co-operation between Xinjiang and Central Asian states. Economic co-operation promotes harmony in ethnic relations, particularly for those ethnic groups residing on both sides of the borders.

3. China and the Central Asian states established diplomatic relations soon after the independence of those states. In the last few years, frequent exchange visits have been made by officials on both sides, including heads of states, as well as by ordinary people such as border residents. Such frequent contacts between two peoples and two governments help facilitate mutual understanding and trust, and promote prosperity and stability across the borders.

There is also some negative impact. The rise of ethnonationalism of titular nationalities of the newly independent Central Asian states has extended its influence across borders into China. For example, the call of the Kazakhstan government for the Kazakhs to 'return home' is undoubtedly an encouragement to the separatists and their activities in Xinjiang. Moreover, the penetration of the increasing influence of Pan-Turkism into Xinjiang also impairs the stability of the region. Islamic fundamentalism and its organizations, such as the Islamic Revival Party in both Tajikistan and Uzbekistan, have engaged in activities that may have serious implications for political stability across the border in Xinjiang.

However, looking back at the last few years, it should be argued that after the disintegration of the former Soviet Union, the independence of Central Asian states has mostly exerted a positive rather than a negative impact on China. Three reasons can be suggested in explanation. First, as argued above, apart from Tajikistan, Central Asia has enjoyed relative political stability. There has been no major ethnic unrest in Central Asia that threatens the stability across the border in China. Second, the Chinese government has positive and practical policies towards the minority peoples. It has paid particular attention to resolving any problems in relationships between Han Chinese and minority groups, as well as those among various minority groups in Northwest China, to prevent any potential conflict. Third, in the last few years, while the Central Asian states have been faced with some economic difficulties, the living standard of Xinjiang has continuously been improved as a result of its opening-up and economic reform. According to official Chinese statistics, for example, the value of Xinjiang's gross domestic product (GDP) rose from 25.2 billion yuan in 1990 to 48.2 billion yuan in 1993, a staggering increase of 91 per cent.[20] The national income of Xinjiang increased from 25.2 billion yuan in 1991 to 29.2 billion yuan in 1992.[21] The economic prosperity and economic development of Xinjiang in the last few years, therefore, have contributed to Xinjiang's stability and at the same time prevented any significant negative impact from Central Asia on Xinjiang's political and economic development.

It must be noted at the same time that compared with many other regions of China, Northwest China, which includes Xinjiang, is still economically underdeveloped and poor. At the same time, it is the region where a large number of ethnic minority groups are residing. To maintain national unity and stability in the region, it would be advisable for the Chinese government to take active measures to promote economic reforms and open up markets in the region and to continue to carry out correct and sensible nationality and religious policies in an effort to prevent any large-scale ethnic unrest. Otherwise, the negative influence of ethnonationalism from Central Asia could impair the stability and national unity of Northwest China in the future.

CONCLUSION

Issues of ethnicity in Central Asia today have their roots deep in history. Ethnic tensions in the region are part of the legacy of Russian colonization and the Soviet domination of the region. The independence of the five Central Asian states changed the ethnic landscape in Central Asia by making the five native nationalities – small minority groups in Soviet times – the ethnic majorities in their respective independent sovereign states. Ethno-nationalist feelings among the five titular nationalities in Central Asia, which had lain dormant and were overwhelmed by Soviet ideology, erupted in full force. Ethnic harmony, however, has been the professed goal of all Central Asian governments in the last few years. Given the complex ethnic composition of Central Asia, inter-ethnic relations are likely to continue to preoccupy Central Asian states in their pursuit of nation-building and of political stability and economic development. While problems in inter-ethnic relations in Central Asia in the last few years have not had any significant impact on national unity and political stability in China's Northwest, ethnonationalism across borders in Central Asia remains a challenge to China.

NOTES

1. All figures in this paragraph are correct in January 1990.
2. Panklatova, A. M., *A Comprehensive History of the USSR* (Chinese edition), Vol. III, pp. 135–7.
3. *Hasakesitan Gongheguo Gaikuang* (A Brief Introduction of the Republic of Kazakhstan), Xinjiang People's Press, 1992, p. 48.
4. *Nezavisimosti*, 12 April 1995.
5. See *Zongjiao Yanjiu* (Studies of World Religions), No. 2, 1993.
6. *Nezavisimosti*, 6 January 1994.
7. See for details *Hasakesitan Gongheguo Gaikuang* (A Brief Introduction of the Republic of Kazakhstan), Xinjiang People's Press, 1992, p. 44.
8. *Sovetskaya Kirgiziya*, 7 December 1972.
9. *Kazakhstanskaya Pravda*, 28 June 1994.
10. *Xinhua News Agency* (Almaty), 7 April 1993.
11. *ITAR-TASS*, 13 November 1994.
12. *Kazakhstanskaya Pravda*, 24 March 1995.
13. *Dongou Zhongya Wenti Yicong* (Studies of Eastern Europe and Central Asia: Translated Materials), No. 4, 1994, p. 55.
14. *Xinhua News Agency* (Moscow), 11 June 1995.
15. See *Zhongya Xinxi* (Bulletin of Central Asia), No. 3, 1995.
16. *Xinhua News Agency* (Almaty), 1 April 1994.
17. *Moscow News*, 26 June 1994.
18. *Erluosi he Dongou Zhongya Guojia Nianjian, 1992–93* (Yearbook of Russia, Eastern European and Central Asian Countries, 1992–93), p. 470.

19. See *Xinjiang Gaikuang* (Facts about Xingjiang), Xingjiang People's Press, 1993, p. 1.
20. *Zhongguo Tongji Nianjian, 1994* (The Statistical Yearbook of China, 1994), p. 35.
21. See *Zhongguo Tongji Nianjian, 1993* (The Statistical Yearbook of China, 1993), p. 40; and *Zhongguo Tongji Niangjian, 1994* (The Statistical Yearbook of China, 1994), p. 38.

5 Russia and Russians in Central Asia

Andrei Kortunov and Sergei Lounev

I. THE RUSSIAN-SPEAKING POPULATION IN CENTRAL ASIA

Each of the Central Asian states has a relatively small population. Only when combined is the population of Central Asian states comparable to that of their neighbours. At the same time these countries were the region of highest population growth in the former USSR: in thirty years the population growth was 260 per cent in Uzbekistan and Tajikistan, 240 per cent in Turkmenistan, 210 per cent in Kyrgyzstan, 170 per cent in Kazakhstan. In comparison, growth in the same period in Russia was only 120 per cent. This growth was mainly among the autochtonous (indigenous) population.

None of the Central Asian states are ethnically homogenous. In the last few years of the lifetime of the USSR, in Turkmenistan and Uzbekistan the titular nationality accounted for 70 per cent of the population. In Tajikistan it was 60 per cent, in Kyrgyzstan 50 per cent and in Kazakhstan about 40 per cent. The emigration of the Russian-speaking population has now increased these proportions. But even in the event of a complete exodus of Russians, the strength of the Uzbek population, significant in all Central Asian states except Kazakhstan, will remain or may even grow.

As a result of the established division of labour between the migrants and the indigenous population, the former are predominantly employed as qualified workers, engineers and scientists. According to the 1989 All-Soviet census in Uzbekistan, where the proportion of locals in modern sectors of the economy is the highest in Central Asia, the percentage ratio between the Russian-speaking and indigenous population was: in science, culture and art 328:100; in information and computing, 250:100; in management 217:100, in industry 126:100, in construction 108:100, and in health care 9:100.[1] The Slavs are practically not represented in the ruling sector of Central Asia. Their interests and the interests of the classes and sections of society that they represent have virtually no reflection in state policies apart from those relating to Russia.

Discrimination affecting the non-indigenous population of Central Asia and its outflow to Russia seriously affects the mindset of the Russian population. The unofficially encouraged departure of Russians and Russian-speakers,[2] accentuated by political instability, lack of prospects, and the decomposition of the highly qualified workforce, was slowly gaining momentum. Although many locals were benefiting from it (through rewards such as free houses and other properties, and career promotions), the minorities (for example, the Tartars, Dungans, and Koreans) who are connected with the Russian-speakers have become discontented. The industries were starting to falter, the quality of education and medical care were deteriorating as well. In 1991 in Kyrgyzstan, the Kyrgyz accounted for eight per cent of the qualified workers and three per cent of engineers and technical cadres. After the departure of the Russians in some areas, many services, like the telephone system, came to a stop.[3]

As opposed to the practice in Latvia and Estonia, discrimination against the non-indigenous population in Central Asia is not conducted at an official level, as the authorities are starting to realize the disastrous consequences of the 'brain drain'. But their activities aimed at containing emigration have a restrictive character. In some areas sales of properties have been banned. In 1992 in Turkmenistan, the sale and exchange of properties by people leaving the country was banned for ten years.[4] In addition to the enormous difference in house prices in Russia and the Central Asian states, the excessive costs of personal containers led to a situation where the forced emigrants appeared in Russia practically without means of subsistence, and had to settle in rural areas, even though the Russians in Central Asia are predominantly city-dwellers.

In all Central Asian republics the non-indigenous population has been systematically forced out of government, industries, education and the higher echelons of the army. At the parliamentary elections in Kazakhstan in 1994 (marked by serious electoral violations), the Kazakhs (who made up forty per cent of the population) won 63 per cent of seats. Eighty per cent of the staff of the Kazak President's office are Kazakhs. Practically only Kazakhs are appointed to senior positions. Whilst the Communist Party of Uzbekistan had forty per cent ethnic Russian membership, the People's Democratic Party of Uzbekistan, which was formed on its basis and is now the majority party in parliament, has only four per cent Russians. None of the twelve Committee chairmen of the Uzbek Parliament is Russian.[5] At the parliamentary elections in Kyrgyzstan in February 1995, Russians won six per cent of seats, Uzbeks nine per cent, while the Kyrgyz, accounting for only fifty per cent of the population, won 85 per cent of the seats.[6]

The Russian language has been consistently forced out. Only in Kyrgyzstan has teaching in the Russian language in schools and universities been maintained at the same level, and no discrimination is allowed against persons not fluent in the state language. The number of newspapers published in Russian is also comparable to the number of Kyrgyz papers. No problems arise with the Russian media, either.[7] In Uzbekistan, the appropriate law allows seven years to learn the Uzbek language. However, since 1993 lack of knowledge of the Uzbek language has been seen as a liability.[8] No literature or scientific and political magazines are published in Russian in Uzbekistan.[9] Moreover, there is no provision in Uzbekistan for Russian to be a means of communication. Kazakhstan refuses to recognize Russian as a second state language, or to call a referendum on this issue, notwithstanding the fact that this is demanded by practically the entire Russian-speaking population and the entrepreneurs of Kazakhstan. Russian is spoken by practically the entire population, whereas only a quarter of the population speaks Kazakh. It is also worth mentioning that teachers teaching in Kazakh receive an extra 15–20 per cent to their salary.[10] In Turkmenistan the Turkmen language is to become the state language in 1996.

For a long time Turkmenistan was the only Central Asian country to have signed a dual citizenship agreement with Russia, something that is demanded by the Russian-speaking population of all former Republics of the USSR. In mid-1995 a similar agreement was signed with Tajikistan. Typically, local authorities oppose this on the following grounds: that a 'dual citizen' cannot be a 'true patriot' of his or her country; that there are ethnic groups which have statehood outside the boundaries of the former USSR; and that the growth of separatist trends is likely. The Kyrgyz President Akayev suggested that dual citizenship be allowed only to the Slavs, as those most affected by the break-up of the USSR.[11] But even this was declined by the Kyrgyz Parliament. Kazakhstan has only conceded a facilitation of change of citizenship for those who move to permanent residence in neighbouring countries.

Only in Kyrgyzstan are the rights of the Russian-speaking population respected. A special decree envisaging practical implementation was adopted there to stop the outflow of the Russian-speaking population from the country. At the same time, Uzbekistan refrains from signing agreements with Russia on refugees and displaced population, and on legal aid in civil and criminal cases. Tashkent resolutely opposed the signing at the CIS summit in 1993 of the Convention ensuring the rights of ethnic, linguistic, cultural and religious minorities, particularly objecting to the clause of the Convention which denounces assimilationist policies towards minorities carried out without their consent.[12]

Given the compact settlement of ethnic minorities, the Central Asian regimes have resorted to specific economic measures. In Kazakhstan all taxes are paid to the Central Government, with the major part of the taxes coming from the Russian-speaking North. But when distributed, most allocations go to the South. The 105,000 Kazakhs who returned from Mongolia and China were settled in the North, and the government provided full financial backing for the settlement.[13] One of the major reasons for moving the capital from Almaty to Akmola is the 'Kazakhization' of the North. The leaders of Russian-speaking communities are arrested from time to time in the Republic.

The process of privatization in Central Asia has also had a distinctly ethnic feature, when the authorities through various manipulations have made sure that the local population get hold of assets and properties. In Kazakhstan, factory workers are practically forbidden to privatize their factories. The majority of factory workers are Slavs. At the same time the rural population, which is mainly Kazakh, received a larger share than the urban population.

Sociological surveys conducted among the migrants show that the main reasons for migration to Russia (not only Russians and Tartars, but Ukrainians, Byelorussians, Jews, Germans and Koreans move there) are: 1. disruption of Central Asia's ties with Russia; 2. the national cadres policy whereby the local population gets all the privileges; 3. lack of quality education for the young; 4. economic difficulties; and 5. grass-level nationalism.[14] Whilst migration from Tajikistan was boosted by the civil war, the recent economic crisis in Kyrgyzstan seems to be the main reason for emigration from the country. Until 1994, job discrimination and grass-level nationalism were among the reasons as well.[15]

In the middle of 1994 the proportion of migrants from Central Asia made up 46.2 per cent of refugees in Russia from the former USSR.[16] Fifteen per cent of Russians have decided to leave Kazakhstan, while another forty per cent are about to do so.[17] In 1993 alone, 365,000 Russian speakers left for Russia.[18] In 1991 98,000 left Uzbekistan, in 1992 the number dropped, but in 1993, through the Russian Embassy, 100,000 left the country for Russia.[19] Many others left on their own. In 1991–1993 more than 100,000 Russian-speakers (ten per cent of the total number) left Kyrgyzstan.[20] In Tajikistan, immediately before and during the civil war, seven thousand Russians were leaving every month, and by 1994 200,000 migrants from Tajikistan were officially registered as refugees in Russia.[21] It should be noted that many of the migrants do not get registered by the local migration services. Only those who have few chances of being well settled in Russia (due to old age or absence of relatives) have decided to stay in Tajikistan. Addressing the Foreign Ministry's Council for Foreign

Policy, then Minister of Foreign Affairs, A. Kozyrev, said that in 1994 the Russian Embassies issued 143,000 Russian passports in Uzbekistan and 76,000 in Kazakhstan.[22]

In areas where the Russians live compactly, the only other form of protest against the discriminatory policies of the authorities is a growth of separatist trends. In North Kazakhstan the population quite openly demands a merger with Russia. These areas had been explored by the Russians from the sixteenth century until 1922, when these areas were transferred to Kazakhstan by the Soviet Government, and many see it as inconceivable that they should be regarded as Kazakh lands in view of the absence of Kazakhs in those areas at that time.

II THE INITIAL STAGE OF RUSSIAN POLICY TOWARDS CENTRAL ASIA

From the end of the 1980s, the average Russian perception of their country was to regard it as a part of the West. The overwhelming majority of the population (as well as the foreign policy elite) proceeded from the view that Russia belonged to the all-European civilization. They strongly advocated making Russia a 'law-based' state, establishing a 'civil society' (ignoring the fact that the process takes dozens of years), and encouraging a rapid modernization based on market reforms. In foreign policy, the public rather quietly accepted the loss by Russia of its major geopolitical role. By and large the public was supportive of priority relationships with Europe and the USA and distancing Russia from Asia. Not much interest was displayed towards partnership with Central Asian states, which were viewed as a 'burden and an alien civilization', particularly because labour productivity differed greatly between Russia and Central Asia and because the Central Asian mentality was heavily based upon the Islamic culture. In the first two years after the break-up of the USSR, Foreign Minister A. Kozyrev did not visit the Central Asian states even once. It was clear that 'Western civilization' was perceived as an ideal model and as an ultimate goal for Russia.

In reforming the USSR, it was believed that if separated from the other republics, Russia would first of all ease its financial burdens. In the late 1980s Moscow's subsidies to the Republics exceeded fifty billion US dollars.[23] According to the IMF, in 1991, subsidies from Moscow made up 44 per cent of Tajikistan's budget, 42 per cent of Uzbekistan's, 34 per cent of Kyrgyzstan's 23 per cent of Kazakhstan's and 22 per cent of Turkmenistan's.[24] Secondly, Russia could avoid demographic pressures. It was estimated that by the end of the twentieth century the population of Slavs in the USSR would have doubled while the population of

Transcaucasians and Central Asians would increase four times.[25] And thirdly, Russia could use fully its own industrial and scientific potential to achieve better economic results and to minimize the influence of traditionalism on the social and political processes, thus accelerating Russia's transition to an 'open' political system and law-ruled state.

Subsequently, the idea of entering the 'European home' was proclaimed in 1991 and made the guiding principle of Russia's foreign policy until the beginning of 1993.

The practical steps taken by Russia to implement this policy – the signing of Byelovezh Agreements 'behind the back' of the Central Asian States, the launching of radical economic reforms without consulting them, the adoption of an exclusively pro-Western foreign policy, and the creation of its own national armed forces – all clearly demonstrated that even after the break-up of the USSR the 'democrats' continued to view Central Asia as having no prospects from Russia's short-term and long-term perspectives. The 'isolationist' policy was accompanied by a slighting and at times racist tone towards the Central Asian civilization, which was treated as unadaptable to an economic and political transformation into a Western model. During 1992 Russian foreign policy almost pointedly ignored the Central Asian states. Those in charge were probably of the view that close political, economic, military and strategic relations with the countries of the region could obstruct Russia's rapid integration into Western structures.[26] As a result, Russia's actions in the region were more of an improvisation than a well-thought strategy.

Summing up the views of the 'Atlanticists' on Russia's future relations with Central Asia, the following conclusions can be drawn:

1 In economic terms, Central Asia is a burden for Russia. The continuation of present economic relations with the countries of the region can lead only to the continuance of the low-efficiency industries of Russia's economy. Russia can easily find alternative sources of required raw material in other regions;
2 A political alliance with the region's authoritarian regimes still sticking to the Communist nomenclature will only discredit the new Russian leadership. Close relations with Central Asia will serve the interests of the conservative opposition and not of the 'democratic' movement;
3 From a military and strategic point of view, Central Asia will always be a source of instability, conflicts and problems, the majority of which are beyond Russia's control. Any military involvement in the region and its inevitable costs will not be appreciated nor accepted by the Russian public.

4 From a civilizational point of view, Central Asia is too far from Russia, and it belongs to a different (Islamic, Eastern, and developing) world. The civilizational incompatibility can not be removed simply by co-operation; and
5 Geopolitically, a focus on Central Asia may needlessly displace Russia's priorities, the most important amongst which is the 'return to Europe' in all senses.

However, the democrats' stance, even at the end of 1991 and the beginning of 1992, did not reflect at all an all-Russian consensus on the building of relations with Central Asia. Moreover, these policies were not shared by the Russian political, economic and intellectual elite. From the very beginning the policy of disrupting ties with Central Asia became a target for criticism by the diverse coalition of its opponents.[27]

Among the opponents of the Yeltsin-Gaidar course were the influential industrial groups who were dependent either on raw materials and semi-processed product supplies from Central Asia or upon the Central Asian market for their products. The disruption of ties with Central Asia was opposed by the majority of the old Communist nomenclature of Russia, which was unable to reconcile itself with the break-up of the USSR. This coalition was joined by many Russian nationalists, who viewed the alliance with Central Asian states as a basis for 'the Eurasian' concept of Russia's national interests.[28] The Russian nationalists were also the first to draw attention to the problems of the Russians and Russian-speaking minorities in the Central Asian region. Even some Russian liberals came out against the Yeltsin-Gaidar policies, accusing the leadership of arrogance, ignorance and political short-sightedness. Many Russian military were critical too, basing their criticism (with good reason) on the fact that the dismantling of Soviet military and strategic space facilities, starting with its Central Asian part was fraught with direct and very serious threats to the defense capabilities of Russia. Although diverse and incohesive, this coalition was too powerful to be ignored.[29]

The Eurasianists' arguments in favour of restoring close relations with Central Asia can be summarized as follows:

1 Russia cannot leave the region without jeopardizing the security of its Southern flank. Attempts to strengthen borders with Kazakhstan would be very costly and probably counterproductive. Therefore, Russia should aim at preserving control over the external borders of the CIS in Central Asia, settle the question of the deployment of Russian troops and military bases in the region, as well as retain the

military infrastructure and equipment making up the integrated system of Russia's military security;

2 Russia cannot sever economic ties with Central Asia without causing the collapse of enterprises and entire areas of Russian industry dependent on raw material and other supplies from the region. In addition, Central Asia is an important market for Russian products which have no demand in other markets. Therefore, trade and economic relations should be preserved, even if this requires subsidizing Russian exports as well as the countries of Central Asia. In the long term, Russia should envisage the establishment with Central Asian countries of a free trade zone, a payments union and then a customs union, a common market for capital and labour and, at the final stage, a monetary union with co-ordinated budgetary, tax, credit and currency policies; and

3 Russia cannot be neutral to ethnic tensions and conflicts in Central Asia, because firstly there are ten million ethnic Russians living in the region, and secondly, the conflicts in the region can directly destabilize the situation in some of the neighbouring regions of the Russian Federation. Therefore Russia should attempt to prevent conflicts in Central Asia, neutralize attempts by third countries to take advantage of regional instability in their interests, and create an effective peace-keeping mechanism built on the basis of the Russian military potential.

The consistent supporters of 'Eurasianism' believed that the system of Russia's foreign policy alliances should be oriented towards, not so much the West, but rather the South. This orientation, according to them, is predetermined by geography, history, culture, and Russia's economic needs, as well as by the ethnic composition of Russia's population. The concept of Russia being 'the bridge' between Europe and Asia, between the Christian and Islamic worlds, between the developed and developing nations logically leads to the assumption that an exclusive orientation towards the West would inevitably mean for Russia a loss of its great power status and its cultural uniqueness, and would make Russia a periphery of the West.

The periphery variant is explained by the fact that Russian society, due to its uniqueness, will never be able, strictly speaking, to become 'European'. It was also asserted that having lost its influence in the South, Russia would inevitably be less important for the West. Therefore it was believed that the Yeltsin-Kozyrev 'Euro-Atlantic' foreign policy orientation was without any prospects, and counterproductive even in its main motivations.[30] The policy of the West, with Turkey as its champion, is aimed at preventing a new hinterland alliance between Russia and the leading Islamic countries, at cutting Russia off from the Persian Gulf, and at obstructing a mutually beneficial co-operation between Moscow and Teheran.[31] This should prompt Russia to treat with the utmost suspicion any Turkish activity in the Central Asian region, as well as possible attempts by the West to enhance its influence here.[32]

It is also asserted that the West, and the US in particular, is objectively interested in maintaining a certain tension in Central Asia and especially in the Middle East, since such instability and the permanent threat of military conflict are the only reliable guarantee of ensuring the military and political presence of the West in the Persian Gulf.[33] Even if Central Asia is not part of the vital interests of the United States, the permanent threat of conflict in this region should allow American diplomacy to keep its allies among the conservative Arab regimes on a short leash.

Nevertheless, as was noted earlier, it was the 'Atlanticists' who determined Russia's foreign policy at its first stage. Central Asia was practically 'forced out' from the Soviet Union. With Central Asia becoming independent in the end of 1991, it required certain steps for the region's ruling elite to legitimize and strengthen its position, to ensure the proper functioning of the economic and social system, to replace the Communist ideology with a nationalist one, and to find the region's place in the international community and international division of labour. In view of Russia's foreign policy behaviour towards Central Asia, the above steps were designed as policies of a continued drift away from Russia.

This explains the introduction by Central Asian states of national languages and national currencies, their curtailing of co-operation with Russia, and their attempts to gain direct access to the world market and to join a large number of international organizations. The cost of the 'drifting away' policy was a grave economic and social crisis that seized all the Central Asian states.

The production system of the Soviet economy, the situation in world markets, the role of Russians and the Russian-speaking population, the consequences of the growth of nationalism and the revival of Islam were all wrongly perceived within the region. The intellectual elite of Central Asia, misled by the Soviet system of prices, was for quite a long time of the view that the republics were plundered by the Centre. In reality, however, the situation was quite the opposite when looked at from the point of view of world prices. In 1987, for example, Russia's exports in world prices exceeded imports by 41,283 million rubles, whilst the Central Asian states were importing more than exporting (Kazakhstan 7,653 million rubles, Uzbekistan 4,362 million rubles, Kyrgyzstan 1,405 million rubles, Tajikistan 1,309 million rubles, and Turkmenistan 105 million rubles).[34]

It was due to the abrupt reduction of Russia's subsidies that the region experienced a decline in investments and funding of the social sphere. The considerable interdependency between all the republics that had developed in the Soviet period was also underestimated. In 1991 intra-USSR trade made up 81 per cent of Turkmenistan's trade, 89 per cent of Kazakhstan's, 90 per cent of Uzbekistan's and 99 per cent of Kyrgyzstan's.[35] The diminution of these trade relations led to an industrial decline in Central Asia. The hopes entertained by Central Asian states for broad international assistance and a significant inflow of capital did not materialize. Although the West did provide economic assistance to the newly independent states, the size of this aid was relatively small. The inflow of capital has also been restrained by political instability and by unclear prospects for the countries in the region, as well as by the weakness of their market infrastructure.

In addition, the search for a common national ideology resulted in the rise of Islam. In April 1992 Islam Karimov went on a pilgrimage to Saudi Arabia. He was followed by other leaders of the Central Asian states. In the Soviet period Tajikistan had seventeen registered mosques. Once the restrictions were removed their number jumped to 2,000.[36] Every village and town district in Uzbekistan rushed to open its own mosque. In Turkmenistan the number of mosques increased from 16 to 163 in the middle of 1994.[37] The rise in religious self-identification was slower in Kazakhstan and Northern Kyrgyzstan.[38]

Nevertheless, the process of Islamization objectively enhanced the role of social groups critical of the local elite which were formed in the Soviet period. The Islamists started vigorous activities in Bukhara, Samarkand, and the Fergana Valley. In Namangan the local imams formed their Islamic militant units. Muslim radicals in Kazakhstan tried to provoke public disorder in Almaty. The radical Islamic Revival Party was notably active in Uzbekistan and Tajikistan.

Realizing the threat to its interests, the ruling elite in Central Asian states began a selective policy of supporting the moderate Islamists and containing and even suppressing the extremist forces. The Islamic Revival Party was banned in Tajikistan and Uzbekistan. The majority of its Tajik supporters fled to Afghanistan. They have gone deep underground in Uzbekistan. The Namangan-based Adolat Islamic Party was banned in Uzbekistan. Some of its members were arrested, whilst others emigrated.[39] The campaign against the fundamentalists was energetically supported by Niyazov and Akayev.[40]

The local population started to bid farewell to its illusions. According to a survey by the Institute of Strategic and Regional Studies under the Office of the President of Uzbekistan, 62 per cent of the population regretted the break-up of the USSR and 70.5 per cent believed life was much better then.[41]

This is why from the end of 1993 the policy started to change. Bilateral and multilateral agreements aimed at restoring the severed links were signed. Russia's financial assistance to the Central Asian states started to increase. The emigration of the Russian-speaking population was discouraged and dealt with. But owing to the ambiguity of Russian policy, management failure in the economic zone of the former USSR and the inertia of nationalism, this policy of the Central Asian states is rather controversial and inconsistent.

III RUSSIAN POLICY IN THE MID-1990S

The economic, political and foreign policy miscalculations committed by the Russian government prompted a gradual transformation of the public mentality. Recently it has been leaning towards a primitive Slavophile ideology, and the concept of the uniqueness of Russia. It believes that the country should head the struggle of the developing and exploited South against the developed and exploiting North. It regards the West as the main threat to Russia, and demands a return to traditional values in governing and developing the country.

At the moment there are at least four concepts of Russia's foreign policy, or four main forms of identification shaping Russia's approach to the post-Soviet space.

The first concept is characterized by narrow nationalism. Russia is seen in its present boundaries with no distinction between 'Near' and 'Far' Abroad. This is shared with some variations by the democratic part of the elite and the public opinion.

The second concept, quite an opposite one, is promoted mainly by the Communists, and envisages a restoration of the USSR as some sort of a union of equal republics, and apparently with the restoration of the subsidies system.

The third concept is elaborated mainly by different nationalistic forces. Some influential members of the national-patriotic camp favour the federal union of only four entities, namely, Russia, Belarus, Ukraine and Northern Kazakhstan. It calls for a union of unequal partners. This is justified by the notion that since Russia will have to subsidize the other members of the union, it should have a dominant role in it.

And finally a fourth concept has emerged recently, which could be branded as 'national-liberal'. It believes in the feasibility of a voluntary union, probably approved by a referendum, of some of the former republics, including Russia, in a form of a Federation based upon a common culture and civilization.

All of these approaches are present (in different combinations) in Russian foreign policy. The constant struggle between these perceptions and the forces subscribing to them, as well as the changing influence of these forces on the executive, makes Russian policies very mobile. It is also responsible for the absence of clear tactical and strategic guidelines and goals with regard to Russian policy towards Central Asia. It should be noted that these perceptions are shared by the elite, whereas the views of the public are very controversial and incorporate quite antagonistic approaches.

From 1993 the Russian government began to link its policy towards Central Asia particularly with the treatment of the Russian-speaking population there. In the course of his visit to Uzbekistan, Tajikistan and Kazakhstan in November 1993, A. Kozyrev pointed out that Russia would be interested in developing mutually beneficial economic co-operation with the region, but would link it to the treatment of Russian-speakers there. The Russian authorities are seriously concerned that the possible migration of eight to ten million Russians from Central Asia to Russia may increase tension at home and consolidate the nationalists. Understandably, the migrants would be very hostile to the nationals of their ex-homelands, as well to the leaders of Russia who would be blamed for the break-up of the USSR.

After sidelining the 'Atlanticists', Russia undertook some steps designed to develop political and military relations with the Central Asian states. The most vivid example of this was Tajikistan. After a six-month period of hesitation following E. Rakhmonov's victory, Russia agreed to sign a treaty of friendship, co-operation and mutual assistance with Tajikistan (May 1993). The key provision of the treaty states that the two parties will come to each other's assistance (including military assistance) in the case of aggression against either of them. Russia soon found itself involved in the Tajik conflict and its border guard checkpoint in Tajikistan was attacked. Previously the opposition had limited itself to blackmailing Russia. The 'democrats/Islamists' declared the Russian-speaking population hostage to the domestic political struggle. A Russian school was occupied in Dushanbe, and a member of the Russian humanitarian mission was captured. Russia had to enter into negotiations with Iran and Pakistan to stop their support of the militant Tajik opposition. Afghanistan received a serious warning from Moscow against provoking or carrying out attacks against Russian troops. The annual spring and summer offensives by the irreconcilable opposition, starting from 1993, caused increasing casualties among the Russian border guards. In 1992 the casualties were five thousand, in 1993 ten thousand, in 1994 sixteen thousand, and in 1995 eighteen thousand.[42]

Russia's change of approach to military and political issues was to a great extent the result of pressure from the Russian military lobby, which had never reconciled itself to the idea of withdrawing all Russian troops to Russia. According to the new military doctrine approved in October 1993, Russia can have military bases beyond its boundaries as well as delegate its troops to peacekeeping operations.

Whilst Russia's influence in Tajikistan was growing, with Rakhmonov choosing to depend practically only on Russia, and a stronger movement in Tajikistan for merging with Russia, Uzbekistan, Kazakhstan and Kyrgyzstan started showing their discontent. In summer 1993 Nazarbayev, with full endorsement from Akayev, proposed to encourage Afghanistan, Pakistan, Iran, Turkey, and Saudi Arabia to get involved in the inter-Tajik peace process. At the same time, Uzbekistan, along with Tajikistan, apprehensive of Islamic fundamentalism, had for a long time refrained from criticizing Russia. This was helped by the fact that the Russian Foreign Ministry was persistently expressing the point that the settlement of the Tajik crisis was impossible without input from Uzbekistan.[43] In March 1994 the first joint military exercises involving armies of signatory states of the Treaty on Collective Security were held in Tajikistan. Russia, Uzbekistan and Tajikistan took part in them. But later in the summer, Karimov called for no more interference in Tajikistan's internal affairs, and advised Russia to abide by the provisions of the Treaty on military co-operation.[44] Uzbekistan also started to put pressure on the Tajik regime to share power with the opposition.[45]

The Central Asian states were also indignant at Russia's attempts in 1993 to force them out of the rouble zone. Russia put forward such strict conditions for membership of the rouble zone that the countries of the region had to introduce their own currencies. The Russian stance was determined by the prevailing arguments that filling the CIS countries up with rubles would lead to hyper-inflation in Russia. In 1994 Russia refused to let Tajikistan rejoin the rouble zone.

It should be said, however, that some of the Central Asian states contributed to the collapse of the rouble zone in 1992 through huge rouble loans given to their enterprises. This, of course, undermined Russia's anti-inflationary measures. Along with that, certain politicians in the region rushed to accuse Russia of 'colonial economic policies' and of plundering of Central Asia's natural resources. It was also popularly believed that other countries would be able to offer Central Asia better economic deals.

Objectively, in the foreseeable future Central Asia is 'doomed' to close co-operation with Russia, although the Central Asian states are trying to distance themselves from Russia. They react painfully to many Russian policies which are regarded as imperialistically motivated, and negatively to the growth of Russia's influence. *But* at the same time they realize that it is Russia that ensures political stability in Central Asia. Even the Afghan-based 'irreconcilable Tajik opposition' accepts this. The Pamiris broadly celebrated the centenary of mountainous Badakhshan's inclusion into the Russian Empire. Russia is also seen as a guarantor of the external borders of the CIS.

The economic needs of the regional countries also prompt them to seek close relations with Russia. Russia's trade in the region is notable. In spite of the decline of trade relations between Russia and Central Asia, in 1992 Russia still accounted for 68 per cent of Kazakhstan's imports, 58 per cent of Uzbekistan's, 51 per cent of Kyrgyzstan's, 48 per cent of Tajikistan's and Turkmenistan's. Russia accounted for 61 per cent of Uzbekistan's exports, 54 per cent of Turkmenistan's, 53 per cent of Kazakhstan's, and 39 per cent of Kyrgyzstan's.[46] In technological terms, Russia and Central Asia are highly interdependent. For example, because of low quality, Central Asian cotton cannot be supplied to the world market, and at the same time the Russian textile industry is tied to Central Asian cotton. On the other hand, Central Asia depends on Russian subsidies. Even though subsidies from Russia have been reduced, they have not been abolished completely. Uzbekistan insists on selling its cotton to Russia according to world prices, but is keen to buy energy and timber from Russia at prices below international levels.[47] Kazakhstan is exempted from paying interest on the loans received from Russia, and Tajikistan receives favourable loans from Russia. Central Asia's huge debt to Russia continues to grow.

The Republics depend on Russia's political and military support, too. Such dependence is not only on Russian military supplies and the presence of Russian border guards, but also on military training and the large number of ethnic Russian officers in the newly created defence forces of Central Asian states who, realistically, cannot be replaced now. The Russian military are also contracted by some Central Asian armed forces, as in Turkmenistan. At the CIS summit in Ashkhabad in December 1993, the Central Asian states signed bilateral agreements with Russia on military and technical co-operation. Russia also agreed to guard Turkmenistan's borders. It should be noted that due to Turkmenistan's special approach to membership in the CIS, the 850 km of Turkmenistan's border with Afghanistan and its 1600 km border with Iran are not treated as the external borders of the CIS. Before Turkmenistan's agreement with Russia, its border guard service was only forty per cent manned, which had allowed Iran to apply pressure on Turkmenistan.[48]

Russia is quite influential in the cultural and ideological senses as well. Practically all non-locals (not only Russians) see Russia as their cultural home. Russia also appeals to the local population who have been educated in Russia, have Slav relatives or have been brought up in the Russian culture. Not surprisingly, it is this group that opposes Islamic fundamentalism most, since it realizes that it will be targeted by the Islamic regimes.

IV FUTURE SCENARIOS

Russia's future role in conflicts in Central Asia is still an unknown derivative of domestic developments in Russia. In view of the complete unpredictability of Russia's future, even in a short-term analysis, ranging from stabilization of the democratic system and the beginnings of economic growth to the prospect of a tough authoritarian regime and complete political chaos and economic collapse, it is hard to predict Russia's future role in Central Asia.

But whatever the regime in Russia, and whatever the economic and political situation, the Russian government will have to choose between several strategies in Central Asia. It is perhaps worth mentioning two possible strategic goals for Russia in the region: preserving the status quo and facilitating the managed transition.

The strategy of preserving the status quo envisages unconditional support to the current regimes in their struggle with the opposition. This strategy can be illustrated by Russia's role in Tajikistan from 1993. This type of strategy is based on the assumption that the authoritarian and semi-authoritarian regimes in the region have a considerable margin of safety, are in a position to control the opposition, and require only limited external support to remain in power indefinitely.

The orientation towards the status quo will be especially attractive if conservatives and neo-Communists prevail in Russia. They are ideologically much closer to Islam Karimov than to Nursultan Nazarbayev. The ideological and political closeness between Russian and Central Asian authoritarianism enables them to co-operate on a broad basis. The only serious obstacle to such co-operation could be authoritarian-related nationalism, both in Russia and in Central Asia.

The idea of preserving the status quo has a theoretical basis as well. Recently the universality of Western norms of democracy has been increasingly challenged. More popular is the theory of 'the clash of civilizations'. Without going into the details of the theory and its drawbacks, it should be noted that it is commonly used to substantiate the expediency and desirability of using 'double standards' when evaluating political developments in various regions of the world. It is also asserted that while democracy is a 'natural' phenomenon for Europe, and therefore needs to be encouraged and supported from outside, attempts to impose democratic norms on countries in Asia and Africa are a useless exercise and should be rejected.

According to the advocates of the Russian 'Monroe Doctrine' and some of 'the Eurasianists', Russia, surrounded by 'quasi-states', has become a logical leader in the post-Soviet space. And since the states of Central Asia cannot be radically transformed from the civilizational point of view, preserving the status quo becomes not only the desirable but also the only possible goal for Russian foreign policy.

Although quite attractive, the strategy of the status quo as a strategy and not as a temporary tactic has doubtful prospects. Attempts to put the political situation on ice against the background of growing social, economic and ecological problems would require tougher methods of suppressing the opposition and more significant outside support. It is now clear that neither the West nor the Islamic world will be prepared to share with Russia the burden of ensuring the status quo in Central Asia. Moscow will have to deal with it single-handedly.

In addition, orientation towards Russia may narrow the political basis of the ruling regimes in Central Asia. If they are seen by their population as Moscow's puppets, receiving not only aid but instructions from the Kremlin, their credibility will be undermined. Subsequently they will be in greater danger of being removed by forces flying the banner of self-determination.

Even if the status quo strategy was to be successful, it would still lead Russian foreign policy to an impasse. The doubtful privilege of policing the new global ghetto would obstruct Russia's integration into global political and economic institutions, would isolate the former Soviet republics even more, and would widen the gap between them and the industrialized world.

Facilitating the changes seems to be a more promising strategy in principle. If the liberal democrats in Russia are able to regain what they lost in Central Asia in the last few years, then supporting the reformers in Central Asia would be a logical continuation of their domestic policies.

In practical terms, implementing such a policy would be an enormous task. It is very difficult to calculate all the possible consequences of 'unfreezing' the political situation: breaking the status quo may lead to a chain reaction of changes, not necessarily leading to liberal democracy and market economy. The radicals, nationalists or fundamentalists may take advantage of the opportunities created by the process of liberalization.[49] It can also be assumed that the external forces keen to export their radical ideologies to the region would exploit the softening of the current Central Asian regimes. It is also not clear how Moscow can influence the neo-Communist regimes in Central Asia so that they concede power.

Understandably, the evolution of the ruling regimes depends first of all on the decisions taken in the region and not in Moscow. The ultimate choice between the strategy of status quo and the strategy of liberalization will be made depending on how a given authoritarian regime views its perspectives. If authorities in Tashkent, Ashkhabad and Almaty realize that the current situation is not permanent, and that changes are inevitable, then they can be expected to follow the course of regulated liberalization. Such a policy would ensure continuity and reassure the forces holding power. They would have the chance of taking part in elections and even winning them, and in the event of a defeat they can still continue to take part in the political process.

But if the ruling regimes consider their current position as stable and unchallenged, they will not be motivated to undertake liberalization. The more likely scenario then would be to ensure the status quo. This would raise the risk of a social and political explosion and the coming to power of the most radical opposition. Attempts to start reforms when the temperature in the society has already reached its highest point are normally counterproductive. They are interpreted by the opposition as a sign of weakness in the ruling regime and only stimulate struggle against the regime.

Nevertheless, Russia's influence on the evolution of the Central Asian states can be considerable. Apparently it would be in both Russia's and Central Asia's interests to stick to an 'enlightened authoritarianism', at least in the medium term, with gradual development of a civil society and market economy, under the patronage of the state. The experience of democratic experiments in Kazakhstan and Kyrgyzstan demonstrates the possibility of transforming the Central Asian societies into Western democratic structures. At the same time, it is important to see economic reforms as a priority without rushing into political changes. In so much as Russia can influence events in Central Asia, it should facilitate this very process.

NOTES

1. *Obshchaya Gazeta*, No. 20–21, 3–9 December 1993.
2. In the first six months of 1990 (i.e. when the USSR was still alive) twenty-three thousand Russians emigrated from Tajikistan. See *Izvestiya*, 5 August 1990.
3. Sitniansky, G., 'Kyrgyzia: Independence Gained, What Next?', in *Asia and Africa Today*, No. 6, 1995, p. 9.
4. *Pravda*, 9 February 1994.
5. *Segodnya*, 2 March 1995.
6. Ibid.

7. *Segodnya*, 6 May 1994.
8. *Segodnya*, 24 December 1993.
9. *Obshchaya Gazeta*, No. 20–21, 3–9 December 1993.
10. *Moscow News*, No. 20, 15–22 May 1994.
11. *Pravda*, 31 March 1994.
12. *Segodnya*, 28 December 1993.
13. *Moscow News*, No. 20, 15–22 May 1994.
14. *Segodnya*, 8 June 1994.
15. *Segodnya*, 6 May 1994.
16. *Segodnya*, 13 October 1994.
17. *Obshaya Gazeta*, No. 20–1, 3–9 December 1993.
18. *Moscow News*, No. 20, 15–22 May 1994.
19. *Segodnya*, 8 June 1994.
20. *Pravda*, 24 February 1994.
21. See *National Doctrines of Russia: Challenges and Priorities*, RAU Corporation, Moscow, 1994, p. 54.
22. *Diplomaticheskii Vestnik*, No. 5, 1995, p. 54.
23. Marnie, S. and Whitlock, E., *Central Asia and Economic Integration*, RFE/RL Research Report, Vol. 2, No. 14, 2 April 1993, p. 34.
24. Some experts find this an understatement. For example, the figure for Kyrgyzstan is suggested as 62.5%. See Sitniansky, G., 'Kyrgyzia: Independence Gained, What Next?', in *Asia and Africa Today*, No. 6, 1995, p. 9.
25. *Moscow News*, No. 25, 19–26 June 1994.
26. See MacFarlane, S. Neil, 'Russia, the West and European Security', *Survival*, Vol. 35, No. 3, Autumn 1993, pp. 7–18; and 'Russian Conception of Europe', *Post-Soviet Affairs*, Vol. 10, No. 3, July–September, 1994, pp. 241–44.
27. For debates on Russia's policy in CIS in 1992 at the Russian Foreign Ministry sponsored conference, see *Mezhdunarodnaya Zhizn*, No. 3–4, 1992.
28. Eurasianism as a philosophical concept should be distinguished from Eurasianism as a political orientation. It has to be noted, however, that the followers of political Eurasianism aspired to be seen as the offspring of the philosophical tradition of Eurasianism. The linkage between the two, however, is debatable.
29. For debates in Russia on relations with Central Asia, see Narochinskaya, N., 'Realizing the Destiny', in *Nash Sovremennik*, No. 2, 1993; and 'National Interest of Russia', in *Mezhdunarodnaya Zhizn*, No. 3–4, 1992. See also Ambartsumov, E., 'Russia's Interests Know No Border', in *Megapolis Express*, 6 May 1992.
30. See for example Pozdnyakov, E., 'Contemporary Geopolitical Changes and Their Influence on Security and Stability in the World,' *Voennaya Mysl*, No. 1, 1993; and 'Russia – a Great Power', in *Mezhdunarodnaya Zhizn*, No. 1, 1993. See also Pleshakov, K., 'Russia's Mission: The Third Epoch', in *Mezhdunarodnaya Zhizn*, No. 1, 1993; Migranyan, A., 'Real and Alleged Ends in Foreign Policy', *Rossiiskaya Gazeta*, 4 August 1992; Stankevich, S., 'The Phenomenon of Great Power', *Rossiiskaya Gazeta*, 23 June 1992; Vladislaviev, A. and Karaganov, S., 'Russia's Heavy Cross', in *Nezavisimaya Gazeta*, 11 November 1992.
31. Even the civil war in Tajikistan is interpreted by this school of thought as inspired by the West or at least advantageous for the West and Turkey. By taking part in the conflict there, Russia is in fact strengthening Uzbekistan's

regional hegemony, with Uzbekistan seen as the main stronghold of Pan-Turkism in Central Asia. At the same time Moscow is complicating its long-term relations with Afghanistan, Pakistan and China, which also suits the strategic interests of the West. See *Nezavisimaya Gazeta*, 13 May 1993.

32. The anti-Turkish and anti-Western views (or at least the apprehensions about the growth of Turkey's and the West's role in Central Asia) are to some extent shared by the Russian Foreign Ministry. In late 1992 the Russian Foreign Ministry drafted a concept of Russia's foreign policy which had a warning to neighbouring countries like Turkey not to try to take advantage of the break-up of the USSR to enhance their own influence in the region, particularly by promoting the formation of religious and nationalistic groupings threatening Russia's security and economic interests. The concept declared that 'in consistency with international law and using the potential of partnership with leading democratic countries, Russia would actively obstruct any attempts by third countries to build up a military and political presence in Russia's neighbourhood'. See 'The Concept of Foreign Policy of the Russian Federation', *Diplomaticheskii Vestnik*, January 1993, p. 8.
33. See Evstafiev, D., *Russia, the Islamic World and the Middle East*, Association of Military, Political and Military History Studies, Moscow, 1992, p. 17.
34. *Argumenti i fakti*, No. 50, 16–22 December 1989.
35. Calculated on the basis of *International Financial Statistics: Supplement on Countries of the Former Soviet Union*, International Monetary Fund, Washington, 1993.
36. *Segodnya*, 14 May 1994.
37. *Segodnya*, 1 June 1994.
38. That Northern Kyrgyzstan is less religious can be illustrated by the fact that 90 per cent of mosque-goers there are Uzbeks, who make up only 1.5 per cent of the population of the Kyrgyz capital.
39. *Komsomolskaya Pravda*, 24 June 1993.
40. *Izvestiya*, 19 March, 1993.
41. *Segodnya*, 16 February 1995.
42. *Segodnya*, 14 April, 1995.
43. *Moskovskie Novosti*, No. 4, 1994, p. 10.
44. *Segodnya*, 25 August 1994.
45. It should be noted that Rakhmonov and the Russian politicians were not reacting adequately either. Even the chief of Russia's peacekeeping forces in Tajikistan, General Valery Patrikeev, put the blame for the aggravation of the situation at the Tajik-Afghan border on the Tajik authorities and the command of the Russian border guard forces. See *Segodnya*, 20 April 1995.
46. *Segodnya*, 2 February 1995.
47. Uzbekistan also claims part of the gold and diamond reserves of Russia which were inherited by Russia as a successor of the USSR. But it refuses at the same time to share the foreign debt of the former USSR. See *Segodnya*, 2 February 1995.
48. *Segodnya*, 6 August 1993.
49. Some analysts believe that even if fundamentalists win at free and democratic elections, it is still a better alternative than their outright victory in a fierce civil war. In the first scenario they will be bound by certain rules of the game, while in the second they will feel free from any obligations or commitments.

6 Islamic Fundamentalism, Ethnicity and the State: the Cases of Tajikistan, Pakistan, Iran, and Afghanistan

Alexander Umnov

INTRODUCTION

Islam, Christianity and Buddhism are the three world religions which have the largest number of believers. The crisis of Marxism – the most influential atheistic alternative of development – caused by the break-up of the USSR underlines once again the importance of the religious and, particularly, the Islamic factor in world politics.

This can be explained by means of two analyses. Firstly, the zones of influence of Christianity and Buddhism are generally stable. In spite of the collapse of the communist regimes in the USSR and Eastern Europe, the process of the revival of Christianity in terms of its scale and influence is not comparable with the current expansion of Islam. The Muslim religion has not only consolidated its position in Central Asia, which was until very recently seen as an inalienable part of the USSR, but is also becoming a significant factor in European history after nearly a 500-year break. This process can be seen in the Balkans and also in France where the rapid growth of the Arab population as the result of the high birth rate and of tides of immigrants makes the prediction of Nostradamus about the country becoming Muslim closer to becoming true.

Secondly, the influence of Islam on public life differs substantially from that of Christianity and Buddhism. Islam, unlike the other two, is not content with the private life alone. Therefore there is a stronger case in referring to the Muslim world as an Islamic civilization than would be in the case of the Christian and Buddhist worlds.

At the same time, the Islamic world, although different from the rest of the world, is not as one. The inner differences and contradictions inside Islam are so strong that some parts of it lean towards closer relations with other civilizations rather than with other parts of the Islamic world. For example, Tatarstan is inclined to ally itself with the Orthodox civilization within Russia. Along with contradictions within the Islamic tradition, another important source of contradictions is the painful entry of the Muslim world into world civilization, which is based on Euro-American civilization.

Up to the end of the 1970s, political science in both the West and the East used to refer to the processes within Islam as a confrontation between modernism and traditionalism, that is, the adaptation of Islam to modern life and resistance to it. However, in practice, as the revolution in Iran demonstrated, a traditional Islamic form can sometimes have a non-traditional substance. This prompted political scientists to introduce the term 'Islamic Fundamentalism'. Although 'Islamic Fundamentalism' is sometimes used as a synonym for traditionalism or extremism or even quite arbitrarily, it definitely has a very specific substance, and plays a very specific role in relations with both ethnic groups and the state.

Islam, as is well known, is divided into two groups: Sunnism, which is followed by the majority, and Shi'ism, followed by the minority. Each of these groups has its own subgroups, and all of the subgroups in Sunnism and Shi'ism have their specific features, based on dogmas and rituals. Each subgroup contains two traditions: popular and theological.[1] The former represents the interests of the families, kin and clans (the so-called 'everyday Islam'). The latter stands above them, representing the interests of the entire society. Both these traditions can interact well only within a subgroup or a group of Islam. At the same time, these traditions often confront each other if they involve different groups or subgroups of Islam.

For example, the theological tradition in Sunnism claims the right of each Muslim to relate directly to God. The clergyman is seen here as an organizer of important public functions such as a collective prayer. These functions can be performed by any Muslim. The theological tradition in Shi'ism requires a mediator between God and man – an authority in Islamic law. Therefore, unlike Sunnism, in Shi'ism the role of interpreting Islam is monopolized by the clergy. As for popular traditions in Sunnism and Shi'ism, although these traditions share the acceptance of saints as mediators between God and man, the other differences in dogma and ritual prevent the coming together of the followers of these two branches of Islam.

In addition to this, in the tradition of the same group of Islam there may be serious differences between the ethnic groups. Those differences are well characterized by a popular saying, 'When a Turkman prays, the Uzbek spits'.

It is known that the Islamic Fundamentalists stand for a radical redistribution of power and property among Muslims in favour of the 'genuine' followers of the Prophet. They stand for returning to the foundations of Islam, i.e. strengthening the theological element at the expense of everyday Islam, and for creating on this basis 'a genuine Islamic' state. However, when it comes to what the foundations of Islam are or what constitutes a genuine Islamic state, the fundamentalists normally have very conflicting views, both with the majority of Muslims and among themselves.

Of particular interest are the religious and political movements in the four countries central to the proliferation of Islamic fundamentalism, namely, Tajikistan, Pakistan, Iran, and Afghanistan. Dominating Iran is the main branch of Shi'ism, whereas Sunnism is the predominant philosophy in Afghanistan, Pakistan and Tajikistan. It has to be noted that because of Communist control, Islam in Tajikistan existed until recently only in a form of popular Islam. The theology was either destroyed in the years of the Soviet control or forced underground or incorporated into the Soviet system through the officially appointed mullahs. It was left with no role to play at the level of social life. In the other three countries the theology has always been active, with its activity directly proportional to the state of the relationship between the local ethnic groups.

ETHNICITY AND STATEHOOD

All the four states mentioned above are multiethnic. In each of them there is an ethnic group which makes up the absolute or relative majority of the population. In Iran it is the Persians, who account for fifty per cent of the population. In Afghanistan, the Pushtuns are about forty per cent. In Tajikistan, the Tajiks are more than sixty per cent, and in Pakistan, more than sixty per cent are Punjabis. The rest of the population in these countries is ethnically quite heterogeneous, with Tajikistan perhaps the least so. Among the minorities in Tajikistan, the Uzbeks stand out distinctly. Pakistan is more heterogeneous, with the Pushtuns, Sindhs and Belujis, whilst Iran has the Azeris, Kurds and Arabs. Ethnically the most diverse is Afghanistan, with a large Tajik population but much smaller Uzbek and Turkman groups.

This ethnic mix in these countries is further complicated by the fact that some ethnic groups reside on both sides of the borders. More Tajiks live in Afghanistan than in Tajikistan and there are more Azeris in Iran than in

Azerbaijan. The Pushtuns, the largest ethnic group in Afghanistan, also constitute a significant part of the population of Pakistan, and play an important political role in that country.

However, the degree of ethnic mix does not determine the degree of strength and stability of a state. More important is the efficiency of the mechanism of inter-ethnic co-operation, which has for centuries ensured the viability of the multiethnic states of the Muslim East, as well as the state of alliances and vassalages between the kin, tribes, communes and clans mutually interested in each other due to geographic and economic reasons – to the extent that the ethnic background became of secondary importance. These traditional groups formed a hierarchical but at the same time very mobile pyramid. The constant struggle between different parts of the pyramid was a result of ambitions for a better place in the pyramid, but the need for the pyramid itself was never questioned.

Although in the 19th and the 20th centuries this mechanism was meticulously dismantled by direct political interference and the introduction of private ownership in those Muslim countries of the East which were able to preserve their sovereignty, in the colonial epoch the mechanism was retained successfully. Iran and Afghanistan are two such countries, whilst Tajikistan and Pakistan belong to a very different group of countries.

The northern part of contemporary Tajikistan – the Leninabad (now Khojand) region – joined the Turkestan region of the Russian Empire in the 19th century. The more backward parts of the Bukhara emirate – the South and the East – remained independent until the 1920s. While in Iran and Afghanistan the interaction between ethnic groups, kin and clans in the framework of one state was a result of domestic politics, in Tajikistan it was shaped by colossal pressure from an external totalitarian system. The role of a common ideology was ascribed to Marxism-Leninism, which was alien to local traditions.

Pakistan (which literally means the 'country of the faithful') emerged in 1947 from the predominantly Muslim-populated parts of British India. Although the struggle for the creation of Pakistan was carried out under the banners of the religious community, the leaders of the movement followed Western political tradition by attributing a modest place to religion. Thus both Tajikistan and Pakistan developed not so much under the local tradition that was common to Iran and Afghanistan, but under the impact of world economy, politics and ideologies.

This explains the varying inner strength of these states. To the Europeans both the Iranian and the Afghani ethnic conglomerates seemed to be very fragile, and prone to collapse under a more or less active foreign interference. In reality, however, such interference led to opposite results. Uniting under the banner of Islam, local societies did not break up into separate ethnic groups, but instead developed into nations. A vivid example of this is the British-Afghani wars in the 19th century. Although (unlike Afghanistan, which preserved independence) Iran became a semi-colony in the last century, this internal inter-ethnic balance was preserved. It is not accidental that the separatist movements in Iran at the time (instigated usually from outside) had little success. The only exception confirming the rule was perhaps the Iranian Kurds. But even here it is not very clear whether their separatism was genuine or only a means of getting a better place within the pyramid.

The experience of the 20th century, with Afghanistan and Iran acquiring full political independence, plainly demonstrated that inter-ethnic cohesion in these countries remains intact. This was confirmed during the years of the Islamic revolution in Iran and the civil war in Afghanistan, provoked by the communist coup and exacerbated by the Soviet intervention and invasion. Pakistan and Tajikistan, on the contrary, lack such a cohesion. The state of Pakistan has fallen apart once. In 1971 the armed struggle by the Bengal-populated Eastern province led to the emergence of a new state – Bangladesh. The viability and the territorial integrity of contemporary Pakistan has also been questioned by influential domestic forces. Many Pushtuns, Belujis, and Sindhs, who make up less than thirty per cent of the population but claim almost three-quarters of the country's territory to be their historic homeland, have been demanding an independent Pushtunistan, Belujistan and Sindh.[2]

SELF-REGULATING MECHANISM AND FUNDAMENTALISM

The existence of a self-regulating mechanism of inter-ethnic integration in Iran and Afghanistan and the absence of such in Tajikistan and Pakistan have played a significant role in shaping Islamic fundamentalism in these countries at the end of the 1970s and the beginning of the 1980s.

In Iran, the rejection by society of the deeply alien secular model of development (which the Iranian monarchy was trying to impose, with the help of the US) made Shi'a fundamentalism at the end of the 1970s a form of self-defence against the excesses of modernization. This was very much helped by the strengthening of the notion of the mediatory role between God and man played by experts in Islamic law, both in the theological and in the popular traditions of Shi'ism. This has allowed the clergy to become the unchallenged leaders of the popular movement.

In Afghanistan the Communists, who came to power in April 1978, introduced small ownership closely linked with the state in their attempts to destroy both the potential and real opposition. This blow to feudal and tribal relations provoked a sharply negative reaction from the population which was neither ready nor keen to embrace these changes.

Due to the confrontation that ensued, in many regions the large feudal ownership was wiped out. It was destroyed by the communists as well as by the field commanders who were re-animating and consolidating the communal forms of ownership. While the agrarian policy of the communists was rejected by the population which regarded them as undermining the foundations of local society, the agrarian policy of the field commanders was welcomed and supported. In this situation Islamic fundamentalism based on the theological tradition of Sunnism received a strong impetus. It approved the changes as a God-desired redistribution of wealth in favour of 'genuine' followers of Islam.

The factual usurpation by the field commanders of the role of secular and spiritual leaders has actually narrowed down the place of popular tradition in Sunnism, treating the clergy as a mediator between God and man, in favour of the theological tradition, which denies such mediation. Because of the tension caused by this, the Afghani fundamentalists became much more interested in having external allies. They chose neighbouring Pakistan and the Pakistani fundamentalists as their main allies.

In trying to compensate for the lack of internal inter-ethnic gravitation, and at the same time to control tightly the few but well-organized fundamentalists in the country, Pakistan opted for a distinct 'Islamic' foreign policy. The problem of Kashmir was chosen as a trump card. The predominantly Muslim-populated former principality was divided after the bloody confrontation between India and Pakistan. Formally New Delhi had the right to the whole of Kashmir, since when British India was divided into two entities the status of principalities had to be determined according to the will of the princes, and not on a religious basis. However, Pakistan always denies the legitimacy of any part of Kashmir merging with India, and has been demanding that the population of Indian Kashmir be allowed to determine their future status through a referendum. At the same time, Pakistan has been denying a similar right to the Pushtuns, in spite of demands by Afghanistan, which has never recognized the legitimacy of the Afghan-Pakistani border.

While dealing with India, Pakistan prefers to refer to the era of the Great Moguls, a Muslim dynasty that ruled most part of the subcontinent. When it comes to relations with Afghanistan, Islamabad normally claims the right of a successor to British India. However, starting from the mid-1970s the 'Great Mogul' legacy started to show in Pakistan–Afghanistan relations as well. As a means of pressure on Kabul, Islamabad started supporting the Afghani fundamentalists, who do not recognise borders between Muslim countries. After the communist coup in Afghanistan in 1978, and especially after the Soviet invasion in 1979, the Pakistani authorities intensified their activities in this direction. At that time the communists and the fundamentalists in Afghanistan were provoking each other into a more active role.

Not surprisingly, the withdrawal of Soviet troops from Afghanistan and the departure of communists from the political scene seriously undermined the strength of local fundamentalism. During the war against the communist regime and the Soviet invasion, the consolidation of fundamentalist forces which stood for rigid centralized institutions based on communal ownership was seen as a necessity prompted by the situation in the country.[3] However after the Mujahedin Government was formed in Kabul this policy met with resistance. More and more field commanders were viewing the fundamentalists as enemies, and their Islamic ideology as even more dangerous than communism.

Against this background, the close relations between the Pakistani and Afghani fundamentalists were seen in Islamabad as negative rather than positive. It is no accident that Pakistani fundamentalists were removed from an active foreign policy role. In its turn this had a reverse impact on the influence of the fundamentalists inside Afghanistan. Subsequently popular tradition in Sunnism started gaining momentum and questioning the authenticity of the fundamentalists' claims about Islam. Today the question is not about fundamentalism becoming a leading force in Afghanistan, but about the place it is going to occupy in the multiethnic structure of the local society, which is going through its worst ever crisis.

As a result of calamities caused by the communist rule, the presence in the country of the Soviet troops and the confrontations between the mujahedins, the demographic balance between the Pushtuns and the non-Pushtuns has changed in favour of the non-Pushtuns, the Tajiks, Uzbeks, Turkmens and others. This is explained by the large emigration of Pushtuns, primarily to Pakistan. The erosion of ancient communal, clan and tribal connections strengthened the ethnic factor. This was exacerbated by the break-up of the USSR and the emergence on the northern borders of Afghanistan of sovereign Uzbekistan, Turkmenistan, and particularly Tajikistan.

FUNDAMENTALISM IN TAJIKISTAN AND AFGHANISTAN

While the totalitarian system in the USSR was becoming senile in the 1970s, relations between the northern, southern and eastern clans in

Tajikistan, which had never been really warm, were becoming even more tense. The Northerners who were mainly recruited in the Soviet period into the party and government elite and some of the Southern clans who received their share of power were meeting with a growing challenge from the East and a large part of the South.

The local Communist Party (also dominated by Northerners) failed to stop the centrifugal trends. The totalitarian control, which had been keeping Tajikistan united, suffered a dramatic decline after the victory of anti-Communist forces in Russia. Such a decline in turn provoked a new wave of inter-clan struggle, which was stopped only when Moscow and Tashkent intervened.

Islamic fundamentalism in Tajikistan, which was initially trying to challenge the clan structure of the society, soon became an instrument of the struggle of the South against the North. This was helped by the fact that in the Soviet period Islam was brought down to a domestic (everyday) level, whilst the absence of theological tradition was depriving the local fundamentalists of an integrating role in the society. In view of the tremendous influence of traditional ties in the country which (unlike in Afghanistan) were not undermined but rather regenerated in the new 'socialist' forms, the local fundamentalists as well as the communists were only an additional leverage in the power struggle between the regional clans.[4]

The explosive situation in Tajikistan is negatively affecting the domestic situation in Afghanistan. In the course of the inter-clan war dozens of thousands of people were forced out into Afghani territory. Their appearance has seriously complicated the local scene, and pressure on the limited resources of the country has increased significantly. The armed groups arriving from Tajikistan were viewed by the field commanders as rivals in the power struggle. This led to a situation where the mujahedins and the local authorities started sending the refugees back to Tajikistan. The latter agreed to return only in groups and in a well-armed state in order to be able to survive, and also to take vengeance. The border is guarded by Russian troops who try to stop these groups from penetrating into Tajikistan. The support to the refugees in crossing the border provided by the Afghani forces escalates the conflict. Naturally, the Afghani, Tajik and Pakistani fundamentalists are trying to score as many political points as possible out of this situation, but the objective realities in Afghanistan, Tajikistan and Pakistan are working against them. Particularly active in this is Islamabad, which has shifted its sympathies for the fundamentalists to the forces of traditional Islam.

Islamabad is prompted in this by the situation inside Pakistan. Millions of Pushtuns who have moved there are not in a hurry to leave, and this leads to growing inter-ethnic conflicts and undermines the territorial integrity of the state. The Pakistani authorities are well aware that only through restoring the inter-ethnic pyramid in Afghanistan with endorsement from traditional Islam can the Afghani Pushtuns be persuaded to return home. In stimulating this process Islamabad has facilitated the formation of the Taliban movement.

The word 'talib', which means a pupil in a Muslim religious school, can be applied to any Muslim who can comprehend but not cleanse Islam. One can be a talib in any branch of Islam as well as a fundamentalist, but while the former respects popular tradition in Islam, the latter is intolerant of it.

The seed sown by Islamabad has fallen on a fertile soil. Having united various forces among Pushtuns ranging from fundamentalists to former communists, the Talibs have taken over more than half of the territory of Afghanistan. The split among the non-Pushtuns (for many of them traditional Pushtun domination is a lesser evil than a fundamentalist revolution or a rule by Tajiks incapable of uniting their country) provides the Talibs with serious chances for final victory.

FUNDAMENTALISM IN IRAN

The strengthening of traditional Islam prevents Islamic revolution, which fundamentalists are prone to, since they are keen to drastically restructure society. At the same time it is wrong to treat the hypothetical victory of fundamentalists in the Middle East as an absolute evil. The policy of contemporary Iran demonstrates this quite well. The formation in that country of a fundamentalist state, still the only one in the world, has enabled Teheran to continue the policy of modernization in such forms as are acceptable to the public.

A combination of the special rights of the clergy and of electoral choice has created in Iran a very solid and flexible system of power; much more democratic than in many countries of the Near and Middle East. Iran does not have the rigid pyramid of power that other countries in the region have. While the assassination of a ruler in those countries can be sufficient to cause changes in domestic and foreign policies, in Iran such an action would not have much impact. The wide range of powers than the Iranian Parliament enjoys finds no comparison in the political systems of Iraq, Saudi Arabia, Syria and even in relatively more liberal Kuwait.

'The human rights violations in Iran', according to an American expert, 'are enormous. But compared to Saudis and Syrians currently co-operating with Americans, are Iranians really the worst in the Near and the Middle

East? The Iranian democracy is in its embryonic state. It is limited, easily annoyed but constitutional, tangible and successive. Do Saudi Arabia, Syria or Egypt have a parliament which could compete with the Iranian? The freedom of expression and particularly political freedoms are often limited and suppressed in Iran but under the surveillance of censors various views in the society, some of them indirectly critical of the clergy, find their way into the media, books, theatre and movies.'[5]

Incidentally, the US-based Freedom House human rights organization, in its report for 1994, did not list Iran among more than twenty states which were rated at the bottom in terms of political rights and civil liberties. The list, however, included Afghanistan, Algeria, China, Cuba, Iraq, Libya, North Korea, Saudi Arabia, Somalia, Sudan, Syria, Tajikistan, Turkmenistan and Uzbekistan.

In the economic sphere, the Islamic regime in Iran has moved away from the initial policy of nationalization to privatization and market reforms. The programme of creating free economic zones indicates Teheran's consistency in this. It is well known that such zones are one of the most efficient ways of converting a centralized economy into a market one. Thus the political system of Iran is in fact much more liberal than that of many countries in the region, and is being supported by an adequate economic base.

As for Iran's foreign policy, it contains nothing that would suggest a forced export of Islamic revolution. Recollections of the treatment of US diplomats kept hostage in Teheran at the end of the 1970s and the beginning of the 1980s, the death sentence imposed on the British writer Rushdi as well as the policy of non-recognition of Israel do not do credit to Iran's foreign policy. Apart from that, Teheran is playing a stabilizing role today, and like Afghanistan, Iran is one of the multiethnic states with the most diverse ethnic groups in the world. The growth of instability in the Middle East and in Central and South Asia after the break-up of the USSR has also been affecting Iran. This could provide some explanations for Iran's policy towards Iraq's aspiration to be reunited with Kuwait, the Karabakh conflict and the settlement of the situation in Tajikistan and Afghanistan.

CONCLUSION

Whilst defending the Tajik-Afghan border, Russia is trying to support and restore (on each side of the border) the mechanism of stabilization and national integration. Iran, where the fundamentalists are in power, has similar interests. So do Afghanistan and Pakistan, where Islamic fundamentalism, either as a religious or a political movement, is not in power, but rather a marginal opposition or semi-opposition force. This controversial role of fundamentalism in one of the most unstable parts of the world refutes the popular notion that with the demise of the Soviet-American confrontation it is this religious and political movement that is the most destabilizing force in the world. Moreover, in some situations fundamentalism can become a stabilizing element of international and inter-ethnic relations, and a means of consolidating liberalism in the parts of world where civilization is incompatible with the Euro-American civilization.[6]

NOTES

1. See Manson, H.J., *Islam and Revolution in the Middle East*, Yale University Press, New Haven, 1988; and Poliakov, S., *Everyday Islam*, N.Y.L., 1992.
2. Harrison, S.S., 'Ethnicity and the Political Stalemate in Pakistan', in *The State, Religion, and Ethnic Politics: Afghanistan, Iran and Pakistan*, Syracuse University Press, 1986, p. 270.
3. See Roy, O., *Islam and Resistance in Afghanistan*, Cambridge University Press, Cambridge, 1988.
4. See Khaidarov, G. and Inomov, M., *Tajikistan: Tragedy and Anguish of the Nation*, St. Petersburg, 1993, p. 21 and p. 84.
5. *Foreign Policy*, 1994, No. 96, p. 77.
6. See Umnov, A., Russia and the South in *Russia Today: A Russian View*, The Leonard Davis Institute for International Relations, the Hebrew University of Jerusalem, Jerusalem, 1994.

7 Population Dynamics in Central Asia and Adjacent Countries from 1960 to 2020

Alexander Akimov

This essay is an analysis of possible future population growth in the Central Asian states and adjacent countries. If a forecast is considered to be the most probable variant of a future, then this analysis is not a forecast. Rather it is a computational experiment which shows potential changes in the population in each country in the region and analyses the importance and results of the population profile changes in the region.

The technique for computational experimentation called algorithmic description of demographic transition, which is aimed at forecasting the population numbers of a country, is presented here by the author. Its short description is presented in an appendix to this essay, and its full description is in the author's book.[1]

Computational experiment in this essay imitates two processes: natural population growth (births surplus over deaths) and international migration. The principal question of the analysis may be formulated as: *What will happen if all the Russian-speaking population (RSP) leave Central Asia?* By RSP we mean Russians, Ukrainians, Byelorussians, Germans and Jews.

The migration of these ethnic groups is significant for Central Asian states and Russia. RSP makes up a considerable portion of the Central Asian population, and a big portion of its skilled labour and professionals. Presently RSP immigration adds to Russia's social and economic problems, but it can be an important inflow of people for the decreasing Russian population. The neighbouring countries of China, Afghanistan and Iran can also be affected by these migrations, because if all RSP leaves Central Asia, then the question arises: who would take their place in the Central Asian economies? Besides, the RSP departure from Central Asia will significantly affect the future population profile of the Central Asian states.

POPULATION GROWTH FROM 1960 TO 1990

The algorithmic description of demographic transition consists of two tables and a graph. To use description for forecasting, one should first describe real population growth in retrospect. The retrospective description embraces two steps:

1 The first is to find the country's interval of the principal social and economic indicators in the algorithmic description, which is the number of people involved in non-agricultural activities as per 1,000 of total population. Graphically the relationship between crude birth and death rates and the number of people engaged in non-agricultural activities per 1,000 of the total population is similar to the relationship of these rates to time according to the theory of demographic transition. The bend point for people engaged in non-agricultural activities per 1,000 of total population is 150 for death curve, and 250 for birth curve.

2 The second step is to derive the demographic patterns for the retrospect. The patterns are the pairs of crude birth and death rates, intrinsic to particular stages of demographic transition. The identification of the pattern for the particular country should be done for comparing the five-year natural increases in population with the patterns increase. The patterns, which are possible for the country at the given interval of non-agricultural activities level, are involved in comparison. The pattern which minimizes the difference between the model and the real increases is considered to be actual for the corresponding period for an individual country.

After the retrospective patterns are found, the population number projections can be calculated by moving along the graph according to the choice made by an expert.

Information sources for population growth and the number of people engaged in non-agricultural activities are the UN and national statistical publications.[2] The results of calculations are presented in Table 1.

HYPOTHESES FOR THE FORECAST

Two forecasts are made in this section. One presents patterns of demographic development up to 2020 for the Central Asian states and all adjacent countries. The other shows migration levels for the Central Asian states and Russia. To forecast the future patterns two sources are used: the sequence of patterns in retrospect from 1960 to 1990 and our projection based on the sequence of patterns.

Table 7.1 Retrospective Population Growth Description by Demographic Development Patterns

	1961–1965	1966–1970	1971–1975	1976–1980	1981–1985	1986–1990			
	Kazakhstan[3]								
pattern	TFS(c)	PTH	BD	PTH	BD				
discrepancy[4]	–0.10	–0.45	–0.96	+0.06	–0.51				
	Kyrgyzstan								
pattern	PEG	TFS(a)	TFS(c)	TFS(c)	TFS(c)	TFS(c)			
discrepancy	–0.04	0.0	–0.86	–0.31	–0.45	–0.80			
	Tajikistan								
pattern	PEG	PEG	TFS(a)	TFS(a)	TFS(a)	PEG			
discrepancy	–1.62	–0.52	–1.42	–0.62	–0.11	+0.68			
	Turkmenistan								
pattern	PEG	TFS(a)	TFS(a)	TFS(b)	TFS(b)	TFS(a)			
discrepancy	–0.27	–0.28	+0.44	–0.11	+0.22	+0.98			
	Uzbekistan								
pattern	PEG	PEG	TFS(a)	TFS(a)	TFS(b)	TFS(b)			
discrepancy	–0.97	+0.36	+0.36	+0.95	+0.18	–0.62			
	Russia								
pattern	BD	PTC	PTC	PTC	PTC	PTC			
discrepancy	–0.94	–0.15	+0.79	+1.15	+1.54	+1.73			
	China								
pattern	TM(b)	BC(l)	TM(b)	ÀÀ(p)	TM(b)	BC(l)	PTH	PTH	PTH
discrepancy	+0.30	–0.07	+0.59	+0.49	+1.14	+0.68			
	Iran								
pattern	TFS(b)	PEG	PES	PES	PES	PEG			
discrepancy	+0.15	+0.73	+0.63	–0.19	–0.19	–1.31			
	Afghanistan								
pattern	TM(b)	BC(l)	TM(a)	TM(a)	TM(a)	TM(a)	TM(a)		
discrepancy	0.0	–0.35	+0.27	–0.19	–0.18	–1.19			

Two main trends for the Central Asian states are worked out. The first is a salvation of demographic trends in fertility and death, the second is a delay of demographic development from the point of view of a transition of demographic patterns, intrinsic to developed nations of the world, as a result of the RSP emigration. This delay is quite possible, because the RSP is the bearer of modern demographic behaviour.

To imitate migration processes two possible evolutions are examined: emigration of the entire RSP, and a cessation of RSP emigration after 1995.

For all the Central Asian states an assumption is made that 80 per cent of emigrants go to Russia and 20 per cent go to the other Commonwealth of Independent States (CIS) and outside the CIS. Emigration statistics from 1991 to 1994 are taken from current publications.

The computational procedure is as follows:

First, the number of population for the last year of the five-year intervals is estimated according to the patterns of demographic development;

Second, the number of emigrants is subtracted from the numbers of population for the Central Asian states and the number of immigrants is added to the population of Russia.

This procedure is rather rough as a computational tool, but it is satisfactory at the initial stage of analysis, when the numerical estimate may not be accurate. The estimate can be improved later with the improvement of forecast hypotheses and computational procedure. The problem is that the complicated procedure needs more detailed information. For instance, the usage of the most commonly used age survival technique needs statistical and forecast age-specific information on population number, birth, death and migration. If there is no such information, or if access to it is difficult, many additional hypotheses are needed to use this technique. We consider that calculations and estimates of this kind, together with the more detailed estimates of migration potential, bi-national marriage rates and other hypotheses, are better applied after the first calculations, based on the simple premises, to ensure control of the most important factors in the computation.

Kazakhstan

In retrospect, from 1970 to 1990, the closest correlation between the real and patterns description of population growth is achieved by PTH and BD patterns. They alternate while BD should follow PTH. This alternation is a sign of instability of the demographic progress in Kazakhstan. Nevertheless, assuming a fertility slow-down and an ageing population, then according to the sequence of patterns graph (see Appendix) these patterns will be followed by a period of stable demographic evolution with low birth and death rates. It is described by the BD pattern. It is a forecast for Kazakhstan after the year 2000. It means that from that time Kazakhstan will have demographic parameter similar to those in Sweden from 1920 to 1970. This pattern was defined for the other Scandinavian countries for the same period, for the East European countries from 1961 to 1985 and in several other demographically developed countries (countries with low fertility and death rates).

If demographic transition slow-down after the RSP emigration occurs, then Kazakhstan's population growth is described by the PTH pattern. This pattern describes the relatively high fertility situation in economically developed countries, where in a generally good economic environment there are social factors pushing the birth rate up. Argentina, Uruguay, Chile, and South Africa in the 1960s and 1970s are the closest parallels of this type of development.

It is in the analysis of emigration that the most eye-catching point is raised. From 1991 to 1994 the number of emigrants increased tenfold. To forecast future emigration, the following assumptions are made: in 1995 emigration growth will continue at the present rate; and after 1995 emigration will be stable during all five-year periods and will be equal to the level of the 1991–1995 period.

If these assumptions are correct, the annual emigration will be 400,000 people in the years to come. The potential emigration from Kazakhstan is estimated as half of its 1990 population of 7.345 million people. During the first five years about one million people will leave Kazakhstan and then every five years about two million people will emigrate from it.

Kyrgyzstan

Population growth in Kyrgyzstan from 1970 to 1990 is described by the TFS(c) pattern which is the final phase of demographic transition in fertility. According to the sequence of patterns graph, TFS(c) pattern should be followed by PTH – the post-transitional pattern with high birth rates. The states whose population growth is also approximated by this pattern are listed above in forecasting hypotheses for Kazakhstan. If an assumption about demographic transition slow-down after the low-fertility RSP emigration is made, Kyrgyzstan's population is described by the present demographic pattern. The present TFS(c) pattern is an accurate long-term approximation for Caribbean states, for example. It describes population growth correctly there from 1961 to 1985.

From 1991 to 1994, about 210,000 people left Kyrgyzstan for Russia. If 1995 emigration to Russia and five-year emigration to all other states is added, the total emigration from 1991 to 1995 will make up 275,000 people. In contrast to Kazakhstan, in 1994 there was a small emigration decline in Kyrgyzstan. That is why the 1995 emigration estimate is not bigger than the average for the period. On the basis of the ethnic structure of the population, the total emigration potential is estimated at 1.1 million people or one quarter of the population.

Tajikistan

Like Kazakhstan, the alternation of demographic patterns in Tajikistan is an expression of demographic transition instability. If the retrospect trend is prolonged, Tajikistan should pass to fertility transition patterns. In the short run this hypothesis is not correct from the point of view of social and economic assumptions which are made for this pattern. In fact, fertility transition patterns imply high levels of economic, social and political well-being in a country. There are no adequate conditions for these demographic patterns in Tajikistan now and they will not appear in the near future. Anyhow, population growth rates there are likely to slow down, principally because of the extremely high population density and natural limits to extensive economic growth. Civil war and general economic crisis add to the severity of the situation. Thus the use of the following patterns for the future demographic growth in Tajikistan (see Table 7.5) is provisional. But there is no alternative to the slow-down of population growth in that country.

The RSP of Tajikistan was about 450,000 people before the civil war started there. From 1991 to 1994 about 190,000 people left Tajikistan for Russia. In 1994 there was decline in emigration compared to 1993. For 1995 emigration can be estimated equal to the average level of the 1991–1994 period. So the 1991–1995 emigration can be estimated as 250,000 people. The last 200,000 people will leave Tajikistan within the next five years.

The RSP emigration cannot influence birth and death rates in Tajikistan significantly because of its low share in the total population. That is why there is no accelerated population growth scenario for Tajikistan.

Turkmenistan

From 1991 to 1994, 39,500 people left Turkmenistan for Russia. The emigration trend is irregular. In 1991 and 1993 between 4,500 and 5,500 people emigrated to Russia each year, while in 1992 and 1994 a much larger of number of between 12,000 and 17,000 people did so annually. It should be mentioned that in 1993 emigration rates and even volumes declined in Turkimenistan. However, unlike trends in Turkmenistan, the emigration volumes remained high in the other Central Asian states, making the trends more consistent.

Keeping the above-mentioned uncertainties in mind, we consider that the most natural assumption for Turkmenistan is a stable annual emigration at the average 1991 to 1994 level. So an annual emigration will be around 10,000 people. The total RSP in Turkmenistan is about 360,000 people. Therefore, if the present trends continue, about 50,000 people will leave Turkmenistan during five-year periods. In this case not all RSP will leave Turkmenistan up to 2020.

In retrospect slow fertility transition pattern was registered in Turkmenistan. We consider that this pattern will remain in Turkmenistan and the transition process will be slow in the foreseeable future. Low RSP share in the total population and low volume emigration make an accelerated population growth scenario for Turkmenistan meaningless.

Uzbekistan

In 1991, the RSP of Uzbekistan was about 1.8 million people. From 1991 to 1994, 326,400 people left Uzbekistan for Russia.

As in Turkmenistan, there was an emigration decline in 1993 in Uzbekistan. If the 1995 emigration to Russia and the whole five-year term emigration to the other states is added, the 1991–1995 total emigration can be estimated at 500,000 people. Such five-year emigration level is forecast for the next three five-year periods and the last 300,000 people of the RSP will leave Uzbekistan between 2005 and 2010.

In retrospect, Uzbekistan's population growth was approximated by a slow fertility transition pattern and the rate of transition was equal to the international average rate for the period from 1960 to 1985.

Prolonging this trend, Uzbekistan can terminate demographic transition in fertility after 2005. We forecast that complete RSP emigration will inevitably slow down demographic transition in Uzbekistan. To reflect this evolution, we elongate the terms of the fertility transition pattern for Uzbekistan.

Russia

In retrospect, the Russian population dynamic is approximated by a post-transitional pattern with stable birth and death rates. It is worth mentioning that the discrepancy between the pattern description and real population dynamics was growing gradually larger from the early to the later periods. Patterns overestimate Russian population in retrospect. If the sequence of patterns is followed, Russia has a significant potential of population growth. But recent demographic statistics show a Russian population decrease as a result of extremely low fertility and growing mortality. So to approximate Russian population dynamics from 1991 to 1995, a natural decline of population pattern is used. It is highly probable that such a trend will continue until 2000. If an economic recovery begins in the near future, better economic conditions may push death rates down and birth rates up. In this case the ageing-population pattern will describe population growth in Russia. A return to the post-transitional pattern with stable birth and death rates is hardly possible because of the ageing of the Russian population during the previous ten years. A high proportion of old people in the population and the widespread one-child-per-family standards will be obstacles to returning to the earlier fertility standards.

In our calculation experiments of imitating the RSP immigration to Russia from the Central Asia, only those immigrants who come directly from Central Asia are involved (see Table 7.2). All other migration to and from Russia is excluded in our calculation.

Table 7.2 Emigration from Central Asia from 1990 to 2020 (in 000)

Year	1991–1995	1996–2000	2001–2005	2006–2010	2011–2015	2016-2020
Total	2,075	3,025	2,825	2,625	1,550	50
including to Russia	1,660	2,420	2,260	2,100	1,240	40

RESULTS OF MIGRATION PROCESSES

Kazakhstan (see Table 7.3)

The RSP emigration will result, first, in qualified workforce losses and, second, in a loss of Kazakhstan's position as a state with relatively high population in the Central Asian region. Two problems will arise. The first one will be how to fill job vacancies by qualified people and the second will be the changing ethnic identity of Kazakhstan in the event of the inevitable immigration of other ethnic groups from neighbouring countries, particularly Uzbeks. High demographic pressure on Uzbekistan and easy-to-cross state boundaries between Uzbekistan and Kazakhstan make the second problem very critical. There are several ways of solving the first problem. Special training programs for Kazakh nationals can be launched or foreign work force can be invited for temporary job in oil fields, metallurgical works and other industrial sectors which are vital for the Kazakh economy.

Table 7.3 Kazakhstan's Population Forecast up to 2020

	1990	1995	2000	2005	2010	2015	2020
	The RSP Emigration and Extrapolation of Demographic Trends						
scenario patterns[5]	BD	BD	PTC	PTC	PTC	PTC	–
emigration[6]	–	1,000	2,000	2,000	2,000	1,500	–
population[7]	16,746	16,600	15,447	14,035	12,569	11,548	11,987
	The RSP Emigration and Demographic Transition Slow Down Scenario Patterns						
patterns	BD	PTH	PTH	PTH	PTH	PTH	
emigration	–	1,000	2,000	2,000	2,000	1,500	–
population	16,746	16,600	15,883	15,111	14,278	13,882	14,955
	The RSP Emigration Stoppage Scenario						
patterns	BD	BD	PTC	PTC	PTC	PTC	–
emigration	–	1,000	–	–	–	–	–
population	16,746	16,600	17,447	18,337	19,272	20,255	21,289

Many countries can provide Kazakhstan with the requisite professionals. Russia, Ukraine, Uzbekistan, and Azerbaijan are the first among them. These CIS countries have workforces which can fill job vacancies in the key industries of the Kazakh economy, which feed national exports such as oil and metallurgy. It should be mentioned that in their immigration policy the Kazakh authorities will have to choose between a highly qualified but culturally strange Slavic labour force and culturally close Uzbek and Azerbaijanian labour with lower qualification.

Second, China and South Korea can be the sources of the much needed skilled labour. Labour forces from these countries will meet fewer national prejudices and raise fewer national fears than the CIS labour force. The Korean labour force will be more expensive but it can work hand in hand with capital imports from Korea. Our hypothesis is that to make the right decision in this situation, the Kazakh authorities will examine the key export potential and then import the labour force to ensure the development of that potential.

To save the ethnic identity of Kazakhstan from the demographic pressures from Uzbekistan, the Kazakh authorities can launch a campaign to attract the Kazakhs to immigrate to Kazakhstan from other Central Asian countries and China. This problem is connected with political aspects of power (army, state officials, as well as electorate), but the Kazakh immigration back home solves no economic problems, because Kazakh-immigrants will be principally from the rural areas.

If Russians and Ukrainians leave the northern territories of Kazakhstan, another problem will arise. They are engaged in corn production, which is a flourishing sector of Kazakh agriculture and an important export item. Local Central Asian nationals have no skills in this field.

Kyrgyzstan (see Table 7.4)

The after-effects of complete RSP emigration from Kyrgyzstan are similar to those in Kazakhstan. There will be no highly qualified workforce and the share of Kyrgyzstan in the total Central Asian population will decrease. As with Kazakhstan, many other issues will be critical for Kyrgyzstan. Kazakh exports are dependent on the RSP labour and their emigration is a threat to Kazakhstan's export sector. While for Kyrgyzstan the survival of the modern urban economy is vital, it is also dependent on the RSP. The RSP here, however, can be replaced by Uzbeks, for instance, because this sector needs lower qualifications.

The problem of demographic potential remaining for national territory control in the easy-to-cross state boundaries environment is not very sharp for Kyrgyzstan because the RSP here is mainly urban settlers.

Table 7.4 Kyrgyzstan's Population Forecast up to 2020

	1990	1995	2000	2005	2010	2015	2020
The RSP Emigration and Extrapolation of Demographic Trends Scenario							
pattern	TFS(c)	PTH	PTH	PTH	PTH	PTH	–
emigration	–	275	275	275	275	–	–
population	4,396	4,579	4,657	4,742	4,834	5,207	5,610
The RSP Emigration and Demographic Transition Slowdown Scenario							
pattern	TFS(c)	TFS(c)	TFS(c)	TFS(c)	TFS(c)	TFS(c)	–
emigration	–	275	275	275	275	–	–
population	4,396	4,579	4,780	5,003	5,248	5,795	6,398
The RSP Emigration Stoppage Scenario							
pattern	TFS(c)	PTH	PTH	PTH	PTH	PTH	–
emigration	–	275	–	–	–	–	–
population	4,396	4,579	4,933	5,314	5,725	6,167	6,644

Tajikistan (see Table 7.5)

In the civil war environment the RSP emigration from Tajikistan is not the most important demographic event, because the rupture of economic life there is mostly caused by warfare. Because of the economic destruction, the fast-growing native population may take the RSP's emigration as good for them, because it provides homes and consumer goods for the local population.

As the civil war comes to an end, qualified labour will become an urgent need for Tajikistan. Of course, a part of the RSP may return to their former jobs at big industrial enterprises which have their own company towns where it is easier to provide homes for them. To return the RSP to big cities will be much more difficult, because their homes will be already occupied by others.

In addition to the RSP labour force, Uzbek and Kazakh specialists may be invited. This variant has advantages and disadvantages as compared with the RSP labour force. Uzbeks and Kazakhs, though newcomers, are culturally close to Tajiks. On the other hand, Uzbeks can be 'received as unfriendly' in Tajikistan. As for the Kazakh labour force, there are enough job vacancies in Kazakhstan. Generally speaking, the problem of qualified labour force will arise in Tajikistan only when foreign investments comes, and investors will have to solve this problem in the way they see as the best.

Another opportunity is orientation to Iran. There are cultural and political prerequisites for it – a common language, and the need for allies in the region, for instance. Besides, growing demographic pressure also makes this scenario probable. High population growth in Iran and a threat of potentially high unemployment there may make job vacancies in

Table 7.5 Tajikistan's Population Forecast up to 2020

	1990	1995	2000	2005	2010	2015	2020
The RSP Emigration and Extrapolation of Demographic Trends Scenario							
pattern	TFS(a)	TFS(a)	TFS(a)	TFS(b)	TFS(b)	TFS(b)	–
emigration	–	250	200	–	–	–	–
population	5,302	5,896	6,636	7,693	8,703	9,847	11,141

Tajikistan attractive to a labour force with middle qualifications in Iran. Moreover, the two are culturally close.

Turkmenistan (see Table 7.6)

The RSP emigration will not influence seriously neither labour market nor demographic potential in Turkmenistan. If emigration goes on at the rates seen during the recent years, it will not cause any disorder to economic life such as in Kazakhstan, Kyrgyzstan or Tajikistan. It will be easy to replace the RSP labour force in oil and gas sector and other industries, because growing gas export revenue brings big money to Turkmenistan, making the country attractive to labour forces from various states.

Table 7.6 Turkmenistan's Population Forecast up to 2020

	1990	1995	2000	2005	2010	2015	2020
	The RSP Emigration and Extrapolation of Demographic Trends Scenario						
pattern	TFS(a)	TFS(a)	TFS(b)	TFS(b)	TFS(b)	TFS(c)	–
emigration	–	50	50	50	50	50	50
population	3,669	4,203	4,823	5,407	6,067	6,814	7,474
	The RSP Emigration Stoppage Scenario						
pattern	TFS(a)	TFS(a)	TFS(b)	TFS(b)	TFS(b)	TFS(c)	–
emigration	–	50	–	–	–	–	–
population	3,669	4,203	4,873	5,513	6,238	7,057	7,792

Uzbekistan (see Table 7.7)

Although the RSP in Uzbekistan is much larger compared to Turkmenistan, the RSP emigration from Uzbekistan will have only limited demographic effects, as in Turkmenistan. However, the economic impact can be greater, though not as great as in Kazakhstan and Kyrgyzstan. The reason is that the most important export sector in Uzbekistan is cotton, and the RSP is not engaged there. The problem of qualified labour in Uzbekistan has a specific feature at the regional level. The fact is that Uzbekistan has the largest qualified labour force and the most efficient

Table 7.7 Uzbekistan's Population Forecast up to 2020

	1990	1995	2000	2005	2010	2015	2020
The RSP Emigration and Extrapolation of Demographic Trends Scenario							
pattern	TFS(c)	TFS(c)	TFS(c)	PTH	PTH	PTH	–
emigration	–	500	500	500	300	–	–
population	20,500	22,134	23,938	25,929	27,633	29,769	32,069
The RSP Emigration and Demographic Transition Slow Down Scenario							
pattern	TFS(b)	TFS(b)	TFS(c)	TFS(c)	TFS(c)	TFS(c)	–
emigration	–	500	500	500	300	–	–
population	20,500	22,694	25,176	27,296	29,837	32,943	36,372
The RSP Emigration Stoppage Scenario							
pattern	TFS(c)	TFS(c)	TFS(c)	PTH	PTH	PTH	–
emigration	–	500	–	–	–	–	–
population	20,500	22,134	24,437	26,981	29,789	32,890	36,313

educational system in the region. Thus potentially Uzbekistan is a supplier of professionals to the other Central Asian countries, while no other Central Asian country can be an adequate source for the market of qualified labour for Uzbekistan. In such circumstances, Uzbekistan can only rely upon out-of-region sources of qualified labour, such as Russia, Azerbaijan (the oil sector) or Iran, China, Turkey and South Korea.

Russia (see Table 7.8)

Presently the RSP immigration to Russia from Central Asia and other CIS countries is a disaster for the Russian federal budget and for social stability in a situation of growing unemployment. There will be little change of this prospect in the years to come.

In the long run, if the Russian economy recovers, the work force will be needed as a factor of economic growth. Immigration may become the only source of wanted labour as long as the Russian population decreases. Under these circumstances the RSP departure from Central Asia to Russia may be explained by the attraction of Russia as a place of higher wages and salaries and higher living standards rather than by factors such as the

Table 7.8 Russia's Population Forecast up to 2020

	1990	1995	2000	2005	2010	2015	2020
Extrapolation of Demographic Trends with No Immigration from the Central Asia Scenario							
pattern[8]	NDP	NDP	ZPG	AP	AP	AP	
immigration[9]	–	–	–	–	–	–	–
population[10]	148,255	144,585	141,007	141,007	142,778	144,572	146,388
Extrapolation of Demographic Trends with Immigration from the Central Asia Scenario							
pattern	NDP	NDP	ZPG	AP	AP	AP	
immigration	–	1,660	2,420	2,260	2,100	1,240	40
population	148,255	146,245	145,046	147,306	151,256	154,396	156,376

government policies of Central Asian states and/or popular nationalism in the region as at present.

There may be another scenario of the RSP emigration development. The RSP may prefer to stay in Central Asia not only if the Central Asian governments stop their policies of pushing out the RSP, but if Russia becomes unattractive. This could happen if the political situation in Russia worsens dramatically with a parallel economic decline. If this happens, the RSP will prefer to stay in politically stable Central Asian countries, even under volatile interethnic conditions. The possible scenarios of instability in Russia are extreme political dictatorship, social disorder, and deep economic crisis.

POPULATION FORECAST FOR CHINA, IRAN AND AFGHANISTAN

The population of China, Iran and Afghanistan has also been forecast by employing the algorithmic description technique. Unlike Central Asia and Russia, migration has not been taken into consideration. Only one version of demographic forecast is used. The reason is that the principal purpose of the present analysis is to examine the relative significance of various demographic trends in Central Asia. Very many changing variables can make analysis extremely complicated. For all three countries a variant is chosen which can be considered medium, if a common demographic classification to minimal, medium, and maximum variants of population growth is kept in mind.

China

For China the principal hypothesis is that it will finish the demographic transition in the near future. The post-transitional pattern with stable birth and death rates, which is typical for developed countries before the ageing of population, is an approximation of China's population growth.

Iran

To describe the future population growth of Iran, a sequence of patterns is chosen which describes slow fertility transition.

Afghanistan

For Afghanistan the chosen patterns describe mortality transition.

The results are presented in Table 7.9

REGIONAL POPULATION PROFILE AND POSSIBLE RELATED PROBLEMS

Migrations and demographic development[11] change the relative weights of an individual country's population in the region. In addition, the age structure of the population is different in these countries. In Russia and, to a lesser extent, in China, the population will be ageing, that is to say that the proportion of old people will increase in the entire population, while in the other countries the proportion of young people will stay high.

In Central Asia the most important change up to the year 2020 will be the unchallengeable position of Uzbekistan as the country in the region with the largest population (see Tables 7.10 and 7.11). In 1960 Uzbekistan was ranking second in terms of population in Central Asia after Kazakhstan, and it became the first in 1990 with 40 per cent of the regional population, while Kazakhstan accounted for 1/3 of the regional population. There have been various projections of the growth of the regional population. The average estimate is that by the year 2020 Uzbekistan's population will be twice as large as Kazakhstan's population. Other projections estimate that Kazakhstan's share in the total regional population will decrease to half of Uzbekistan's share. Kazakhstan may account for only between 18 per cent and 26 per cent of the total.

Another important change will be the rise of Tajikistan's share in the regional population from 10 per cent in 1990 to 13 or even 16 per cent in

Table 7.9 Population Forecast for China, Iran and Afghanistan up to 2020

	1990	1995	2000	2005	2010	2015	2020
	China						
pattern	PTH	BD	BD	PTC	PTC	PTC	PTC
population[12]	1,133,683	1,221,299	1,283,597	1,349,073	1,400,425	1,453,735	1,509,074
	Iran						
pattern	TFS(a)	TFS(a)	TFS(b)	TFS(b)	TFS(c)	TFS(c)	
population	56,857	65,913	76,411	86,452	97,812	107,993	119,233
	Afghanistan						
pattern	TM(b)	TM(b)	TM(O)	TM(O)	TM(O)	TM(O)	
population	17,638	20,200	23,135	26,820	31,091	36,043	41,784

Table 7.10 Central Asian Population Profile in 1960 and 1990

	1960		1990	
	Population (000)	Share in the region(%)	Population (000)	Share (%)
Kazakhstan	9,755	40.83	16,746	33.09
Kyrgyzstan	2,131	8.92	4,395	8.68
Tajikistan	2,045	8.56	5,302	10.48
Turkmenistan	1,564	6.55	3,669	7.25
Uzbekistan	8,395	35.14	20,500	40.50
Total	23,890	100.00	50,612	100.00

2020, according to some projections (see Tables 7.10 and 7.11). More than that, Tajikistan's population will practically double from 5.3 million people in 1990 to 11 million in 2020.

Thus such changes in relative weight in Central Asian population will first stimulate competition for regional economic and political leadership between Kazakhstan and Uzbekistan; and second, will result in uncontrolled immigration of Uzbeks and Tajiks to Kazakhstan, because the size of the rural population in these two states is close to natural ecological limits or, perhaps, already over those limits; and third, will either lead to further internal conflicts and violence in Tajikistan as a means of redistribution of limited land resources or force large-scale emigration from Tajikistan, especially to Uzbekistan, producing acute conflicts between these two countries.

As for the proportion of the Central Asian total population to the population of the adjacent states, great changes will take place here too (see Tables 7.12 and 7.13). In 1960 the Russian population was five times greater than the Central Asian one. In 1990 this proportion decreased to three times. In our projection, in 2020 the Central Asian population will be equal to half the Russian population. This can be a serious demographic pressure on Russia from the South. The pressure can be both peaceful and aggressive. Immigration can come to both Russian cities and the countryside.

The successful fulfilment of demographic transition and the ageing of population in China will naturally decrease the proportion of its population to the Central Asian one, but the initial great difference in the numbers of population will make these changes unimportant.

Table 7.11 Projections of Central Asian Population Profile in 2020

Country	Scenario 1 population (000)	(%)	Scenario 2 population (000)	(%)	Scenario 3 population (000)	(%)
Kazakhstan	11,987	17.54	14,955	19.58	21,289	25.59
Kyrgyzstan	5,610	8.21	6,398	8.38	6,644	7.99
Tajikistan	11,141	16.30	11,141	14.58	11,141	13.39
Turkmenistan	7,524	11.01	7,524	9.85	7,792	9.37
Uzbekistan	32,069	46.93	36,372	47.61	36,313	43.66
Central Asia Total	68,331	100.00	76,390	100.00	83,179	100.00

Scenario 1 - The RSP Emigration and Extrapolation of Demographic Trends
Scenario 2 - The RSP Emigration and Demographic Transition Slow Down
Scenario 3 - The RSP Emigration and Stoppage

Table 7.12 Proportion of Population in Central Asia and Adjacent Countries in 1960 and 1990 (in 000 and %)

	1960		1990	
	Population	Excess[13]	Population	Excess
Russia	119,046	498	148,255	293
China	657,492	2,752	1,133,683	2,240
Iran	20,301	85	56,857	112
Afghanistan	10,775	45	17,638	35

Table 7.13 Projection of Proportion of Population in Central Asia and Adjacent Countries in 2020 (in 000 and %)

	Scenario 1 Population	Excess	Scenario 2 Population	Excess	Scenario 3 Population	Excess
Russia	156,376	229	156,376	205	146,388	176
China	1,509,074	2,208	1,509,074	1,975	1,509,074	1,814
Iran	119,233	174	119,233	156	119,233	143
Afghanistan	41,784	61	41,784	55	41,784	050

Scenario 1 - The RSP Emigration and Extrapolation of Demographic Trends
Scenario 2 - The RSP Emigration and Demographic Transition Slow Down
Scenario 3 - The RSP Emigration and Stoppage

More important will be Iran and Afghanistan's growing roles. In 1960 the Iranian population was smaller than that of Central Asia; in 1990 it became already slightly larger. By 2020, it will be about 1.5 times greater than the Central Asian one, according to our projections. At the same time the total population of Iran and Afghanistan combined will be greater than the population of Russia (see Tables 7.12 and 7.13)

Thus along the southern borders of Central Asia two population pressure centres are emerging: Iran and Afghanistan. The situation is different in these two cases. Iran has a common border with Turkmenistan which has a small population. Turkmenistan's northern neighbour is Uzbekistan, which will have a large population by 2020, too. Because of the easy-to-cross boundaries situation, Turkmenistan could become an area of competition between Iran and Uzbekistan. The competition could take various forms, ranging from competition between Uzbeks and Iranians in the labour market to armed conflicts between the two states, Uzbekistan and Iran.

Afghanistan also has borders with Turkmenistan, but it has hardly become a player there. Northern Afghanistan may become a place of severe competition and even struggle, but it would be a competition between peoples rather than states, because the region is home to Uzbeks and Tajiks. Afghanistan's expansion to the north is quite possible, but potentially the direction of demographic expansion is the opposite. Tajikistan's countryside is already overpopulated and Tajiks may try to migrate to Afghanistan's northern regions. At present this scenario seems to be improbable, because of the domestic situation in Afghanistan. However, when the civil war in Tajikistan and Afghanistan is over, it may become possible if Tajikistan's population growth stays high and the standard of living grows closer in these two countries.

So demographic pressure on Central Asia from the South and growing internal demographic pressure in Uzbekistan and Tajikistan make the North (Kazakhstan and Russia) potential places of immigration from Uzbekistan and Tajikistan. This is a potential source of both conflict and co-operation.

APPENDIX: ALGORITHMIC DESCRIPTION OF DEMOGRAPHIC TRANSITION

The algorithmic description of the demographic transition used in this essay consists of two tables and one graph. They describe:

- the sequence of patterns;
- the possible lifetime of each pattern; and
- the rate of population increase under each pattern.

Patterns are the pairs of crude birth and death rates at different stages of demographic transition. We use the acronyms in this essay to describe these demographic patterns as follows:

PTMF – pre-transitional as to mortality and fertility

TM(a) – mortality transition (initial phase)

TM(b) – mortality transition (middle phase)

TM(c) – mortality transition (the last phase)

PETM – population explosion during mortality transition

TM(b)BC(h) – birth control during mortality transition, (middle phase) in a country with high birth rates

TM(b)BC(I) – birth control during mortality transition, (middle phase) in a country with low birth rates

TM(c)BC(h)h – birth control during mortality transition (the last phase) in a country with stable high birth rates ('h' is not changed)

TM(c)BC(h)l – birth control during mortality transition (the last phase) with declining birth rates ('h' becomes 'I')

TM(c)BC(I)l – birth control during mortality transition (the last phase) in a country with stable low birth rates ('l' is not changed)

TM(c)BC(I)d – birth control during mortality transition (the last phase) in a country with declining initially low birth rates ('l' is declining)

PEG – great population explosion

PES – small population explosion

TFR – rapid fertility transition

TFS(a) – slow fertility transition (initial phase)

TFS(b) – slow fertility transition (the main phase)

TFS(c) – slow fertility transition (the last phase)

PTH – the post-transitional pattern with high birth rates

BD – birth rate decline

PTS – the post-transitional pattern with stable birth and death rates

AP – the ageing of population

ZPG – zero population growth

NDP – natural decline of population

Note: 'TM' is mortality transition; 'PE', population explosion; 'TF', fertility transition; and 'BC', birth control. '(a)', '(b)', '(c)' refer to the phases of patterns.

NOTES

1. Akimov, A., *The Global Population: Looking Ahead*, Nauka Publishing, Moscow, 1992.
2. These include *Demographic Yearbook*, UN, N.Y., various years; *Statistical Yearbook UN*, N.Y. various years; *Yearbook of Labour Statistics*, ILO, Geneva, various years; and *1990 Statistical Handbook: States of the former USSR*, The World Bank, Washington D.C., 1992.
3. This is a period of large-scale immigration to Kazakhstan from many other Soviet republics; patterns are aimed to describe closed population, so they cannot be used to describe population growth in Kazakhstan without addi-

tional information about migration, but this analysis adds nothing to the accuracy of later periods description which are more important for the forecast.

4. 'Pattern' here is an index of the pattern which describes the five-year population increase with the minimal discrepancy. Please refer to the appendix for the full names and numerical characteristics of patterns. 'Discrepancy' here is the discrepancy between calculated number of population and a real one described in percentage terms.
5. 'Patterns' here refrers to the patterns' indexes for five-year terms, beginning from the year mentioned in the column. Patterns' full names and parameters are presented in the Appendix.
6. Emigration is emigration of the RSP during a five-year term, which ends in the year mentioned in the column (in 000).
7. Population is the mid-year population (in 000).
8. As in footnote 4.
9. Immigration here is immigration of RSP from the Central Asian states.
10. As in footnote 7.
11. By 'demographic development', we mean demographic transition from high birth and death rates via period of high birth and low death rates (demographic explosion) to low birth and death rates and then to a slight death increase as a result of population ageing while the birth rate stays low.
12. As in footnotes 5 and 7.
13. Excess is excess over the population of Central Asia expressed in percentage terms.

Part III
Economic Agonies

8 Central Asia's Transition to a Market Economy: An Analytical Comparison with China

Zhuangzhi Sun

The independence of Kazakhstan, Kyrgyzstan, Tajikistan, Turkmenistan and Uzbekistan in the former Soviet space of Central Asia in 1991 was followed by intense efforts of nation-building by those newly independent states. Economic reform and transition to a market economy are an indispensable part of such efforts. In the last five years, all five have announced and started to implement their ambitious programmes for economic reforms. Market-oriented economies are emerging in Central Asia. This essay is a preliminary analysis of the background, the international and domestic context, the process and social conditions of economic reforms in Central Asian states. On the basis of this analysis, a comparison between the Chinese experience and economic reforms in Central Asia is also provided, wherever appropriate.

THE BACKGROUND

The political dynamism for Central Asian states to make their commitments to a transition to a market economy has been provided largely by the break-up of the Soviet Union. Boris Yeltsin's decision in December 1991 to dissolve the former Soviet Union without prior consultation with the five Central Asian republics caught the Central Asian leaders by surprise. The ramifications of such a political decision for the economic life in Central Asia are significant. The Central Asian republics had to accept their complete independence as sovereign states. At the same time, although unprepared, they had to face the economic realities that independence imposed upon them.

The break-up of the former Soviet Union did not immediately cut off economic links between Central Asian states and other former Soviet republics and the Russian Federation. It nevertheless fragmented a formerly integral national economy into fifteen small national economies. The immediate effect was the breakdown of central planning and the disruption of inter-republic trade and payment mechanisms. Falling production output followed as a result of the abrupt dissolution of supply-demand relations in the Soviet economic framework. Central Asia as well as other republics also lost the budgetary transfer from Moscow, which had been used to subsidize the economy in the region in Soviet times.

The fragmentation of the Soviet economy helped to expose the distortions in the Central Asian economies, such as a highly monopolistic market structure, and single-product economy. This is probably because they were never meant to be integral, self-sufficient national economies. For the same reason, none of the former Soviet republics had either national institutions or experience to manage a national economy. There were neither credible economic institutions nor expertise. Now they suddenly found themselves in a difficult position. They not only had to manage and develop a national economy without national institutions; they also had to rescue their economies from the depth of crises. The agenda for economic reforms, it could be argued, was forced upon the newly independent Central Asian states very much by a political dynamism that was out of their control. Stabilizing first the economic situation and then building and developing an integral national economy became the double thrust of economic reforms in Central Asian states immediately after their independence. The very viability of their states depended on the successes of economic reforms.

Economic reform in Central Asia, on the other hand, has to deal with the economic legacies of the Soviet Union. In order to have a better understanding of the background of the economic reforms in Central Asia, we need to look in some detail at the Soviet economic legacies in the region.

Before the end of 1991, when the Central Asian republics declared their independence, the economic development in the region was largely distorted. The market infrastructure and mechanisms were largely absent. The production structure was monopolistic. Economic production in the region was forced to 'specialize' in Soviet times. To promote economic development in Central Asia and to balance regional economic development, the Soviet government had relocated some industries to Central Asia. This created an irrational distribution of industry in the region and distorted economic structure, both of which were not, to say the least, conducive to cultivating the use of natural resources and the market. At their independence, all Central Asian republics could be said to have a single-product economy, with processing industries lagging far behind. There was another distortion in the Central Asian economies. Under the command economy in Soviet times some heavy industrial giants with advanced technology had been bundled together with backward agriculture and animal husbandry in Central Asia.

The former Soviet Union was the birthplace of the command economy. Central Asia in Soviet times was arguably a 'beneficiary' of such a command economy. For example, between forty per cent and seventy per cent of manufactured and other consumer goods for Central Asia were allocated by Moscow from the Russian Federation and other republics. With the help of the central plan and substantial financial subsidies from the central government in Moscow, the Central Asian economies had developed by leaps and bounds. That, however, created a heavy economic dependence of Central Asia on other economies in the former Soviet Union, especially that of the Russian Federation. After their independence, the Central Asian republics still depended on members of Commonwealth of Independent States (CIS), particularly Russia, to supply them with some raw materials and most consumer goods. In 1994, Russia still provided 61 per cent of imported goods for Kazakhstan. Uzbekistan at the same time purchased seventy per cent of its consumer goods from Russia and Ukraine. In 1993, industrial output of Uzbekistan dropped more than ten per cent, largely because Russia failed to fulfil its contracts to provide raw materials for Uzbekistan industries.

The 'division of labour' in Central Asia under the Soviet economic system therefore continued to preoccupy those concerned with the reconstruction of Central Asian economies after their independence. To overcome problems brought about by the forced specialization of Central Asian economies in effect calls for the radical transformation of the economic structure and economic system of Central Asian states. While such a restructuring can only be sustained with a large input of capital, the Central Asian states could no longer look to Moscow for any financial help. Foreign investment and financial assistance from international economic organizations, as we will see later, are slow in coming into Central Asia. Lack of capital for restructuring the economy compounded the difficulties of economic reforms in Central Asian states.

There is another legacy that has severely constrained the process of economic reforms in Central Asia. Years of domination by the Soviet command economy not only deprived the Central Asian republics of any infrastructure for a market economy; it also kept the living standards low in the region. Ordinary people and government officials alike had a poor understanding – or no understanding at all – of market and the market economy. There was also severe shortage of economic expertise to guide the reform process.

Equally importantly, it should be pointed out that for Central Asian states, economic reforms have had to be carried out in the process of nation-building. Before 1991, the governments of Central Asian republics were no more than local administrative authorities of the Soviet government in Moscow. They had to listen to Moscow in their political orientation and economic and social policies. Historically, until 1991, Central Asia did not have independent nation-states as we understand the term today. Nation-building therefore has been the first priority on the political agenda of all five Central Asian states. The transition to a market economy has been in fact incorporated as an indispensable part of the nation-building. Economic reforms, however, often bring about the disruption of economic life, which in turn affects political stability. In this sense, economic reforms are also a political challenge to all five national governments of the newly independent Central Asian states.

At their independence, therefore, all five Central Asian republics were faced with similar problems and daunting challenges in economic development. They all had to build a self-sustainable national economy out of the economic legacies of the former Soviet Union. They all had to rectify the existing distortions of their economies. For this purpose, all of them embarked on economic reforms aimed at eventual transformation of their economies into market economies.

What, then, can we learn from comparing Central Asia and China? At the start of their reforms, both Central Asia and China were faced with the same challenge: i.e. how to reform the Soviet-style command economies. In many ways, the success or failure of economic reforms in both cases would decisively affect the legitimacy of the governments concerned. They also encountered similar problems when they initiated economic reforms. In both Central Asia and China, the lack of capital for investment was forbidding. The state-owned enterprises had obsolete equipment, backward technology and primitive management. They presented major obstacles to economic reform. In both cases, the productivity of agriculture was very low and agricultural reforms were central to the national programme of economic reform. The reforms had also to correct problems such as the irrational distribution of industries, the underdevelopment of services sectors, and severe shortages in the supply of consumer goods. In addition, the abuse of the social welfare system and heavy state subsidies had to be stopped. In a word, the major goals of economic reforms in

Central Asia and in China are the same: that is, to transform the command economy into a market-oriented one.

Economic conditions such as economic potential, labour force conditions, and socioeconomic structure in Central Asia and in China at the time when their economic reforms were initiated are, however, widely different. Behind the launch of economic reforms in Central Asia and in China is a different political momentum, too.

As we mentioned earlier, the political momentum for radical economic reforms in Central Asian states was provided by dynamic political developments largely outside the control of Central Asian states. The economic reform agenda was dictated by the break-up of the former Soviet Union. The volatile political and economic situation in Russia continued to influence, sometimes decisively, the pace and the orientation of economic transition in Central Asia. In contrast, the political momentum for Chinese economic reforms was largely generated from China's domestic politics. The consensus reached at the Third Plenum of the Eleventh Central Committee of the Chinese Communist Party (CCP) in 1978 decided and also sustained the general orientation of guided economic reforms and the gradual opening of the Chinese economy. In the last seventeen years, China's international environment has rarely decided either the pace or the orientation of economic reforms in China.

In socio-economic terms, China (the third largest country in the world) has a large population. Eighty per cent of its labour force at the beginning of the economic reforms was working outside the state-owned economies. Its geographical location also gives China some geo-economic advantages to exploit for reforms. These conditions made it possible that while restructuring its economic system, China could seek to develop its economy at a reasonable pace. Central Asian states, however, are landlocked and limited in their economic manoeuvrability. For example, 93 per cent of Tajikistan is mountains and hilly areas; only three per cent is arable land. Kyrgyzstan, on the other hand, is poor in natural resources, and drought has been a perennial problem for Turkmenistan. Moreover, China by 1978 had already built up an integral and self-sustainable national economy managed by a set of credible, though not so competent, national economic institutions. None of the Central Asian economies was, at the time of the break-up of the former Soviet Union, either integral or self-sustainable. Credible national economic institutions were non-existent in all new states.

More importantly, although the Central Asian states and China are both agrarian societies in the sense that agriculture accounts for a large percentage of the national economy and that the rural population is much larger than urban population, agriculture and rural population have played different roles in the process of economic reforms. In China, the first breakthrough in economic reforms was initiated in agriculture. The introduction of the household responsibility system and the dismantling of the commune system were unexpectedly successful. Surplus labour from the rural areas in China has also provided ready human resources in the rapid economic development of Chinese urban areas. In comparison, the main components of the rural economy of Central Asian states belonged to state-owned sectors before independence. Agriculture in Central Asia had been already largely mechanized. Peasants and farmers were beneficiaries of the state welfare system. Their living standard was much higher than Chinese peasants before China's economic reforms. They were better educated, too, with illiteracy rate at almost zero. In their respective transition to a market economy, these socioeconomic conditions have sometimes conditioned, if not determined, the pace and the orientation of economic reforms in both China and Central Asian states.

THE PROCESS

Although in the late 1980s the Soviet leadership started economic reforms in the former Soviet Union, those reforms nevertheless did not have any significant impact on the remote and economically underdeveloped regions such as Central Asia. In Uzbekistan, agricultural reforms did achieve some results, particularly after the Soviet government decree in 1987 legalizing the private-owned farms. In general, large-scale and comprehensive economic reforms arguably did not start in Central Asia until 1991. Even before the Central Asian republics declared their independence, it was already clear that the reforms started by the Soviet government had a clearly-defined goal of guiding the transition towards a market-oriented economy by emphasizing the ownership reforms. Already in 1991, a large number of government decrees on price reforms and privatization had been promulgated and put into effect. In early 1992, the Russian government experimented with its radical reform programme of 'shock therapy' and liberalized prices. Some Central Asian states followed suit. The governments of Kazakhstan and Kyrgyzstan decided to try the 'shock therapy' approach in their economic reforms. Other three Central Asian governments were also heavily influenced by the Russian reform programme. Economic reforms in all five Central Asian republics in this period focused decisively on price reform and privatization as the main mechanisms of the transition to a market economy.

In 1992, economic reforms in five Central Asian republics proceeded, however, at a different pace and with different emphasis. Kazakhstan and Kyrgyzstan, for example, decided on wholesale privatization and made comprehensive plans to implement the privatization programme. Already in June 1991, the Kazakh government had mapped out a strategy for privatization with three stages. In 1992, it was claimed that the privatization in Kazakhstan had overtaken the plan. The three stages were redefined as two stages: all state-owned enterprises were to be either privatized or corporatized through first the 'small-scale privatization' stage, leading to the 'mass privatization' stage. Under the influence of the Russian reforms in 1992, the governments of Kazakhstan and Kyrgyzstan also liberalized eighty per cent to ninety per cent of their retail prices. In contrast, the governments of Uzbekistan and Turkmenistan took a more cautious approach. Both stated clearly that they would not embark on a comprehensive privatization programme. Their short-term goal was to develop 'diversified ownerships in the economy'. In 1992, Uzbekistan carried out a limited privatization programme in commercial sectors, service sectors as well as in urban residential property, while delaying privatization in industries. In agriculture, the government of Uzbekistan drew lessons from the Chinese experience. Reforms started with organizing household farms and cooperatives. Land was not up for sale, but for lease in rural areas.

In 1993 and 1994, radical economic reforms in Kazakhstan and Kyrgyzstan encountered serious problems. Many government reform policies could not be implemented, mainly because with the accelerated rate of rising inflation, an economic crisis was in the making for the two countries. In 1994, the GDP of Kyrgyzstan decreased 25 per cent from that of 1993. Sixty per cent of the state-owned enterprises had to stop production. The unemployment figure rose to 300,000. The collection of tax revenue reached only 58 per cent of the goal. There was a huge deficit in the government budget. In 1993, the rate of inflation in Kazakhstan was an unprecedented 3,000 per cent. In comparison with 1990, the prices of consumer goods in Kyrgyzstan rocketed 2,027 times, and in Uzbekistan 1,473 times. In view of such a situation, both the Kazakhstan and the Kyrgyzstan governments had to slow down the pace of their transition to a market economy. Both governments readjusted their reform programme and strengthened state intervention in the economy. In 1994, inflation in Kyrgyzstan was brought down to 5.5 per cent from 25.4 per cent in 1993. Uzbekistan and Turkmenistan, on the other hand, continued their gradualist approach to their transition to market economy, with an emphasis on the state's role of regulating and controlling the market. The Turkmenistan government even reverted to the practice of a state-controlled pricing system: the prices of some commodities which had been liberalized earlier were again set by the government. Economic reforms in Tajikistan started to gather pace only after the civil war ended. Its transition to a market economy has also encountered a number of problems.

In only a few years, the transition of Central Asian economies to a market economy has made some progress, in spite of all the difficulties and problems encountered. In general, the economies of Kazakhstan and Kyrgyzstan have been marketized more than others. For example, in 1988, only twenty per cent of produce from enterprises in these two countries was sold directly to the market. The rest went to the state and was sold by the state. In 1993, in contrast, seventy per cent of enterprise produce as sold directly to the market. The state order system was largely scrapped. To take another example, in 1993, de-nationalized and privatized enterprises made up 25 per cent of the total in Kazakhstan and 22 per cent of the total in Kyrgyzstan. Most of them were small commercial businesses in catering and other tertiary industries. In early 1995, private ownership increased to account for fifty per cent of the national economy in both countries. A securities market was also emerging. In Uzbekistan, in 1994, there were more than 49,000 private enterprises and businesses. The statistics show that private ownership accounted for sixteen per cent in industry, 25.2 per cent in construction and 82.4 per cent in commerce. Turkmenistan was also implementing a privatization plan in 1995. More than 2,000 state-owned enterprises were to be privatized, of which 1850 were commercial and catering businesses.

Agricultural reforms provide an interesting comparison. Reforms in Uzbekistan started with agriculture. To transform the existing socio-economic relations in rural Uzbekistan based on agricultural collectives, the Uzbekistan government first transferred the right of use of fifteen per cent of the land to private farmers. The purpose of this was to introduce a new ownership and new management system into the agriculture in Uzbekistan, with the state in control of the process. In early 1995, state ownership in agriculture decreased to ten per cent. Collective ownership rose to fifty-four per cent, and private ownership of sideline production rose to thirty-five per cent. In general, agricultural reforms in Central Asian states seem to have followed a similar path, beginning with a change of ownership and management system by contracting out the land for the farmers to till on a long-term basis. Some agricultural products were to be sold to the state according to an agreed price in the contract, while the others were sold freely on the market.

Agricultural reforms in China differ from those in Central Asia in many ways. The most important difference is that although both Central Asian and the Chinese reforms deal with the problem of micro-economic management of the land, agricultural reform in China did not, in its early stage, try to solve the problem of ownership. The agricultural reform in China had a well-defined goal. After the Third Plenum of the Eleventh Central Committee of the CCP in December 1978, the household responsibility system was implemented, which instilled a new vitality into the agriculture. Agricultural reforms in Central Asia, however, started with changing the ownership system and took such a reform as a permanent solution of agricultural production. The problem is that it is precisely the disputes about the privatization of land in rural areas that have impeded further reforms in agriculture in Central Asia. Because of the mechanization of agriculture in Central Asia and because of its existing irrigation system, it is impractical to make a single household the basic agricultural production unit as embodied in the household responsibility system in China. On top of that, there is another daunting problem for agriculture in Central Asian states, particularly for three states, Uzbekistan, Kyrgyzstan, and Turkmenistan: the structural transformation of agriculture is imperative to reduce the cotton-producing area and to increase the growth of grain crops. To realize such structural transformation while implementing the privatization programme further aggravated the difficulties of agricultural reforms.

For another comparison, in the mid-1980s, economic reforms in China dealt with the problem of redistribution of natural resources. Those reforms successfully promoted the vigorous development of non-state-owned enterprises. The rapid growth of non-state-owned enterprises has proved to be valuable in extending economic reforms in China. For one thing, non-state-owned enterprises created new wealth and ensured the continued growth of the economy as a whole. For another, labour-intensive township enterprises helped correct the structural distortion of the national economy brought about the previous government strategy to develop heavy industry first. Again, non-state-owned enterprises became the experiment site to prepare for the marketization of large and medium-sized state-owned enterprises in China. In contrast, reforms in Central Asia were started on the premise that private ownership would lead to a market economy. The denationalization programme promoted and enforced by the Central Asian governments, however, has not so far provided such impetus as was expected by those governments for any breakthrough in a smooth transition to a market economy. The principal reason is that although private ownership is a necessary condition for a market economy, it does not and cannot automatically lead to a market economy. In other words, transition from a command economy to a market economy in Central Asia involves much more than just the transformation of ownership. In Central Asia, privatized enterprises have been pushed onto the market when the market itself has yet to develop operational mechanisms and competent institutions for fair competition. Further, macro-economic conditions in Central Asia still seriously constrain the growth of any non-state owned sectors in the economy.

Macro-economic conditions in Central Asian states have in fact been repeatedly brought to the edge of crisis ever since their independence and the start of economic reforms in 1991. In 1992, following the Russian experiment with 'shock therapy', some Central Asian states were forced to liberalize in a few weeks prices of between seventy per cent and ninety per cent of their consumer goods and production materials. That created a chaotic situation in macro-economic control and management by the newly independent states. The inclusion of Central Asian states into the rouble zone seriously constrained the Central Asian states' initiatives for currency reforms and fiscal and monetary policies. The structural distortions of the Central Asian economies, on the other hand, have yet to be corrected. Indeed, because of the deteriorating situation in macro-economic conditions, some Central Asian states, notably, Kazakhstan and Kyrgyzstan, vacillated between an unregulated and a controlled transition to a market economy in their reform orientations. In 1993 to 1995, Central Asian states started to issue their own currencies, which seem to have reduced pressures of the crises in their macro-economic management on the reforms.

In contrast, China has adopted a completely different strategy in reforming the management of its macro-economy. China's approach to price reform is certainly more cautious and gradualist. Price reform in China started as early as 1984; after ten years, in 1994, the prices of about eighty per cent of its consumer goods and production materials were decided by the market. During the decade from 1984 to 1994, China first used and then tolerated the 'dual-track' system policy in its price reforms. Such a policy encouraged the growth of the non-state controlled sectors in the economy and at the same time ensured relative stability in the state control of the macro-economic conditions. It could be argued that in the reform period, the macro-economy of China has had to deal with many problems – but it has not been plunged into crisis, partly because of its sustained economic growth and partly because China has implemented a credible fiscal and monetary policy compatible with its economic development.

Another interesting example is China's enterprise reforms. These were started from what could be called the 'periphery': that is to say, the sectors which had already existed outside the state-owned economy were pushed on to the market first. Although such a strategy slowed down the pace and the process of economic reform, it nevertheless quickly expanded the non-state-controlled economy and helped alleviate the crisis conditions of the state-owned medium-sized and large enterprises. It also allowed time and space for necessary experiment and preparations for the reforms of the state-owned enterprises. In comparison, enterprise reforms in Central Asia were almost forced on them. There was neither time for the Central Asian states to experiment nor was there any careful planning. Enterprise reforms in Central Asia have been largely carried out in a disorderly manner. The relative small scale of the non-state-owned economy also ruled out the possibility of starting reforms from the 'periphery'.

The weakness of the non-state-owned economy in the rural areas has constrained the economic reform process in Central Asian states in yet another way. For example, Kyrgyzstan had taken a great interest in China's experiment with the development of township enterprises in rural areas. However, social conditions and economic development in rural China are radically different from those in rural Kyrgyzstan. For one thing, the rural economy in China was largely outside the state-owned sector. For another, there was sufficient surplus labour to sustain the risks of developing township enterprises. Those two vital conditions were not present in Kyrgyzstan's rural economy.

At present, the Central Asian governments attach great importance to stabilizing their economies. They are making efforts to adjust the pace and to reorient their emphasis in their economic reforms in search of new breakthroughs. Looking back at the reform process in China and in Central Asia, it is clear that China's reforms from the very start were carefully planned, the reform strategy emphasized a gradual transition, and reform policies were planned and implemented according to the changing conditions of the Chinese economy. The existing institutions played a vital role in introducing, executing and managing the reform process. In contrast, Central Asian states had to embark on a rapid transition to a market economy as a result of their unexpected independence. There was neither time nor space for them to plan their reforms, nor did they have any credible national economic institutions to manage the reforms. It is therefore not surprising that there was no well-defined and realistic strategy of economic reform in the Central Asian states. Hesitation and vacillation in implementing the reform strategy followed. Considerable progress, however, has so far been made in economic reform in Central Asia. For example, the privatization of residential properties has made impressive headway; and meaningful experiment has been carried out in ownership reforms – whereas in China, the privatization of residential properties is still half-hearted and ownership reforms now lag behind the Central Asian states.

THE INTERNATIONAL CONTEXT

Central Asia's transition to a market economy was an experiment in a unique international environment. As discussed before, the political development as seen in the sudden dissolution of the former Soviet Union forced the economic reforms agenda on the newly independent states. Such a political development, however, could hardly break the economic dependence of Central Asia on other republics of the former Soviet Union, particularly Russia. More intriguingly, the dissolution of the former Soviet Union turned overnight inter-republic economic dependence within the former Soviet Union into international dependence and interdependence among independent sovereign states.

It is important to note that economic development in Central Asia had been subject to the central planning of the former Soviet Union until 1991. It is equally important to point out that the Central Asian economies were constructed as part of the Soviet economy and were not meant to be individual integral national economies. Economic links had been fostered among Soviet republics with Moscow not only as the central planner, but also as the central co-ordinator. This legacy has now been turned into a significant component of the international context of Central Asia's transition to a market economy. There are other factors to be reckoned with. International economic organizations such as the International Monetary Fund (IMF) and the World Bank became involved in the economic reforms in Central Asia after the Central Asian states became members of both organizations in 1992. Such an international context provides constraints as well as incentives for the transition of Central Asian states to a market economy.

When the agenda of economic reforms was forced on the Central Asian governments, they had to face a grim economic situation created as much by the unexpected break-up of the former Soviet Union as by the Soviet economic legacy. To overcome that legacy and to build a national economy, the Central Asian states have pursued a multi-strand strategy to improve their international environment. As the first main component of this strategy, they seek active participation in regional economic co-operation and integration, including economic integration with other CIS economies. Kazakhstan and Kyrgyzstan, for example, joined Belarus and Russia in signing an agreement of 'deeper integration'. On the other hand, as early as 1992, five Central Asian states joined the Economic Co-operation Organization (ECO), consisting now of ten Muslim nations and encompassing a large area from Central Asia to the Middle East. In 1994, an agreement to establish a Central Asian economic space was signed by

Kazakhstan, Uzbekistan, and Kyrgyzstan. Kazakhstan has also signed an agreement with Russia and Belarus on a unified customs.

Second, Central Asian states have vigorously developed trade links with many other countries beyond the CIS framework. Foreign trade is seen as an engine for domestic economic recovery and growth. In 1994, significant trading partners for Central Asian states beyond the CIS included Turkey, Iran, China, the United States, Britain, Germany, and the Netherlands. The main exports from Central Asian states consist of such commodities as coal, petroleum, cotton, wool and gas. Main imports into Central Asian states are foods, machinery and consumer goods. It was reported that in 1994, four Central Asian states, Kazakhstan, Kyrgyzstan, Turkmenistan and Tajikistan, had trade surpluses – respectively US$ 580 million for Kazakhstan, US$ 24 million for Kyrgyzstan, US$ 78 million for Turkmenistan, and US$ 2 million for Tajikistan.

Third, they have opened their economies to foreign investment to attract foreign capital and technology and management expertise. For that purpose, Central Asian governments have enacted legislation and announced various preferential policies for foreign investment. Free trade zones have also been established. Let us take Turkmenistan as an example: by 1994, Turkmenistan had signed more than 280 joint-venture agreements for the exploration of petroleum and gas, involving an investment total of US$ 3 billion. Kazakhstan has signed agreements with Chevron for joint exploration of its oil fields in the Tengiz region. Joint ventures with French, German, Turkish, and Chinese capital have also been established in Kazakhstan.

Fourth, all five Central Asian states have obtained membership in key international economic organizations such as the World Bank and the IMF. That enables Central Asian states to obtain loans for restructuring their economies. More importantly, it makes the expertise of these two important global economic organizations available to Central Asian states in planning their economic reforms. By the end of 1992, the World Bank, for example, had produced various reports on Central Asian economies, providing advice for their economic reforms.

It should be argued that in the last five years, through the efforts of the Central Asian states, the international environment of the Central Asian economies has been more favourable to their transition to a market economy. Problems, however, still abound.

First of all, regional economic co-operation and integration in Central Asia and with the CIS states has not proceeded smoothly. Economic crises in Central Asian states created economic conditions which were not conducive to economic integration. Furthermore, nationalistic feelings among

Central Asian states stood in the way of meaningful economic co-operation among the CIS states. Central Asian leaders complained time and again that economic union with Russia was not only dominated by Russia but was also made favourable to Russian interests. On top of this, there were substantial disagreements among Central Asian leaders as to the necessity and the orientation of economic integration in Central Asia in particular and more broadly among the CIS states. Uzbekistan's President Karimov openly criticized Kazakhstan's President Nazarbayev's proposal for a Euro-Asian Union. Turkmenistan, on the other hand, refused to sign the agreement of economic integration of Central Asia, reluctant to share the wealth of its rich natural resources with other states.

Secondly, all five Central Asian states are land-locked, with no seaports within reasonable distance. The railway system is yet to be fully developed. Such geographical conditions continue to impose serious constraints on foreign economic co-operation in the Central Asian states, particularly trade. For example, Kazakhstan has rich deposit of petroleum, and Turkmenistan is rich in gas supply. They have also found investment partners for the exploration of these natural resources. The transport problem, however, defies a simple solution. Turkmenistan exports an average of eighty per cent of its gas production annually, mostly to Europe by renting the Russian pipelines for transportation. For Turkmenistan, however, making use of the existing Russian pipes means that it is subject to the goodwill of Russia. In the last few years, Russia has often put pressure on Turkmenistan to sell its gas to CIS states at a price thirty per cent lower than the world market price. Worse still, many CIS states could not pay for their use of Turkmenistan gas. It is estimated that in 1994 CIS states owed Turkmenistan US$ 1.5 billion gas money. To construct another pipeline is also problematic. On the one hand there is the investment, which involves billions of dollars. On the other hand, the new pipeline has to go either through Iran, which is hostile to the West, or through areas with no political stability, such as Afghanistan. The shortest route therefore is not the easiest one,

Thirdly, the foreign investment environment is far from satisfactory, and can hardly attract enough urgently needed foreign investment. Although the Central Asian states have instituted a good deal of foreign investment legislation, it is still insufficient. It is reported that only ten per cent of foreign investment contracts signed were actually implemented. Taxes on joint ventures are still high, and various taxes are not well-regulated nationwide. In Kazakhstan, many economic policies were announced by presidential decree. In the three years from 1991 to 1994, more than 500 decrees were issued. Often, later decrees cancelled policies decided in earlier decrees. This has increased the risks of economic and trade activities initiated by foreign investment in Kazakhstan.

Fourthly, political instability, hyper-inflation and deteriorating productivity in Central Asian states further deter international capital from entering Central Asia. It is true that the World Bank and the IMF have provided some loans but these are mainly for assisting the structural reform of Central Asian economies. Other international loans have been promised but have not materialized. The Kyrgyz President Akayev signed US$ 550 million loan agreements with European governments on his visit to Europe in 1994. At the beginning of 1995, however, the Kyrgyz government had not received any of these funds. International financial interests have also promised Turkmenistan support, but only one fifth of the contract value was realized in Turkmenistan's foreign investment.

Fifthly, technicians and skilled workers have emigrated in significant numbers out of Central Asia. After independence, the Russians and the Russian-speaking population feared reverse discrimination in Central Asia. Many of them migrated to Russia and other CIS states. Because they had been the intellectual and technical force behind the Central Asian economies, their emigration compounded the problem of the shortage of technical expertise in Central Asia. This in turn affects the capability of Central Asian states in engaging in international economic co-operation.

In comparison with Central Asian states, the international context of China's economic reforms is radically different. China did not have any macro-economic crisis when the reforms were launched at the end of 1978. China's diplomatic relations were at its best since 1949. China also joined the World Bank and IMF in 1980. Although China was a closed economy before 1978 with limited trade links with the world economy and with no participation of international capital, the Chinese economy was not so distorted as the Central Asian economies. Political stability in China further enabled the Chinese reformers to cultivate favourable elements in China's international environment for economic reforms.

More importantly, perhaps, the economic dynamism of East Asia, Japan and the four small 'dragons' provided China with both models and dynamism for rapid economic development. The overseas Chinese quickly instilled not only capital but also expertise to make the Chinese economy dynamic. China had also the advantage of economy of scale. China's cheap labour and its market attracted a large percentage of foreign direct investment into China. As a regional political power, and increasingly also an economic power, China has much more room to manoeuvre than the Central Asian states. If it is true that Central Asian states cannot compare with China in this aspect, they could at least draw on China's experience in opening its economy and in opening up special economic zones. Further economic cooperation between China and Central Asia would facilitate economic reforms in both China and Central Asia.

THE SOCIAL CONDITIONS

In terms of social conditions, the transition to a market economy in Central Asia was started without adequate support or sufficient preparation. The break-up of the former Soviet Union and ensuing rapid political changes in Central Asian states threw Central Asian societies into disarray. Independence, although long yearned for in Central Asia, came as a shock to the Central Asian peoples. Because the agenda of economic reform was forced upon Central Asian leaders, they did not have time even to try to prepare and mobilize the society behind the reforms. In other words, the reforms had to be carried out regardless of existing social conditions. Eventually, it has been proved that social conditions also present an obstacle to a transition to a market economy.

A transition to a market economy involves more than economics. The redistribution of resources has an important impact on the redistribution of interests, of benefits and of wealth. Such redistribution will in turn affect social mobility, social status and, in the end, social relations in a society. The transition to a market economy is therefore a complicated social engineering process. In his book 'Kazakhstan's Future Depends on the Unity of Thought of the Entire Society', Nazarbayev asserted that 'important reforms aimed at the social and economic transformation of one country often have close links with complicated ideological changes'. He believed that in Kazakhstan, the most fundamental and most vital basis upon which the growth of a market economy could be sustained was yet to be created. He argued that the social orientation of present-day society in Kazakhstan came largely from tradition. The economic reforms could therefore only establish a 'market economy which is society-oriented with the co-existence of multiple ownerships'.

It must be pointed out that the command economy was first imposed by the Soviet government on a largely nomadic and agricultural society in Central Asia in the 1920s. The transformation of Central Asia from a feudal economy to a socialist economy was completed in just a few years. Thereafter, economic activities in Central Asia, such as production and exchange, had all been dictated by arrangements made in Moscow. The distribution of resources was completed through the command plan. Central Asia therefore had little experience in the capitalist market economy. Even the basic relationship between supply and demand was alien to the political economy of Central Asia in Soviet times. It is difficult, for example, for Central Asian leaders and peoples alike to accept the principle of evaluating products, personnel, and enterprises on the basis of their competitiveness.

Furthermore, the patriarchal clan system, and in some cases Islamic tradition, condition the understanding of markets and the market economy by the general public. The dominant tradition and many other subcultural traditions are not compatible with the concept of a market economy. Ethnic diversity and conflicts between ethnic groups affect social cohesiveness, which is vital for any success in economic reforms.

The growth of markets should be synchronic with the development of a society. A new system is often distorted or slow in establishing itself largely because of resistance from the society. Central Asia could be said to have jumped from a feudal society to a socialist society. For many years, it was public ownership and a command economy that Central Asia was subject to. Naturally, people had little understanding of private ownership and had doubts about privatization. There was considerable resistance initially to the ownership change through the auction, renting and issue of stocks. Cultural resistance to privatization and other reforms makes the transition to a market economy a 'passive action' in Central Asian states.

Culturally, societies in Central Asia are unique. They are all between East and West. The Czar's conquest of Central Asia was followed by Soviet domination. As large numbers of Russians, Ukrainians, and Germans moved into urban areas in Central Asia, major cities in Central Asian were quickly 'Europeanized'. In rural areas where titular ethnic groups in Central Asia today are living, tradition reined. Such a contrast between urban centres and rural areas offers an explanation as to why Central Asian states could not in practice meaningfully implement the economic policies which had been proved successful in Russia and Turkey. The rise of Islam and a large-scale emigration of Europeans from Central Asia after independence indicate a revival of the Islamic culture in Central Asia. Such a culture, which is rooted in the natural economy, is not necessarily an ally to market economy.

In the current discussions on Central Asia's transition to a market economy, denationalization and privatization are very often used to measure the progress of economic reforms. It is an often neglected fact that social conditions have become an obstacle to further reforms, and there is a cultural explanation for it. In 1994, in Kazakhstan and Kyrgyzstan, the privatization of residential properties was nearly complete. In Kyrgyzstan, ownership reforms claimed to have denationalized and privatized ninety per cent of the previously state-owned sector. At the same time, such reforms encountered strong resistance. Many reform policies could not be carried out effectively, largely because the inertia of tradition, the opposition of the traditional interests and the uncertainty of the transition all combined to condition people's attitudes towards the reforms.

The social conditions for the start of economic reform in China are different from those in Central Asia in several respects. First of all, as many Chinese economists argued, the seeds of a prototype capitalist economy were first sown in the Ming and Qing dynasties in China. In the second half of the 19th century, China was forced to open to trade with the West. Sustained contact was established between East and South China with the outside world. Under the impact of the West, national capitalism also grew in difficult conditions. In short, commodity exchange and market economy were not entirely unfamiliar to China and to many Chinese, particularly in East and South China. China's strategy (to open its coastal areas first) therefore accords with socioeconomic conditions in China. In the last sixteen years, the successes of economic reforms in the coastal areas have provided a sustained momentum for further action.

Secondly, social cohesiveness is much stronger in China. Although China claims to have 54 nationalities, the Han Chinese population is dominant at about ninety per cent. Ethnic diversity in this context does not pose severe problems for Chinese reforms. Regional cultural differences do exist. But they do not divide people in their support for reform. Regional economic disparity, on the other hand, has not created social resistance to economic reforms in the less developed regions.

Thirdly, the so-called gradualist approach ensures that reforms have been carried out in relatively stable and supportive social conditions so as to avoid any devastating impact on the society. One of the important arguments for a gradualist approach is that such an approach would win time to prepare and mobilize the whole society for the support of new reform initiatives. The gradualist approach seems to have worked well to cushion the impact of economic reforms on social conditions in China.

CONCLUSION

Although the economic reforms agenda in Central Asian states has been forced on them by radical political changes in the former Soviet Union, all five Central Asian states have achieved successes in various degrees in their transition to a market economy. As China's new neighbours, economic reforms in the Central Asian states are important and interesting to China for two reasons. One is that they could draw lessons from each other's reform experience in their attempted march towards a market economy. The other is that as both China and Central Asia have embarked on such a historical transition, the success or failure of their reforms will determine the prospect of a common economic prosperity for China and Central Asia.

REFERENCES

1. He Wei and Wei Jia (eds.), *Zhongguo Zhumin Jingji Xuejia Lun Gaige* (Prominent Chinese Economists on Economic Reforms in China), Beijing Press, Beijing, 1992.
2. Lu Nanquan et al. *Erluosi, Dong Ou, Zhong Ya Jingji Zhuangui de Xuanze* (Russia, Eastern Europe and Central Asia: Towards Transition to a Market Economy). China Social Sciences Press, Beijing, 1994.
3. Wang Pei (ed.), *Zhong Ya Siguo Gaikuang* (An Introduction to Four Central Asian States), Xinjiang People's Press, Urumqi, 1993.
4. *Dong Ou Zhong Ya Yanjiu* (Journal of Eastern European and Central Asian Studies), various issues, 1992–1995.
5. *Guowai Shehui Kexue Qingkuang* (Bulletin of Social Sciences Research Abroad), no. 2, 1995.

9 Central Asia: Towards Ethnic Harmony Through Openness and Reform?

Alexander Salitsky and Vladimir Fisyukov

It is undeniable that present economic and social conditions in the Central Asian countries are quite complex, but this does not mean that they cannot be analysed within the framework of international comparisons and the appropriate theoretical approach. Presuming that the region still belongs to what can be called the post-Soviet area, we would like first of all to draw some necessary distinctions useful for the understanding of processes under way in the Russian Federation (RF) and neighbouring independent states. Then we will try to apply them to the situation in the Central Asian republics, taking into account their special position in the former USSR and current new factors, both internal and external.

There is much discussion regarding 'reforms', both in the RF and in Central Asia. To our minds it is too early to apply this kind of definition to the political tremors and ethnic and social shocks of the last four/five years in any of the states mentioned above. Understanding the term 'reform' as a synonym of gradual, step-by-step improvement of micro- and macroeconomic management, we prefer to keep it reserved for future assessments. At present the 'reformers', 'democrats', 'liberals' and many other labels are just self descriptors of certain political forces struggling for power, publicity and easily convertible resources of the economy, mainly property, fuels and raw materials. Among other disputes, one of the most fierce is the conflict between Moscow and local authorities, including those in the newly independent republics. The object of these activities in the RF and elsewhere is the redistribution of products – not modernization of the economy itself – another sign of real reforms being neglected or ignored.

According to studies conducted in 1994 in Central Asia and regions of the RF, about sixty per cent of the population regard poor performance of the economy as the main cause of ethnic conflicts in the post-Soviet area. The next (in importance) cause indicated by the respondents was the local authorities' poor (unjust) management practice.[1] We agree with these assessments. We would also like to stress one factor which is vital for ethnic stability – openness of economy and society.

Openness is very important from a socio-psychological point of view, bringing to nations the feeling of being a part of humanity. It also provides a positive attitude towards foreign culture, including goods, technologies, management and ideologies. What is actually happening in terms of economic theory in Russia, and to some extent in the Central Asian republics, is not yet a reform, but an abrupt, sometimes chaotic opening of the economy to the outside world, with a very strong participation of the bureaucracy in the process. The whole movement is not thoroughly researched here yet, but there is the rich experience of neighbouring China (PRC), which at the beginning of the 1980s had the same problem of adaptation to the market of a large, centralized and previously half-isolated economy containing a huge proportion of heavy industry and military industrialized complex (MIC). The Chinese pattern of initial experiments in opening for seven to eight years followed by the reform in industry starting in September 1985 is very effective. We would argue that Russia and the Commonwealth of Independent States (CIS) as a whole may follow that general path, but possibly with more dramatic steps and fluctuations. For example, a probable return to power in the RF of left-wing forces will not necessarily mean the end of 'reform' – quite the opposite: it could become the beginning of a real reform process, based on the experience of China's opening. Certain reservations for such a turn of events should be kept in mind.

The Chinese behaviour in the first years of the open-door policy provides striking similarities with today's Central Asia: ambitious appeals to developed countries and major financial institutions, special economic zone euphoria, 'strategic coincidences' with the US, a 'petroleum boom', the commercialization of relations with the developing countries, to name but a few. However, the Chinese, after a period of large-scale appeals and 'sweet dreams', managed to forget their ambitions and started the opening process based upon pragmatism, self-reliance and the gradual introduction of foreign industrial expertise. Billions of man-hours spent on experiments and a thorough study of foreign procedures brought about the industrial reform of 1985 and the consequent rapid growth and creation of a powerful export machine. The principal change brought by the initial period of openness can be seen from the table below.

None of the countries in Central Asia, nor Russia, have so far achieved the Chinese level of 1985–86 in the export of manufactured products. Export-led growth as the only way out looks highly improbable for these states. This does not mean, however, that the Chinese experience should

Table 9.1 China's Export Pattern(%)[2]

Year	1985	1986
Raw Materials and Fuels	50.7	36.4
Manufacturing Output	49.3	63.6

be neglected. Too many basic features coincide, and the Chinese economy certainly does not only consist of the export-led sector.

It should also be noted that the period of 1985–86 was marked by a sharp rise in technology import to China (US$ 4.5 billion in 1986, compared to an average of US$ 1 billion in 1981–84).[3] Thus, modernization and industrial reform followed the opening with a decent time-lag of eight years. It is therefore quite essential to have only modest figures of investment and technology acquisition at the first stages of opening. This is what is now being observed in the RF and Central Asia. Also important is that from 1986 the tightening-up of currency and joint-venture activities regulation went together with a rapid growth in export and foreign investment, ignoring some grumbling in the West about China 'closing its doors'.

Both trends mentioned above lie far ahead (if they are possible at all) in Central Asian development. Nevertheless they provide us with some understanding of how the Chinese model of opening can start 'working' in Central Asia, bringing a sound economic base to ethnic harmony. It is one of our central arguments in this essay that the Chinese model is appropriate for Central Asian states.

Taking the Chinese experience of open policy into account we would like to indicate also that although Central Asia now definitely lags far behind, some of the Chinese achievements may prove very productive for the Central Asian region's co-operation with foreign countries. Basic features of the region are very similar to those that the Chinese had in the initial stages of their open policy. Generally, the Chinese experience clearly shows that labour-intensive branches of the economy, services and light industry, agricultural processing industries and some other businesses are much easier to reconstruct in the course of co-operation with foreigners.

Some participation of international business is already registered in these sectors in Central Asia. Available facts and figures clearly show that the process has started. For example:

- In Kazakhstan, among two thousand registered joint ventures, 492 are operating, mainly in services. One of the largest ventures in labour-intensive manufacturing is a factory, with Chinese participation, producing vacuum flasks;
- The reconstruction of twelve cotton cleaning factories was agreed between Tajikistan and Turkey in July 1994;
- A cotton processing plant was proposed by Mitsui to Uzbekistan in a package with some other labour-intensive projects in August 1994, and the total number of joint ventures registered in Uzbekistan reached 1300 in 1995. Of that number, there were 288 operating joint ventures. The main investors are Afghanistan, Turkey, the US and China;
- Some Russian observers believe that since 1994 the economy of Central Asia has increased in diversity.[4]

The distribution of the technology package acquired by the Chinese in the course of the open policy was marked by the large number of end-users (10,000 for US$ 18 billion accumulated as foreign investment in 1988, and even more modest figures for individual projects in the middle of the 1980s). The respective figures for Central Asia now show the same trend, providing definite hopes. Huge projects prevail, however, in Kazakhstan and Turkmenistan, mainly orientated towards local energy resources. Kazakhstan is famous for its Tengiz project, while Turkmenistan in 1994 started the construction of a gas pipeline to Pakistan through Afghanistan territory and is actively seeking gas markets in the Middle East.

Using China's schedule of opening for comparison, we should note that at present Central Asia is somewhere in 1980–82 at best. Acquaintance with the world and the international economy has started. The fruits are however yet to be reaped, though not in such a distant future as two or three generations from now, as some pessimistic 'reformers' now claim, who are puzzled by the fact that the world 'market' is not a magic spell removing at a stroke all the troubles of the 'very bad socialist past'. Besides, the economic crisis is still developing in Central Asia, and the foreign investment mentioned above improves the general picture only slightly, if at all. Mainly the crisis is caused by the loss of the Russian market and supply (the last was ten per cent to twenty per cent higher than at the end of the Soviet era).

Due to evident geographical factors, it may also be noted that opportunities for massive opening and reform in Central Asia can come (not taking the West into account) from three basic directions: China, Russia and the Muslim countries. But the optimum from our point of view is perhaps a combination of Chinese-style reform with a certain reopening to

Table 9.2 Goods flows in and out of Central Asia (1988, %)[5]

	Import in local consumption (including other USSR)	Export in local production (including other USSR)
Uzbekistan	24	18
Kazakhstan	20	12
Tajikistan	29	21
Turkmenistan	29	22
Kyrgyzstan	28	21

Russia which could alleviate many ethnic problems relatively quickly. This view is shared by leaders with a sound economic background – Prime Minister Kazegeldin of Kazakhstan, for example.[6] Some reasoning for such a point of view may perhaps be found in the more friendly environment (in economic terms) in Russia than in other neighbouring states with more rigid economies, and also is already shared in RF migrants from Central Asia, who are sometimes remarkably successful in their economic activities.

The model described above is certainly not considered as an alternative to the use of other foreign capital. Quite the opposite; the scheme may seriously promote equal and wide-ranged openness to the outside world.

Russia is the nearest source and represents a great opportunity. At present 65 per cent of Kazakhstan's foreign trade is with the RF, while in Turkmenistan, the respective figure is 55 per cent. Russia's actual progress in opening is also of clear value to Central Asia, though it is not without mistakes and bottlenecks. The main trouble within the Russian economy now is a sharp deficit of capital-digesting capacity and easily modernized branches (with adequate human resources) and a lack of investment in this sector. Heavy industry kills rapid opening in many regions. The problems with heavy industry are the same in China, particular in its North-Eastern provinces. They, as well as the Russian Urals, Siberia and part of the Russian Far East provide a clear example of the great scope of problems in a slow drive to the opening of heavy industry. That applies also to a certain extent to the Central Asian economies. In Central Asia, however, patterns of rapid opening up based upon agricultural growth is much easier than in the RF, due to a much larger proportion of rural and semi-rural population, with one evident exception, Kazakhstan, where a large share of heavy industry exists. Certainly there is an imperative need for the restoration of a normal international environment, including ties with former republics of the USSR where easy markets can be found for the first products of their opened economy. Mutual complementarity still exists in the post-Soviet area, though it is under constant deforming pressure from local and central politicians.

Unfortunately, in the relations between former Soviet republics, political and even personal (at high level) attitudes clearly prevail now upon the approaches based on economic considerations. These attitudes and false contradictions are sometimes supported by the current US administration, which seems to neglect the existing trend towards economic reintegration of the post-Soviet area. Local leaders often tried to escape the 'evil' socialist history by conflicting with Moscow and humiliating the Russians left in their states. They seem to be unaware of the simple truth that such conflicts could not improve their economy, which had become artificially disconnected from that of Russia. Moscow's leaders are no better in this respect. Thus, one of the available resources and opportunity of opening up has been ignored by both sides.

Under the constant pressure of economic and social crisis, the authorities in Central Asia usually regarded all ties with Moscow as temporary, perhaps justly claiming than the ruling team in the Kremlin was corrupt. That was why some militant Islamic ideas or concepts of total isolation from Russia looked, at the beginning of the 1990s, rather appealing to a part of the local public, and even received a certain support from scholars both in and outside the RF.[7] The situation has changed somewhat for the better now. It is clear for many in Central Asia and Russia that the present national leaders are poor economic managers.

Meanwhile, corruption at local levels testifies to the fact that the post-Soviet area remains more of a united whole than is widely presumed. Major improvements of economies in the region therefore are very likely to happen within one and the same historic period, with Central Asia as a whole perhaps lagging slightly behind and with Kazakhstan as a possible leader in the drive toward openness and modernization. In fact, Central Asia has in some places even higher levels of corruption, due to large-scale opportunities for speculation in exports and imports, bribing (whilst re-exporting) of illegal immigrants, and the flourishing arms and drugs trade, especially in Kyrgyzstan, the most 'democratic' society in the region. To our mind, Adam Smith's idea of the main source of wealth of nations is sometimes totally forgotten by local businessmen and authorities, simply because many of them have easy access to power, black money or natural resources and are simply incapable (the opposite to the emerging business community in the European part of the former USSR) of the fair development of economic projects.

The disputes with Moscow under various slogans thus include a great deal of personal conflict, economic speculation and political blackmail. For example, obtaining a better bargaining position in the CIS is an idea which, for some reason, has been nurtured slowly by the Kremlin and Nazarbayev, with definite differences in the approaches of each side. Moscow wants power in Kazakhstan, and Nazarbayev wants support for his own power in the same place. The recent 95 per cent referendum vote for Nazarbayev does not mean much. Any success of his government needs to be supported by effective economic and social management. Its present quality of such management may be assessed by one fact: the monthly salary of a shop assistant in Kazakhstan is about US$ 8. In Tajikistan, however, people have not had their salaries at all for a year and a half.

The Eurasian origin of the USSR, certain religious dualism and national tolerance of the former superpower, its achievements in keeping the country from ethnic conflict (sometimes simply by ignoring them, sometimes by placing the Russians in Central Asia in the position of a minority as a focus for local displeasure and thus cementing various nationalities by providing them with a common 'enemy')-all are now almost lost as means of settling these conflicts. Indeed, too much has already been lost in political disputes and as a result of the massive and growing outflow of Russians and other minorities, including Germans, Koreans, Caucasians, and Greeks, from the region.

The registered refugees are only the tip of the iceberg. Actual numbers are much higher, but with roughly the same distribution between the republics. Meanwhile, more and more dangerous conflicts within the Muslim population inside Central Asia are appearing, with different ethnic

Table 9.3 The Number of Refugees Registered[8]

Year	1993	1994
Tajikistan	65,448	134,046
Uzbekistan	3,247	21,613
Kyrgyzstan	897	20,971
Kazakhstan	283	7,948
Turkmenistan	54	504

groups trying to fill up the power vacuums left by the Russians. The origin is usually economic. However, after developing the conflict, the parties tend to forget economics and transform the conflicts into wide ethnic disaster. Titular nationalities do not prevail absolutely in any of the Central Asian republics. In many places rich mixtures of nationalities share small areas of territory.

One million Uzbeks live in Tajikistan, and two million Tajiks live in Uzbekistan, for example. As can be seen from the above table, Tajikistan has seen the most serious situation, which has not only forced out the Russian minority but also many specialists of Tajik origin who did not belong to traditional conflicting groups (clans). A nation with a population of 5.6 million has had 300,000 people killed and about 700,000 forced into fleeing as refugees from the beginning of the conflict. Ethnic conflicts have also taken place in Kyrgyzstan (northern and southern clans), Uzbekistan and Kazakhstan (Novii Usen, Ust-Kamenogorsk, Issik). Turkmenistan looks the most stable place in the region.

Sometimes internal conflicts in Central Asia are 'exported' to Russia together with the outflow of new migrants. Such conflicts are now widespread in the Astrahan and Volgograd regions.

On the question of economic ties between Russia and Central Asia, it is essential to restore a normal system of economic relations between enterprises in Russia and in Central Asia which are at present experiencing many additional difficulties due to artificial limitations at RF and local levels of authority. Rather typical is the grain situation for the Russian Far East. The region buys the product from the US at US$ 240 per ton with Kazakhstan's grain available at US$ 80 per ton.[9] Disputes on prices of fuel, transport, raw materials and corresponding scandals unfortunately draw public attention away from the more urgent task of good management of the available resources, a gradual rise in the quality of their processing, and an increase in world-standard output – that is, the main economic content of open policy and modernization. Instead, some very suspicious contracts appear with long-term obligations of Central Asia for deliveries of raw materials and fuel to various destinations. As an example the Tengiz project can be mentioned. A fifty per cent share of the project is held by Mobil Oil, which is 'unprecedented', according to British observers.[10]

Another inflammatory factor is the rise of enormous transport tariffs, which stimulate the break-away of Central Asia in real economic terms both from other CIS countries and from the whole European Community. We abhor such a policy, an essential result of which is the disintegration of the post-Soviet economic space in the global economy. Another problem is communications with exorbitant tariffs. The Kremlin may become an absolute loser in these games, as the improvement or creation of alternative transport and communication facilities has been singularly seriously treated by Central Asian governments among their economic targets. Part of the Istanbul-Beijing railway is completed, the whole road capacity may start in 1996. Another large project initiated in 1994 by China, Pakistan, Kazakhstan and Kyrgyzstan provides new roads to connect the Karakorum highway with the two capitals of the Central Asian republics.

We should stress that in no way are we against the self-supported, and to a great extent economically independent, development of Central Asia. As the Chinese experience shows, the dual model of self-reliance combined with opening is sometimes the only way out. Moreover, in the late 1980s we were trying to persuade our policy makers in Moscow of the inevitability of a much more independent economic structure in Central Asia than in other maritime and border regions, with the idea of creating an export zone there aimed at South Asia and the Middle East. There was one qualification: it was considered as a stage in preparing the future globalization of the world and Soviet economy.[11]

The second opportunity in the development of opening for Central Asia is China. However in 1994 there were no signs of great progress in mutual relations: trade went down and was far below the levels expected even a year before. With Kazakhstan, the PRC's major trading partner in the region, the volume of trade hardly reached US$ 300 million. We may recall the very optimistic forecasts on possible Chinese involvement in the reconstruction of Central Asia, but now the situation has altered dramatically, and Beijing has adopted a 'wait and see' position.

Some scholars attribute this attitude to the PRC's own problems with Muslim minorities in the Northwest and even fears of Islamic consolidation spreading into China. The same fears are sometimes expressed by Russian academics, who assume that one of the potential dangers is the political and then geographical convergence of Tatarstan (the autonomous Volga republic) with Kazakhstan.[12] The question therefore is: which country's geopolitical mentality is at present better prepared for an Islam-backed Central Asia: Russia or China? However, we think that the question itself is purely academic. There are no signs (in real terms) of actual integration of any kind in Central Asia and its surrounding regions. Among the reasons supporting such an argument are the growing openness of the Islamic world itself, the wide variety of models of future strategies within Muslim countries, ethnic tension in the region itself, and personal conflicts between Central Asian leaders.

The RF and China are not competitors in Central Asia at present. What is more, both countries are potentially interested in the development of opening and economic reform in the region. Russia would like to keep its access to South Asian and Middle Eastern markets through Central Asia and could benefit easily from the restoration of normal ties with the region's economies. On the other hand, China is able to provide reform experience in a more realistic guise, and it can also provide some Central Asian republics with access to markets in the Asia-Pacific region, getting certain benefits from joint processing of the region's raw materials and agricultural products. Instead, the economy of the region has suffered a lot due to the uncontrolled importation of Chinese goods, which not only killed off half of the demand of the RF for cotton but is also obviously killing potential garments, footwear and other light industries in Central Asia.

Maybe there will be more competition for influence in Central Asia between China and the RF in the future. At present, however, there are no indications of such. Both sides react to each other calmly, even co-operate in military contacts in the border areas, and continue to hold multilateral talks on the border issues with regard to the western section of the former USSR border with China. The main reason is perhaps the situation in the region per se. It is too disquieting to get seriously involved in. Other reasons lie in the low investment capacities of the RF. It should therefore be noted that the real escape from the present situation will inevitably carry some extent of self-reliance in Central Asia, possibly upon a large scale.

Isolation even from neighbouring markets will certainly diminish the chances for reform and opening in the near future. Nevertheless it should be optimistically stressed that China, which has successfully developed a flourishing foreign trade, was a society of self-isolated communes only twenty years ago. To a certain extent the tradition of self-reliance is not lost even today. Self-sustained growth with traditional social backing is, we argue, one of the most practicable choices for many areas in Central Asia. Eventually this can also bring national harmony. At the same time, large-scale economic isolation can be viewed as a temporary solution. Some islands of massive opening may appear, as was the case in China, and to some extent the RF, with Tashkent and Almaty as the nearest candidates.

Relations with China are bringing modest but permanent progress in the opening of Central Asia. But it is far below expectations. Certainly some protectionist measures are necessary both in the RF and Central Asia, and preferably simultaneously.

At present, it is quite disturbing to note that the continuing disintegration driven by opportunist economic motives and personal ambitions at the time when open economic policy in the entire post-Soviet economic space could start bearing fruits. Some domestic investors in the European part of the country are already prepared for projects in Central Asia, and have received enough training for that through productive contact with the West. But tariffs, and conflicts between present leaders, stop them, as well as European entrepreneurs, from both western and eastern countries. Indeed, restructuring and reconstruction, after a more reasonable inicep-tion, could, before long, become a 'native-born child' throughout the whole post-Soviet economic area. It would be very stupid to terminate this pregnancy.

One of the basic features of China's open policy during its first stage was a search for appropriate, proportionate partners among the nations of the world. That is why some huge projects with Japanese industrial giants, the World Bank and the US were not started in the 1980s.

Paradoxically, some optimal country partners for Central Asia, from the point of view of their size and industrial pattern, are situated in Europe. Their expertise in labour-intensive processing with world-class quality could be very helpful. Besides, they are not direct competitors with each other in the Russian, Middle East, Pacific Rim and other markets. To a certain extent Europeans are really interested in friendly co-operation and the step-by-step transfer of technology to Central Asia's enterprises. However, that promising partnership may remain only as a dream, due to the actual economic and infrastructural isolation of Central Asia. This situation shows how easily prospective global links may be destroyed by certain Russian ministries.

At the same time it is short-sighted to expect the same (as the European) attitude from Muslim, Chinese and Korean businesses, which traditionally treat the area as a pure resource and cheap labour base, though some corrections in their policy may appear with time. So far the actual isolation of Central Asian economies seriously diminishes the choice of partners for their development.

Some problems also lie in the low flexibility of heavy industry in the area, which includes weapons production facilities. Theoretically, their transfer to the world market should be in the form of 'conversion', or partial use of some divisions for output of components and/or spare parts of foreign orders. Not much has been achieved in this sector, and production management as a whole is still far from the stage of a waiting and fulfilling the orders of marketing departments. Occasional sales of home-made weaponry in the region do nothing to solve the problem. Solutions (at least partial) can be reached only in a much better social and political environment, both domestically and internationally. While Russian participation is crucial, the RF has not enough experience of its own yet. Industrial modernization badly needs an initial investment push to start as a practical project.

The region lacks necessary political conditions for effective use of the human resources available in the opening and reform. Life in the former USSR provided some training in this respect, including knowledge of foreign languages and generally high literacy levels. The Russians and other minorities could easily add to that potential. The opportunity to get them engaged still exists, though it was much greater when the region belonged to the USSR. Now even in Ukraine, where the basis of economic and scientific self-reliance is much more profound, there is much discontent regarding the breakaway from Russia and losses in human ties.

Technical knowledge from traditional centres in Russia has already become very expensive, due to transport and communication problems. The same is true of project management expertise, which is available in Moscow in modest quantities. Another major loss is the access of local administrations to collections of research and experience on world economy and politics in Moscow and St Petersburg, now better adapted to practical co-operation with foreign nations. To no extent does this apply to the ideas of 'reformist' and 'democratic' do-gooders. Fortunately, Central Asia managed to avoid some traps like 'privatization', 'free prices' and other inventions of economic adventurers like Gaidar, Yavlinsky, and Chubais.

Russia and some areas in Central Asia are nearing the historic point where their opening may start working in a more productive way. It may coincide with the appearance of the first popularly elected President of the RF in 1996, or it may come later with his activities. He may well perform better both economically and socially than the present one, irrespective of declared ideological values. He will just use some fruits of openness which are already ripening in the RF and around it. Accordingly, it would be better for the West to forget, for a while, its preference for words such as 'reform', 'democracy', and 'private property', and monitor instead the substance of opening in the RF and Central Asia in real economic and social terms. That, to our mind, makes even more urgent the need for international studies of the present Central Asian opening, its nature and orientation in comparison with what has happened in China or is happening in the RF. Success in researching the topics mentioned above definitely depends upon its scope and adequate theoretical approach.

However, even modest statistical analyses of local data, combined with the interviews with experts used in this article, can provide valuable guidelines. Small ad hoc meetings with inhabitants of Central Asia have added dramatic details to the generally gloomy picture of incompetent leaders stifling the opening and reforms and starting ethnic conflicts instead. But that cannot last for long. Nationalism, both Russian and local, is clearly discredited in the eyes of the population of the former USSR. Leaders like Nazarbayev, with a clear appeal to the population based upon the 'global approach' opposing the regionalism of authorities with a local mentality, both in Central Asia and in the Kremlin,[13] are becoming winners of public support due to the rising status of opening throughout the post-Soviet area. To some extent, that corresponds to other observations on the nature of ethnic conflicts.

International assistance in the essential progress of Central Asia's opening including a certain reintegration with other CIS countries is also vital now, because the region sees very fast population growth, with the birthrate around five per cent annually.[14] A lack of productive employment there in the future could easily bring new soldiers to militant clans with unpredictable consequences for global stability.

NOTES

1. *National Doctrine of Russia: Problems and Priorities*, RAU Corp, Moscow, 1994, p. 34.
2. *Guoji Maoyi*, (International Trade) Beijing, 1987, No. 5, p. 52.
3. *Guoji Maoyi*, 1987, No. 7, p. 51.
4. Data collected from TASS daily issues.
5. *National Doctrine*, p. 59.
6. *Interview to BBC*, 24 April 1995.
7. Sheregi, F. E., 'Prospects for the Development of Russian Ethnic Consciousness', in *Herald of Russian Academy of Science*, No. 1, 1995.
8. *Russia in the Mirror of Reforms*, Report of Independent Institute of Social and National Problems, Moscow, 1995, p. 51.
9. *Russian TV News*, 24 May 1995.
10. *BBC*, 17 April 1995.
11. *The Pacific Region in the 21st Century*, APN, Moscow, 1989.
12. Stepanov, V. V., 'Hotbeds of Interethnic Tension: Reality and Forecast', *Herald of Russian Academy of Sciences*, 1994, No. 4, p. 300.
13. Nazarbayev, N., 'Countries and Peoples Will Return to the Path of Integration'. *Nezavisimaya Gazeta*, 12 April 1995.
14. Shirokov, G., 'Russia and the West: State and Civil Society', Report to International Conference sponsored by Friedrich Ebert Fund.

10 Sino-Central Asian Trade and Economic Relations: Progress, Problems and Prospects

Qingjian Liu

In the wake of the break-up of the former Soviet Union, five Central Asian republics, Kazakhstan, Kyrgyzstan, Tajikistan, Turkmenistan and Uzbekistan, declared independence. Because of Central Asia's strategic location between Europe and Asia, and because of the potential of Central Asian economies and their natural resources, the independence of these five Central Asian republics significantly affects the regional geopolitics and geoeconomics in its own ways. Political instability in these newly independent states further underlines their importance in international relations of the region.

Of the five Central Asian states, three are China's new neighbours along the long frontiers of its Northwest. Kazakhstan, Kyrgyzstan, and Tajikistan share more than 3,000 kilometres of common borders with China.[1] The other two republics, Uzbekistan and Turkmenistan, are close by, though they do not border with China. Further, all five Central Asian republics are located between two great powers, China and Russia. Political, strategic and economic relations between China and these Central Asian states therefore are not only important for the national and regional security of these countries; they also have significant implications for peace and stability in Asia and in the world.

In China's international relations with Central Asian states, trade and economic relations occupy an important position. After their independence, all five Central Asian states have seen a rapid growth in their trade with China. Economic and technical co-operation between China and Central Asian states has also expanded. On the other hand, there are some problems and constraints in bilateral trade and economic relations. This essay examines the progress, the problems and the prospect of this relationship. It argues that there are both opportunities and challenges for China and Central Asian states in further developing this relationship.

I PROGRESS

Economic and cultural contacts between China and Central Asia have a long history which could be dated back to the Silk Road more than 2,000 years ago. The Silk Road played its historical role in promoting economic, trade and cultural exchanges between China and Central Asia as well as Europe. After the establishment of the People's Republic of China in 1949, Sino-Soviet trade took off. With Sino-Soviet trade making up more than sixty per cent of China's foreign trade in the 1950s, there was a brief period of flourishing economic relations between China and the Soviet republics in Central Asia. As the Sino-Soviet relations deteriorated after 1960, trade between China and Central Asia rapidly declined. In the late 1960s and the 1970s, even the traditional border trade totally ceased.[2]

It was not until the early 1980s that the Sino-Soviet relations began to improve. In April 1982, the Ministry of Foreign Trade of China and the Soviet Ministry of Foreign Trade formally exchanged a note, agreeing to resume border trade between the two countries. In January 1986, the Chinese and the Soviet governments again exchanged a note, in which both sides agreed that traditional border trade between China and the Soviet Union along their common borders in China's Xinjiang Uighur Autonomous Region should be resumed. Also in 1986, the former Soviet Union decentralized its foreign trade authority. All Soviet republics were empowered to deal directly with foreign countries for trade. In June 1988, an agreement on local trade was signed between the Chinese and the Soviet governments. The agreement stipulates that local authorities of the Chinese provinces, autonomous regions and municipalities can develop trade and other economic relations directly with their counterparts in the Soviet republics, and vice versa.[3] With a series of inter-governmental agreements, economic exchanges and trade between China and Central Asia had increased notably. However, any progress was extremely limited. For example, in 1990, China's trade with Kazakhstan, the largest economy among the five Central Asian republics, was only 85 million roubles, which was just two per cent of Kazakhstan's total foreign trade of that year.

The independence of Central Asian republics in 1991 has significantly changed this picture. The economic and trade relations between China and Central Asian states have since witnessed fundamental changes in the following four aspects.

Rapid Growth of Bilateral Trade

According to official Chinese statistics, in 1992, China's foreign trade with five newly independent Central Asian states was a total of US$ 475 million.

That is more than ten times that of 1990. Of this total, China's trade with Kazakhstan accounted for US$ 380 million, twenty per cent of Kazakhstan's foreign trade in 1992.[4] China became Kazakhstan's premier trading partner in that year. In the same year, China's trade with Uzbekistan amounted to US$ 52.52 million; with Kyrgyzstan, US$ 35.48 million; with Turkmenistan, US$ 4.5 million, and with Tajikistan US$ 2.79 million.[5]

In 1993, China's trade with five Central Asian states continued to grow to a total of more than US$ 600 million. The annual increase rate was 31 per cent. The growth rate for each Central Asian republic, however, varies greatly. For example, Sino-Tajikistan trade increased more than three times, whereas Sino-Uzbekistan and Sino-Turkmenistan trade increased only 3.3 per cent. Of the five, Kazakhstan remained the largest trading partner with China. Its annual trade was US$ 434 million. (See the following table.)

The picture of China's trade with Central Asia in 1994 was more complicated. The total trade stood at US$ 577 million, which was five per cent less than in 1993. In particular, China's trade with Kazakhstan came substantially down to US$ 335 million, 22 per cent less than in 1993. Sino-Tajikistan trade also suffered a big decline. The total bilateral trade in 1994 was only US$ 3 million, falling back to its 1992 level. The decline of Sino-Kazakhstan trade could be attributed to several factors. Most importantly, it was because both countries were making trade policy adjustments in 1994 which led to drastic changes in import and export commodity composition in bilateral trade. On the other hand, exports of some shoddy consumer goods made in China to Kazakhstan in 1993 seriously damaged the reputation of Chinese exports. Sino-Tajikistan trade suffered mostly because the civil war in Tajikistan seriously disrupted its domestic production. As a result, Tajikistan had serious problem with its exports supply.

Table 10.1 Sino-Central Asian Trade, 1992–1993 (in million US dollars)

Country	1992			1993		
	Imports	Exports	Total	Imports	Exports	Total
Kazakhstan	141.2	227.1	368.3	263.0	171.7	434.7
Kyrgyzstan	16.64	18.85	35.49	65.87	36.55	102.4
Uzbekistan	13.63	38.89	52.52	11.45	42.80	54.25
Turkmenistan	0.41	4.09	4.50	0.80	3.85	4.65
Tajikistan	0.80	1.95	2.75	5.87	6.48	12.35

Sources: *Zhongguo Duiwai Jingji Maoyi Nianjian, 1994–5,* p. 472 & *Zhongguo Tongji Nianjian,* 1994, p. 514

On the other hand, China's trade with Uzbekistan increased substantially to US$ 123 million, an increase of 128 per cent. China's exports to Uzbekistan increased 20.2 per cent, while China's imports grew a staggering 530 per cent! China's trade with Turkmenistan also saw a substantial increase, reaching US$ 11 million – a 142.3 per cent increase. While China's exports to Turkmenistan dropped 4.5 per cent, its imports increased 847.9 per cent. At the same time, trade with Kyrgyzstan in 1994 saw only a moderate 2.7 per cent increase. The Sino-Kyrgyz trade was US$ 105 million in that year.[6]

Diversified Trading Channels

China's trade with Central Asia used to be dominated by border trade. In the mid-1980s, when the Soviet government decentralized its foreign trade and empowered the Soviet republics to conduct trade with their neighbouring countries, Chinese provinces in the Northwest, particularly the Xinjiang Uighur Autonomous Region, started local trade on a small scale with some Soviet republics in Central Asia. After the Central Asian republics declared their independence, China quickly seized the opportunity to start developing bilateral trade at both the state and local levels. Over the last few years, various diversified trading channels between China and Central Asian states have been carefully nurtured. Diversified trading channels are important for both China and Central Asia to expand bilateral trade because of the nature of the traditional trade, the constraints imposed by geography and the severe limitations of transportation means in the region. Border trade, local trade, border residents markets, and tourist purchases have all been developed. They complement bilateral trade at the state level. According to some incomplete Chinese statistics, border trade and local trade between China and Central Asian states in 1992 were over US$ 300 million, three times as much as the total of Sino-Central Asian trade in 1991.[7]

Two particular trading channels are worth mentioning: border residents markets and tourist purchase.

Border residents' markets is a convenient way of conducting small-scale trade along China's borders with Central Asian states. In 1993, Dulata, a trading port in the Yili Prefecture of the Xinjiang Autonomous Region, opened nine border residents' markets for trade. In less than six months' time, more than fifty thousand people visited those markets, which sold goods worth more than RMB 120 million yuan.[8] In a remote trading town of Horgosi in Xinjiang, a border residents' market was launched in August 1992. In the first few months, the monthly purchase on this market averaged RMB 500 thousand yuan.[9]

Tourist purchase has become another new and interesting trading channel between China and Central Asian states. Yilin, renowned as the 'Flower City north of the Great Wall', was the first city to develop tourist purchase as a trading channel. With its convenient geographical location and a good transport service across the borders, Yilin quickly became a hot spot for tourist purchasers from the CIS states. In 1991–1992, it saw an average of 200 tourist purchasers and tourist traders each day and the average purchase per month was over US$ 200,000. In 1992, after the State Council decided that Yilin be given a provincial level of authority in conducting its foreign trade and enjoy preferential policies as applied to four border cities and towns in the Northeast, tourist purchase as a trading channel further flourished. Urumqi, the capital of the Xinjiang Uighur Autonomous Region, followed suit. According to statistics compiled by the Xinjiang regional authorities, in 1993 alone more than 400,000 tourists from Central Asia and Russia visited Urumqi and made purchases of more than RMB 1 billion yuan.[10] In 1994–1995, tourist purchase from Central Asia has been extended to other parts of China. The Almaty–Beijing flight has made large and medium-sized cities in Northern China easily accessible to Central Asian tourist traders.

It should be mentioned here that China's trade and economic relations with Central Asian states have now been developed well beyond Xinjiang and more broadly beyond China's Northwest. In fact, more than twenty Chinese provinces and autonomous regions have established various trading and economic relations with Central Asian republics. Even Chinese enterprises in Hong Kong started to develop economic co-operation with Central Asia. For example, in 1995, Yizhou Enterprise Group Ltd of Hong Kong was negotiating with groups in Kazakhstan to build a commercial city across the Sino-Kazakhstan border near China's trading port of Horgosi, in the hope that this city could be eventually developed into an international free trade market.

Expanding Economic and Technical Cooperations

In the last four years since the independence of the five Central Asian republics, economic and technical co-operation between China and these states has continuously expanded both in scale and in scope. According to the official Chinese statistics, at the beginning of 1993 there were only 95 Chinese joint ventures in Central Asia. A year later, that figure went up to 453. They were all in three Central Asian states, Kazakhstan, Uzbekistan and Kyrgyzstan. Of the 453 Sino-Central Asian joint ventures, 313 were in Kazakhstan, 75 in Kyrgyzstan, and 65 in Uzbekistan.[11]

Statistics from Kazakhstan about Sino-Kazakhstan joint ventures differ widely from Chinese statistics. During Premier Li Peng's state visit to Kazakhstan in April 1994, President Nazarbayev claimed that there were 150 Sino-Kazakhstan joint ventures, while Premier Tereschenko said there were 170.[12] In April 1995, the Kazakhstani embassy in Beijing claimed that by then there were 200 Sino-Kazakh joint ventures. The probable explanation for this wide discrepancy is that during 1994 the Kazakh government started to 'clean up' Kazakh-foreign joint ventures and deregistered a large number of non-manufacturing and exceptional joint-ventures.

The Chinese Premier Li Peng's state visit to the Central Asian states in April 1994 marked an important signpost in the development of economic and technical co-operation between China and Central Asia. More than twenty inter-governmental agreements on bilateral economic and technical co-operation were signed during the visit. For example, on 23 April 1994 six intergovernmental agreements were signed between China and Kyrgyzstan, including an agreement of a loan of RMB 50 million yuan offered by China to Kyrgyzstan, and an agreement on establishing a mixed economic and trade committee between the Chinese and the Kyrgyzstan governments.[13]

The delegation led by Premier Li Peng was accompanied by a large group of Chinese entrepreneurs. That was the first time that a visiting head of Chinese government had been accompanied by such a group.[14] Meanwhile, in Central Asia, the Chinese entrepreneurs signed a number of agreements, contracts and letters of intent with their counterparts in Central Asia. China contracted to purchase cotton from Uzbekistan and chemical fertiliser from Kyrgyzstan, and to exchange textiles for chemical fertiliser with Kazakhstan. Letters of intent covered such areas of co-operation as construction, metallurgy, TV assembly lines, and food processing. In Turkmenistan, discussions of a possible pipeline to transport natural gas from Turkmenistan through China to Japan were initiated.[15] As a follow-up to Premier Li Peng's visit to Kazakhstan, early in 1995, the Kazakhstan government sent an economic delegation to China. During the visit, the Chinese and the Kazakhstan governments further discussed their co-operation in metallurgy, chemical fertiliser and tractor manufacturing, prospecting, petroleum exploitation and refining.

Facilitating Communications

The importance of communications facilities in developing international trade and economic co-operation at the end of the twentieth century needs no emphasizing. Central Asia and China's Northwest share the same severe geographic constraints for developing international economic relations. Both Central Asia and China's Northwest are located in inner Asia and are completely landlocked. The distance from Urumqi to Lianyungang, the closest seaport on China's east coast, is more than 4,000 km. On the other hand, none of the five Central Asian states has a seaport or is even close to a seaport. Means of transport and other communications facilities are therefore vital in developing trade and economic co-operation between Central Asia and China.

The second Euro-Asian continental bridge – the railway trunk linking Lianyungang in China in the East with Rotterdam in the Netherlands in the West – had been under construction for many years. It was completed just months before the Central Asian republics declared their independence. In July 1991, this transcontinental railway began a period of trial operation. From 1992, it was made fully operational. The railway has brought China and Central Asia much more closely together. Since its operation, it has become the main means of transport between China and the Central Asian states. The railway port of Alataw Pass, which sits on the Sino-Kazakhstan border, is now the largest railway port in Northwest China. It is designed to have the capacity to handle 3.5 million tons annually in the short and medium term and 5.9 million tons in the long term. Already in 1992, the freight passing through this railway port reached over one million tons. 1993 saw a further increase in the freight handling of this port.[16] In September 1994, Kazakhstan became the first among five Central Asian states to sign an inter-governmental agreement with China for the use of Lianyungang port for the two-way transport of goods between Kazakhstan and the Asia-Pacific region.[17]

The importance of the building and operation of the second Euro-Asian continental bridge for Central Asia as well as China can be seen in two aspects. On the one hand, it goes right through Northwest China to East China and connects Central Asia with Lianyungang on the East China sea, one of China's main freight ports. Such a transport line will surely have a positive impact on the economic and social development in both China and Central Asian states. It will also facilitate trade and economic exchanges between China and Central Asia. On the other hand, it has also greatly improved transportation facilities between Central Asia and East Asia, including such countries as Japan, Korea and the Southeast Asian states, thus facilitating trade between these two regions in Asia.

Opening trading ports and constructing necessary facilities in those ports are indispensable in developing trade and economic co-operation between China and Central Asia. By 1994, the Xinjiang Uighur Autonomous Region had already opened 14 land and air trading ports to China's neighbouring states sharing common borders with Xinjiang. Eight of them are to the Central Asian states and the rest to Russia. The three most important of them, i.e. Horgosi, Alataw Pass and Tuerduote, are the passageways to Kazakhstan and Kyrgyzstan. The Alataw Pass road trading port complements the railway port there and mainly serves the border trade.[18]

What is particularly worth mentioning is the re-opening and development of the Horgosi trading port. Horgosi is one of the oldest land trading ports in China opened for foreign trade. It was first established in 1860 for Sino-Russian trade. After 1960, with the deterioration of Sino-Soviet relations, the Horgosi port was closed. Only in 1983 did it begin to function again. Before the opening of the Alataw Pass railway port, Horgosi was the most important trading port of Xinjiang in its trade with the former Soviet Union. In 1991, freight passing through Horgosi was more than 200,000 tons. The total trade through Horgosi reached over 100 million Swiss francs. On the other hand, Horgosi also became a major passenger port. In 1990, with the start of the Horgosi-Panfeilov one-day tour, more than fifty thousand tourists from the former Soviet Union visited Horgosi. In 1991, the State Council sanctioned the opening of Horgosi to passengers and tourists from countries other than the former Soviet Union.[19]

Telecommunications facilities have also been steadily improved between China and Central Asia. Most significant of all, in 1992 China and Central Asia and some European countries negotiated and decided to build jointly a Euro-Asian optical fibre communication system which would connect China with Central Asia and Europe. It was also stipulated that the communication system should be completed by the year 1996. In 1994, China had already completed the construction of its section within the borders of China and put it into a trial operation. When this system is completed, it will play an important role in telecommunications between China, Central Asia and Europe.

II PROBLEMS

As has been argued above, trade and economic relations between China and Central Asia have seen some steady and impressive achievements since the independence of the former Soviet republics in Central Asia. This is not to say that there are no problems in bilateral trade and economic relations. In fact, a number of problems and constraints have seriously troubled trade and economic co-operation between China and Central Asia in the last few years and may hamper further development of bilateral economic relations in the future. Some of these problems and constraints are the legacy of history, whereas some others are new. For both China and Central Asian states, earnest attention should be paid to dealing with these problems and constraints jointly in an effort to overcome them. Only in so doing can trade and economic relations between China and Central Asia develop further in the interests of all the states concerned. The problems that constrain the development of Sino-Central Asian economic relations, I would argue, are mainly as follows.

Antiquated Trading Practices

Up till the time of this writing, trade between China and Central Asian states has been mostly conducted in the form of barter trade, whether border trade, or local trade, or state trade. Barter trade had been adopted in Sino-Soviet trade relations because of historical circumstances. This primitive and antiquated trading practice has now become incompatible with and inadequate for international trade at the turn of the 21st century. Barter trade has a number of constraints and limitations. Firstly, what is bartered has to be mutually acceptable if a deal is to be successfully made. Secondly, imports and exports have to be carefully balanced. It makes international settlement very difficult. Thirdly, this trading practice is at odds with market economy which both China and Central Asian states are trying to build in their countries. It seriously constrains any manufacturing enterprise in its independent participation in foreign trade and international economic exchanges. After a few years' practice, both China and Central Asian states have clearly realized that this antiquated trading practice poses a great obstacle to the rapid expansion of bilateral trade and economic relations. Given the shortage of foreign exchange, particularly in Central Asian states, China is actively seeking a transitional way to change this practice. For this purpose, the Chinese governments have offered a number of loans and short-term credits in *Renminbi* to Central Asian states. China firmly believes that practices in Sino-Central Asian trade should also be eventually converted to full compatibility with the norms and rules of international trade.

Limitation in Economic Cooperation

In the last few years since the independence of Central Asian states, Sino-Central Asian economic relations have been dominated by trade. It is true that a number of inter-governmental agreements have been signed, which shows the willingness of both sides to engage actively in economic and technical co-operation. Actual progress in implementing those agreements is, however, still limited. Although China has started a number of joint ventures in Central Asia, most of them are in the restaurant and garment industries and in the setting-up of trading outlets. These joint ventures are generally small in scale and low in technology. It should be admitted that some of these joint ventures have helped to alleviate the severe shortage of daily necessities at a time of economic crisis in some Central Asian states. In the longer term, they should not be, however, the mainstream of bilateral economic and technical co-operation. Furthermore, those joint ventures do not represent the comparative economic and technological advantages that China and the Central Asian states possess.

Because of historical distortions in Soviet times, Central Asian states have mostly what could be called 'single-product' economies in structural terms. They are rich in mineral and agricultural resources. They are also advanced in some sectors such as metallurgy. This is their comparative advantage. The economic development strategy of Central Asian states aims therefore at transforming their economic structure by developing their capability and technology in processing mineral products, petroleum, natural gas and agricultural products. In correcting the distortions in their economic structures, Central Asian states are also in dire need of developing a food processing industry, an electronics industry and other light industries for consumer goods production. China has a comparative advantage in these aspects and can help Central Asian states develop those sectors. In many aspects, the potential of economic and technical co-operation between China and Central Asian states is yet to be fully exploited.

Inadequate Investment Environment in Central Asia

After declaring their independence, the Central Asian states were anxious to develop and expand their external economic relations and to attract foreign investment and technology. This is partly their strategy to transform their economies into market economies. It is also partly a strategy to alleviate the economic dilemma that Central Asian states have been faced with after their independence. Domestic economic conditions were, however, not conducive to their economic opening, particularly their efforts to attract foreign investment. The systemic transformation of the Central Asian economies had just been started. The woes of such a transformation, such as the choice of a model and transitional methods, troubled all five Central Asian economies. In fact, in the first two years of their independence, deep economic crises and deteriorating financial conditions were common features of Central Asian states. As a result, domestic investment declined sharply. Moreover, the inability of Central Asian states to deal effectively with their economic problems created disorder in many aspects of domestic economic activities.

It must therefore be argued that economic, legal and political conditions in Central Asian states are far from adequate to attract foreign investment. Firstly, although a number of laws and regulations have been made by Central Asian states on foreign investment and foreign economic relations, there are still much more to be desired. Further, because of the domestic political situation and economic conditions in Central Asian states, most governments either did not or could not strictly implement those laws and regulations in conducting their foreign economic relations. Joint ventures therefore could not be guaranteed legal protection in conducting their economic activities. Secondly, because of historical circumstances, some Central Asian states have had to rush to issue their own currencies. This has led to rising inflation and rapid depreciation of those currencies. Consequently, economic conditions further deteriorated. Such a situation causes many problems for Central Asian states to make their international settlement in foreign trade and other economic exchanges without delay and without default. Thirdly, banking and other financial institutions have only limited and primitive facilities in dealing with foreign investment and other forms of foreign economic co-operation. This has been compounded by the primitive telecommunication systems in the region. Fourthly, other service sectors, such as hotel and transport facilities, are far from adequate. Last but not least, there is a historical legacy. All five Central Asian states had been subject to the planned economy for more than seventy years. There are also ethnic cultures and traditions to consider. These historical legacies have seriously conditioned their outlook on the market economy and their adaptation to norms and rules of international economic co-operation.

Poor Quality of Trading Personnel

The problem of poor training and unprofessional behaviour of personnel conducting Sino-Central Asian trade has two facets. Although China has opened up its economy for more than sixteen years, the inland frontiers have been open for only a little more than five years. The opening of China's Northwest frontier is even more recent. Moreover, the opening of these land frontiers put the landlocked and economically backward areas overnight at the forefront of China's economic opening. From the very beginning, there has been a serious shortage of qualified foreign trade personnel. Even the existing foreign trade personnel at the time of opening were not properly trained and had to adapt themselves to this unprecedented opening. There have been reported cases in which foreign trade personnel in China's Northwest have practised extortion and racketeering. In 1993, partly owing to the poor training of trading personnel, a large quantity of shoddy consumer goods were exported to Central Asia from China. These incidents have seriously damaged trade relations between China and Central Asia.

For Central Asian states, such a problem is more daunting. All five Central Asian states have just started to conduct their own foreign trade and economic relations independently. In the government departments, there has been a shortage of managerial personnel familiar with the market economy and international trade. The trading personnel, on the other hand, do not have sufficient knowledge of the norms and standard practices in international trade and economic exchanges. Some do not even know how to conduct foreign trade. The Kazakh President Nazarbayev openly admitted that this is a serious problem Kazakhstan is faced with. This is indeed one of the obstructions to the expansion of Sino-Central Asian trade and economic relations.

Chaos in Border Trade

As is well known, with the opening of China's land frontiers from the Northeast to the Southwest, China's foreign trade with its neighbouring countries has grown rapidly. In border areas, there was once a situation in which every household conducted trade across the borders. One consequence of this situation is chaos in China's border trade. For two years in 1992 and 1993, there was little adequate management of trade along China's increasingly porous borders in its Northwest. The momentum of the opening and the overnight booming of trade was such that it was impossible even just to have legitimate traders in border areas registered in good time. Neither was it possible for China to establish customs facilities and commodity inspection services in most of trading ports. Profiteering and wheeling and dealing once dominated the trade across the borders. Profiteers in China and in Central Asia ganged up to take advantage of the chaotic conditions in border trade. As border trade came to dominate bilateral trade between China and the Central Asian states, it has eroded and sidelined the major trading channel between states, i.e. state trade. Such chaos has already troubled bilateral trade relations between China and Central Asian states.[20] The sharp decline of trade between China and Kazakhstan in 1994 could be partly attributed to this.[21]

III PROSPECTS

In simple terms, the prospect of Sino-Central Asian trade and economic relations is promising. There is great potential to be cultivated by both sides in advancing their trade and economic relations. In many areas, Chinese and Central Asia economies are mutually complementary. Economic co-operation is not only possible but also desirable for all. Further, there are historical opportunities for both China and Central Asia at the dawn of the 21st century. Therefore, the discussion of the prospect for Sino-Central Asian trade must start with elaboration of opportunities and challenges presented to Central Asia and China in their economic relations.

Historical Opportunities

Historical opportunities in Sino-Central Asian economic relations have been created by the sea changes in international relations in general and in the recent development of Sino-Central Asian relations. Firstly, there have been frequent high-level state and governmental visits between China and Central Asian states. This has been complemented by more frequent visits by trade and economic delegations and groups at all levels. In April 1994, Chinese Premier Li Peng elaborated the basic Chinese policies on developing Sino-Central Asian relations and expressed the sincere desire of China to cultivate trade and economic relations with Central Asian states. More importantly, the signing of a Sino-Kazakh treaty delineating their mutual borders solved the long-standing nagging problem of border disputes.[22] That has paved the way for further economic co-operation between China and Kazakhstan. Border negotiations between China and Kyrgyzstan and Tajikistan are now an ongoing process.[23] Such favourable political conditions signal new opportunities for both sides to develop trade and economic relations on the basis of equality and mutual benefit.

Secondly, in Sino-Central Asian relations, 'geoeconomic relations' are becoming predominant. Expanding and sustaining trade and economic relations has become the most important issue in bilateral relations. From the Chinese perspective, this has also become the foundation upon which friendly neighbouring relations between China and Central Asian states can be built. China therefore hopes to develop its trade and economic relations with Central Asian states on the basis of equality and mutual benefit. Ideology should not interfere in state-to-state relations. Any nation's choice of social system and developmental model should be respected. The dominance of 'geoeconomics' in Sino-Central Asian bilateral relations could also be seen in the number of agreements signed between China and Central Asian states on trade and economic co-operation.

Thirdly, Central Asian states have since their independence decided to transform their economies into market economies. Opening their economies has become an important aspect of this transformation. It is therefore imperative for Central Asian economies to cultivate the international markets and to expand their foreign economic relations. For China, on the other hand, after more than sixteen years of opening and reform, it is the socialist market economy that is the final goal of China's economic reforms. China also needs to expand and further develop its foreign economic relations. China and Central Asian states, therefore, converge in their need to develop their international economic relations. Such a convergence provides opportunities for more bilateral co-operation.

Fourthly, Central Asian states have decided on a strategy of comprehensive opening to the outside world in an effort to meet the desperate need of severe domestic economic conditions. It is natural and understandable that the focal point of their opening should be to Russia. Central Asian states have, however, also regarded China as an important partner in implementing their strategies of economic opening. This is mainly because of two factors. One is that China and Central Asia are closely bound geopolitically and geoeconomically. The other is that China's experience in economic reform and opening may provide some useful lessons for the Central Asian states which are also trying to reform their centrally planned economies.

China's opening to the outside world is also comprehensive. In particular, China has put special emphasis in recent years on the opening of its Northwest and its land frontiers. That has radically changed the strategic orientation and pattern of China's opening. The strategy of '*Donglian Xikai*' (Integrate with the East and Open to the West) implemented in China's Northwest emphasizes the opening of its West to Russia, Central Asia and to West Asia. It also stresses that the opening of the West must try to make full use of the economic advantage of China's South and East coastal regions.[24]

China and the Central Asian states therefore are presented with historical opportunities in advancing their trade and economic relations. The further development of these relations is compatible with the interests of China and of Central Asian states.

Favourable Conditions for Economic Cooperation

Because of the geographical proximity of China and the Central Asian states, and because of their historical and cultural contacts, there exist conditions conducive to developing bilateral economic relations.

Firstly, there is the question of geography. Geographical proximity between China and Central Asian states means that transportation and telecommunication costs in conducting trade are low. Information about the markets in the region is easily accessible. It is also easy for trading personnel to get first-hand knowledge of the markets. As a result, it is possible to achieve high efficiency in bilateral trade. In fact, both China and Central Asian states have been making efforts to improve their transportation and telecommunication systems, and to open more trading ports so that further advantage of their geographical proximity can be taken.

Secondly, there is ethnicity. China's Xinjiang Uighur Autonomous Region and other Northwest provinces are inhabited by many groups of people of different ethnicity. For example, there are Uighurs, Kazakhs, Uzbeks, Tajiks, Kyrgyzs in the region. They are actually of the same ethnicity as the principal ethnic groups in the Central Asian states.[25] Because of this, they share the same language, the same religious beliefs, the same traditions and the same customs. They also feel that they belong to each other. It is therefore easy for them to communicate with each other, and to establish mutual understanding and mutual trust. This is particularly important in trade. Such a rare advantage should be fully cultivated in developing bilateral trade and economic relations.

Thirdly, there is the nature of the Chinese and Central Asian economies. They are mutually complementary. The Central Asian economies generally have a distorted structure. While these economies have comparatively developed sectors of mining and animal husbandry, their processing industries, such as the textile and food industries, are particularly underdeveloped. It is in these industries that China has developed a comparative advantage in technology and in management. Therefore, China can help the Central Asian economies in these sectors. On top of that, one of the imperatives of Central Asian economies is at present to correct the distortions of their economic structures created during the Soviet years. They are anxious to develop light industries, food processing and domestic appliance manufacturing. China's technology in making light industrial machinery, food processing machinery and domestic electronic appliances can satisfy the needs of Central Asian economies in the short and medium terms.

On the other hand, China has a considerable number of large-scale manufacturing enterprises that were built with the assistance of the former Soviet Union, mostly in the 1950s. Many of them are located in China's Northwest, in Shaanxi and Gansu provinces in particular. Most of them have been and are undergoing a process of technological upgrading. The Central Asian economies can provide these enterprises with technologies and equipment for this purpose. Moreover, in the last few years, the economic development of China's Northwest has seen strong momentum since the Chinese government decided to speed up the exploration of the economic potential of the region. The Central Asian states are in a very good position to conduct economic and technical co-operation with the region by supplying Northwest China with necessary technologies and equipment.

Strategic Position of Central Asia and Its Impact

Five Central Asian republics declared their independence upon the collapse of the former Soviet Union. They have become independent sovereign states in the international community. This simple fact has changed dramatically the strategic importance of Central Asia. Needless to say, a Central Asia of five independent sovereign states is a geopolitical and geostrategic reality radically different from a Central Asia as part of the Soviet Union controlled directly from Moscow. Equally important is the fact that its special geographical location also determined its role as a land bridge in economic exchanges between Asia and Europe. Coincidentally, it was around the time of the declaration of independence of the Central Asian states that the second Euro-Asian railway which goes right through Central Asia was opened to traffic. That further emphasizes the particular role of Central Asia as a land bridge in Euro-Asian economic relations.

With the opening of Chinese economy, Europe has become one of China's major markets. The second Euro-Asian railway (the second Euro-Asian continental 'bridge', in the Chinese phrase) provides a convenient transportation line for Chinese goods to enter Europe. As the railway goes through Central Asia, particularly Kazakhstan, it will at the same time promote China's trade and economic co-operation with Central Asian states. At the same time, Europe, especially the Western European economies, is turning its attention to Asia, particularly to China and other East Asian and Southeast Asian countries. They are bound to use this land bridge to get into China and other East Asian countries. That should promote co-operation between Europe and Central Asian states. The Euro-Asian railway, as the new Silk Road, plays a double role in promoting economic co-operation between China, Central Asia and Europe.

Regional Economic Association and Its Role

In the 1990s, the regionalization of the global economy is a hallmark in the international economic relations. For the Central Asian states, which just gained their political independence and were faced with a grim economic situation, forming an economic association for economic co-operation is important. Of course, the Central Asian states must rely on themselves to stabilize and to develop their national economies. But regional economic co-operation is also indispensable. Soon after their independence, the Central Asian states joined the Economic Co-operation Organization (ECO).[26] As early as the beginning of 1993, the heads of the Central Asian states met in Tashkent and expressed their strong desire to form a 'Central Asian common market'.[27] In July 1994, the Presidents of three Central Asian states, Kazakhstan, Uzbekistan, and Kyrgyzstan, held a summit meeting in Almaty. On the top of their agenda was the need to push through measures aimed at implementing their agreement made earlier in the year to create a common economic zone. Agreements on setting up a common bank and joint ministerial councils were signed for that purpose.[28]

The participation of Central Asian states in regional economic organizations and the formation of close economic relations among Central Asian states reflect a simple fact: like many states in other parts of the world, the Central Asian states see regional economic co-operation as vital to the revival and development of their economies. This could also be seen as a means by which Central Asian states can try to improve and consolidate their geopolitical and geoeconomic positions. The main purposes of such regional economic association, it must be argued, are to help each state stabilize its economy and to try to get out of the economic crisis without too much dependence on the others. Close economic association also enables the Central Asian states to speak with one voice so as to increase the influence of Central Asia, particularly these three states, in the CIS. However, because there are presently some political and economic conflicts among the three states, it is not easy to implement quickly and effectively any decisions and procedures towards forming a productive regional economic association.

China sees the economic development and co-operation of Central Asian states as beneficial to China. Economic co-operation promotes regional economic stability and prosperity, which in turn promotes political stability. China is now concentrating on its economic reforms and development. It needs a stable and peaceful international environment, particularly along its peripheries. Besides, regional economic co-operation among Central Asian states should strengthen the economic capacity of Central Asia as a region. That should also create more opportunities for trade and economic co-operation between China and Central Asia.

Challenges of the 21st Century

In the last decade of the 20th century, there have been revolutionary changes in international relations. The bipolarity since the end of the Second War has gone. New political divisions and new economic groups are forming. World history is now at a critical juncture. As we move towards the 21st century, the global political and economic systems are likely to see more radical changes and to become a multipolar world.

At the beginning of its transformation to a multipolar world, the international system has already manifested some new features. In the first place, economic factors are becoming more and more important in international relations. Secondly, Asia has become more and more important in world politics and in the global economy, largely because of the dynamic development of Asian economies and the relative political and societal stability of Asian countries. Thirdly, the United States and other Western countries have been gradually yet steadily transferring the main thrust of their international trade and economic activities from the Atlantic to the Pacific rim. Fourthly, it is widely expected that in the 21st century, Asia-Pacific is going to be the most dynamic region in the global economy. That is why many politicians and scholars worldwide have pronounced the 21st century as the 'Pacific century'.

Why does the world have such a favourable opinion of the Asia-Pacific economies? Mainly it is because of the rise of Asia-Pacific in the last twenty years. The economic take-off of Japan was closely followed by the rise of the 'four little dragons', Korea, Hong Kong, Taiwan and Singapore. After more than sixteen years of economic reforms and opening, the Chinese economy is also taking off. The dynamics of Asian economies have been generated by the economic take-off of countries in the region. In the last ten years, the newly industrializing countries (NICs) in Asia have achieved an average annual growth rate of eight per cent, far higher than that for developed nations in Europe and in America. The Chinese economy has also made impressive achievements since its reforms and opening. In 1994, China's GDP reached RMB 4,380 billion yuan. To put this in a comparative perspective, while this is 11.8 per cent higher than that of 1993, it is 13.6 times that of 1978. In 1994, the total of China's foreign trade was US$ 236.7 billion. That is an increase of 20.9 per cent on 1993, but is more than ten times that of 1978.[29] From 1979 to 1993, China approved more than 174,000 foreign joint ventures. and foreign direct investment realized in these joint ventures amounted to US$ 60.04 billion. In 1993 alone, China approved 80,000 foreign joint ventures and realized a total of US$ 25.7 billion in foreign direct investment.[30] In absolute terms, the foreign direct investment China attracted in 1993 was only second to the United States.

Judging from the present economic situation in the Asia-Pacific area, its economies are likely to expand further in the 21st century. Trade will become even more important in national economic development. More foreign direct investment will be poured into these economies. It is these dynamic developments and prospects that require developed countries in Europe and in America to adjust their economic strategy towards Asia-Pacific.

The United States has clearly realized the dynamics of Asian economies. Taking advantage of its Pacific identity and geographic proximity to the region, it has already begun actively to expand its market share in Asia. At the beginning of 1994, US President Bill Clinton stated that the United States should become the 'formal partner of Asian development'. Of the ten major markets that US government claims that it intends to cultivate in the near future, four are located in Asia, namely, China, Korea, Indonesia and India. The German government pledges to give 'strong support' to any initiatives from private sectors to march into Asia. It has also decided to increase its direct investment in Asia in order to open and occupy new and promising markets. France initiated a programme to speed up the French investment in Asia in February 1994 and called for a 'firm transfer toward Asia'. It has made Singapore its bridgehead to spearhead its breakthrough of the China market. Australia began to shift its economic focus to Asia. In 1992, the Australian government made a new policy of 'merging into Asia', determined to change its dual identity of 'physically in Asia, but mentally in Europe'. In September 21 1994, the New Zealand prime minister personally initiated the Asian 2,000 Foundation aimed at expand New Zealand trade and economic relations with Asia. Japan, as an economic superpower, used to concentrate its foreign direct investment in Europe and North America. In recent years, there has been increasingly intensive call for it to 'return to Asia'. It is clear that all the economic powers, whether European, American or Asian, have without exception tried to identify and occupy their positions in the evolving Asian economic system.[31]

The important shift of economic policies of developed countries in Europe and in America towards Asia is likely to give new impetus for the development of Asian economies. This also means a new opportunity for Asian economies to develop. At the same time, the surge of European and American capital flow into Asia will have great impact on Asian economies. This is therefore a serious challenge to Asia as well. As member economies of Asia, both China and Central Asian states are faced with the same question: how to meet this coming challenge in the 21st century? The prospect of Sino-Central Asian trade and economic relations lies in how China and Central Asian states answer this question. The challenges and the opportunities for Asian economies in the 21st century require both China and Central Asian states to make joint efforts to expand their trade and economic relations, to open up more areas for economic and technical co-operation and to strive for common prosperity.

NOTES

1. Kazakhstan has 1700 km of common border with China, Kyrgyzstan, about 1000 km, and Tajikistan, more than 400 km.
2. See *Dangdai Zhongguo Duiwai Maoyi* (Contemporary China's Foreign Trade), Vol. I, pp. 257–63.
3. Ibid, pp. 264–6.
4. According to the Kazakhstan President Nursultan Nazarbayev, Sino-Kazakh trade in 1992 was US$ 430 million, 22 per cent of Kazakhstan's foreign trade. *Xinhua News Agency*, 12 Oct. 1993.
5. *Zhongguo Duiwai Jingji Maoyi Nianjian*, 1994–5 (Yearbook of China's Foreign Economic Relations and Trade, 1994–5), p. 472.
6. Figures of China's foreign trade with Central Asian states in 1994 are provided by the Ministry of Foreign Trade and Economic Co-operation.
7. See Gong Xinhan et al, *Bianjing Maoyi Shiwu Shouce* (A Practical Handbook on Frontier Trade), p. 212.
8. RMB, Renminbi, is the Chinese currency. At the time of this writing, the exchange rate between RMB and US dollar is US$ 1=RMB 8.3.
9. *Beijing Review* reports that in 1992 'over 1.5 million tons of goods and more than 500,000 people' passed in and out of the trading ports of Xinjiang Autonomous Region. See 'Border Trade Reaches New Stage', *Beijing Review*, 31 May-6 June, 1993, p. 19.
10. See *Zhongya Yanjiu* (Central Asian Studies), No. 4, 1994, p. 16.
11. The above figures are provided by the Ministry of Foreign Trade and Economic Co-operation. There are some discrepancies in the available statistics about China-funded ventures in Central Asia. According to *Guoji Shangbao* (International Business News), in 1994, there were 450 such ventures. *China Daily* however reported in September 1995 that there were only 350 China-funded ventures in Central Asia. See *Guoji Shangbao* (International Business News), 20 April 1994 and *China Daily*, 12 September 1995.
12. *Renmin Ribao*, 28 April 1994.
13. The six agreements are an agreement on a loan offered by China to Kyrgyzstan; an agreement on establishing a mixed economic and trade committee between the Chinese and the Kyrgyzstan governments; an exchange

of notes on goods and materials given as gifts to Kyrgyzstan by China; an agreement on cultural co-operation; an exchange of instruments on the ratification of a consular treaty between the two countries; and an agreement on co-operation between the China Council for the Promotion of International Trade and the Kyrgyz Council of Industry and Commerce. See *Renmin Ribao*, 24 April 1994.

14. *China Daily*, 15 April 1994.
15. For further details of those contracts and letter of intents, see *Renmin Ribao*, 18–30 April 1994.
16. The Alataw Pass is now the largest trading port in Northwest China.
17. Already in June 1992, the first passenger express began to operate between Almaty and Urumqi. See Tian Zengpei (ed.), *Gaige Kaifang Yilai de Zhongguo Waijiao* (China's Diplomacy since Its Reforms and Opening), p. 319.
18. See Gong Xinhan et al, *Bianjin Maoyi Shiwu Shouce* (A Practical Handbook of Frontier Trade), pp. 212–60.
19. For more about the opening of Horgosi, see Zheng Xinke et al, *Bianjin Maoyi Zhinan* (A Guide to Border Trade), pp. 345–7. See also Gong Xinhan et al, *Bianjin Maoyi Shiwu Shouce* (A Practical Handbook of Frontier Trade), pp. 221–3.
20. As mentioned earlier, Sino-Kazakh trade declined from US$ 434 million in 1993 to US$ 335 million in 1994.
21. This is also a major reason for the decline of Sino-Russian trade in 1994.
22. The Sino-Kazakh border agreement was signed during Premier Li Peng's visit to Kazakhstan in April 1994. It was ratified by the Kazakhstan Parliament in October 1995.
23. Regular meetings on border negotiations have been conducted between the Chinese delegation and a delegation of four CIS states, namely Russia, Kazakhstan, Kyrgyzstan, and Tajikistan since the collapse of the Soviet Union. By April 1995, altogether fifteen rounds of talks have been held. See *Renmin Ribao*, 25 April 1995.
24. For more details, see *Zhanzai Gaige Kaifang de Zuiqianlie* (At the Forefront of Opening to the Outside World), Xinjiang University Press, 1994.
25. For example, there are about one million Kazakhs in China's Xinjiang Autonomous Region.
26. At present, ECO has ten member states, namely, Turkey, Iran, Pakistan, Afghanistan, Kazakhstan, Uzbekistan, Kyrgyzstan, Tajikistan, Turkmenistan, and Azerbaijan. All of them are Muslim countries in West and Central Asia.
27. *Nezavisimozti*; 27 February 1993.
28. The summit discussed all-round co-operation among the three, covering political, social, military affairs, as well as economic development. An interstate council was created consisting of the presidents and the premiers of three states. Under this interstate council, there are to be a council of premiers, a council of ministers of foreign affairs and a council of minister of defence.
29. *Renmin Ribao*, 10 March 1995.
30. The contract value of foreign investment in the period of 1979–1993 was US$ 217.22 billion. The contract value for 1993 alone was US$ 110.85 billion. See Ma Hong and Sun Shangqing, *Zhongguo Jingji Xingshi yu*

Zhanwang, 1993–4 (Economic Situation and Prospect of China, 1993–4), pp. 323–4.

31. 'Xifang de Xin Yazhou Zhengce' (New Asian Policies of the West), *Renmin Ribao*, 30 March 1994.

Part IV
Strategic and Security Issues

11 Security Issues in China's Relations with Central Asian States

Guangcheng Xing

With the disintegration of the former Soviet Union, Central Asia has emerged as a region in its own right, a region whose strategic importance can hardly be overemphasized. China has vital strategic interests in Central Asia, mostly because it shares long common borders with three newly independent Central Asian states, Kazakhstan, Kyrgyzstan, and Tajikistan. The frontiers of China's Northwest have been traditionally perceived as the most vulnerable to defend. It is probably only natural that in the last five years, China has put security concerns at the top of the agenda in its relations with Central Asian states. These concerns include measures to safeguard the security interests of China, ways of enhancing regional security regimes, and steps to take towards cooperative arrangements to foster mutual trust in security matters.

It could be argued that to maintain regional security and to safeguard the strategic interests of all countries in the region are two common goals that have been pursued by both China and Central Asian states in the last five years. This essay examines four aspects of security relations between China and Central Asian states from the Chinese perspective. The four aspects are (1) the nuclear security issue; (2) border disputes; (3) defence and military cooperation; and (4) Central Asia and multilateral security arrangements. Before elaborating on those four aspects, it is necessary to discuss briefly China's defence and security policies.

I CHINA'S DEFENCE AND SECURITY POLICIES

China has adopted very clear national policies and principles towards regional security. Such policies and principles have been followed consistently since the economic reforms and opening in China in 1978. Speaking to the UN Conference on Disarmament and Security Issues in the Asia-Pacific Region in Shanghai in August 1992, the Chinese Foreign Minister Qian Qichen emphasized that China advocated the establishment of a just, rational, and stable international political and economic order on the basis of five principles of peaceful co-existence. Qian Qichen also emphasized the need for China to achieve a long-term peaceful and stable international environment, in particular such an environment in China's surrounding areas, so as to implement the economic development strategy for the modernization of China. China would continue to follow an independent foreign policy of peace. The overarching goal of Chinese foreign policy was to safeguard regional and world peace. To pursue friendly and good neighbourly relations with all surrounding countries, he said, was 'a set state policy'.[1] It goes without saying that such policies and principles apply to China's security relations with Central Asia.

China's military policy and strategy are defensive in nature. The Chinese government has strictly controlled its defence spending at the lowest level possible just to ensure its national security.[2] In fact, it could be argued that it is tailored to meet the minimum needs of China's national defence. The Chinese government has consistently pursued such policies, not only out of economic considerations. More importantly, it is because China does not seek any special interests either in the world or in the regions surrounding China. In the last few years, the 'China threat' theory has become popular. It claims that as the Chinese economy develops, its military will expand. China will try to fill the 'power vacuum' in Asia-Pacific. China has always refuted such a claim. At the 48th General Assembly of the UN in 1993, Qian Qichen stated that such a claim is 'entirely groundless': 'China is an important force for safeguarding the peace and stability of the world.' Qian also argued that the limited defence capability that China had developed was purely for self-defence. China was among the first countries to convert the defence-related industries to civilian production. China's military spending was the lowest among the major powers. Qian further claimed that there was not a single Chinese soldier overseas; neither did China have military bases abroad. As China was concentrating on its economic development, it needed a long-lasting peaceful international environment, and particularly long-lasting peaceful relations with all its neighbours.[3]

II THE NUCLEAR SECURITY ISSUE

One of the fallouts of the disintegration of the former Soviet Union for Central Asia was to make Kazakhstan a quasi-nuclear power. As one of the five declared nuclear powers, China watched very carefully the changing attitudes and policies of the newly independent Kazakhstan towards the nuclear weapons in its possession, especially in 1992 and 1993. China is naturally concerned about the possible emergence of another nuclear state along its borders. As a declared nuclear power, China has repeatedly made its commitment to no first use of nuclear weapons and no-use of nuclear weapons against non-nuclear states or nuclear-free areas. It acceded to the Non-Proliferation Treaty in 1992, and committed itself to the Comprehensive Test Ban Treaty in 1996.

Ambiguous Attitude of Kazakhstan Towards Nuclear Weapons in Its Possession

As we noted above, Kazakhstan was left as a quasi-nuclear state as a result of the disintegration of the former Soviet Union. Nuclear weapons, it could be argued, were forced upon Kazakhstan as part of the Soviet strategic deployment. Nevertheless, at the disintegration of the Soviet Union, Kazakhstan inherited part of the Soviet nuclear arsenal, which included 104 SS-18 long-range ballistic missiles (each carrying 10 warheads). Kazakhstan also hosted two strategic missiles launch sites at Derzhavinsk and Zhangiz-Tobe, and one strategic bomber airbase with 40 Tu-95 Bear bombers stationed there. The former Soviet Union also built a nuclear test zone at Semipalatinsk in Kazakhstan.

After the disintegration of the former Soviet Union, the Commonwealth of Independent States (CIS) countries reached the Agreement on Nuclear Weapons and Their Control signed at Almaty on 21 December 1991. By late January 1992, all tactical nuclear weapons were withdrawn to Russia from Kazakhstan. For a while, though, whether Kazakhstan would give up totally its nuclear-weapon status remained unclear.

In February 1992, the Kazakh President Nazarbayev claimed during his visit to India that 'Kazakhstan's nuclear threat perception evolved from the nuclear arsenals in possession of Russia, China and the United States'. He also claimed that 'in the principle of parity, Kazakhstan would be prepared to destroy its nuclear warheads provided the USA, Russia and China agreed to follow a similar course.'[4] In early 1992, President Nazarbayev also made the assertion that Kazakhstan had the right to join the nuclear club and that Kazakhstan should keep its nuclear weapons because of its unique geopolitical position between Asia and Europe.[5] Although Kazakhstan signed the Lisbon Protocol of the START Treaty in May 1992, committing Kazakhstan to a non-nuclear status, in early 1993, Kazakhstan, together with Ukraine, raised the question of their right of control of nuclear weapons still deployed in their territories at the CIS summit in Minsk.

The ambiguity and sometimes contradictory positions of Kazakhstan on the nuclear weapons in its possession might be explained by the Kazakh leaders' desire to highlight Kazakhstan's international status, and by its intention to use nuclear weapons in its possession for bargaining with the West. It was probably also because, faced with crises and conflicts among CIS states, Kazakhstan wished to play the nuclear card to strengthen its position within CIS.

The ambiguous attitude of Kazakhstan towards the nuclear weapons in its possession, particularly in 1992 and the early 1993 was not only a concern for China. More importantly, it was a concern for the West, and in particular the United States. The Western countries put a lot of pressure on Kazakhstan to give up its nuclear weapons. The American leaders made it clear that unless Kazakhstan made clear and unequivocal commitment to being a non-nuclear state, Kazakhstan could not expect either any American support of Kazakhstan in international affairs, or any economic aid from the West, including economic and technical co-operation. For the newly independent Kazakhstan, both an amicable relationship with the West and economic aid and technical cooperation from the West were extremely important for state-building. It was under the pressures of the West that Kazakhstan eventually made its unequivocal commitment to being a non-nuclear state. There are two other reasons. One is that the nuclear policies of three former Soviet republics in possession of nuclear weapons, namely Belarus, Kazakhstan and Ukraine, were mutually reinforcing. Belarus from the very beginning had committed itself unconditionally to removing all its nuclear weapons to Russia. Ukraine also made a similar commitment conditionally, though it continued to play its nuclear card in order to gain more concessions from both Russia and the United States. The other is that Kazakhstan eventually got explicit security pledges from all three most concerned nuclear states, the United States, Russia and China. Such security pledges included the undertaking that none of them would target their nuclear weapons at Kazakhstan and that none of them would use nuclear weapons against Kazakhstan after Kazakhstan removed all nuclear weapons from its territory. Indeed, the key reason why Belarus, Kazakhstan and Ukraine were willing to accede to the Non-Proliferation Treaty is because all nuclear powers were willing to give them security assurance.[6]

Kazakhstan ratified START I Treaty in July 1993, and in February 1994, acceded to the Non-Proliferation Treaty as a non-nuclear state. The removal of nuclear weapons from Kazakhstan began in earnest in late

1993. By February 1994, the last four of the 40 heavy bombers were withdrawn to Russia. In March 1994, Kazakhstan also handed over half-a-ton highly enriched weapon-grade uranium to the United States. By the end of May 1995, all nuclear warheads in Kazakhstan were transferred to Russia.

China's Nuclear Security Assurance to Kazakhstan

On 24 May 1995, the Kazakh Foreign Ministry announced that all nuclear weapons deployed on the territory of Kazakhstan in the Soviet era had been either transferred to the Russian territory or destroyed.[7] Shortly before Kazakhstan became a nuclear-weapon-free state, on 8 February 1995, the Chinese government issued its security assurance to Kazakhstan. In a brief announcement, the Chinese government stated,

> China fully understands the desire of Kazakhstan for security assurance. The Chinese government has unconditionally undertaken not to use or threaten to use nuclear weapons against non-nuclear states or nuclear-weapon free zones. This long-standing principled position also applies to Kazakhstan.
>
> The Chinese government urges all nuclear-weapon states to undertake the same commitment so as to enhance the security of all non-nuclear-weapon states, including Kazakhstan.'[8]

III BORDER DISPUTES

Border disputes had been a perennial problem in the Sino-Soviet relations. In the late 1960s, armed conflicts broke out along the Sino-Soviet borders. For many years until the late 1980s, tensions and military confrontations along the Sino-Soviet borders were hallmarks of Sino-Soviet relations. China and the former Soviet Union restarted their high-level talks on border disputes in the late 1980s. The Sino-Soviet summit in May 1989 gave further momentum to those ongoing talks.

The disintegration of the former Soviet Union has, among other things, changed the context of ongoing negotiations for the settlement of disputed borders. China's border disputes with the former Soviet Union now became China's disputes with four independent states, Russia, Kazakhstan, Kyrgyzstan and Tajikistan. How to settle the border disputes with the newly independent Central Asian states became an important aspect of China's security relations with Central Asia. It could be argued here that one of the main thrusts of Chinese foreign policy towards post-Soviet

Central Asia has been aimed at settling those territorial disputes through negotiation and mutual accommodation. It is an integral part of China's search for the security of its Northwest frontiers.

The disintegration of the former Soviet Union was widely perceived as presenting both new opportunities and new challenges for China in continuing its negotiations for the settlement of border disputes. It presents new challenges, for example, because China now has to negotiate with four states, rather than just one country. In Central Asia, through which the Western section of the former Sino-Soviet borders runs, China has to negotiate with three states and deal with different demands from those states. It presents new opportunities partly because the newly independent Central Asian states have little historical baggage as far as the border disputes are concerned. They could blame Imperial Russia or the Soviet Union for that. Moreover, the three newly independent Central Asian states bordering with China may be more willing to negotiate for the settlement of border disputes because in their state-building efforts, it is desirable to have regional peace and stability.

China then moved quickly to affirm with the three Central Asian states the basic principles in their negotiations. These include (1) respect of results already achieved in Sino-Soviet negotiations; (2) existing treaties as the basis of negotiations; (3) settlement in accordance with the established rules of international law; (4) mutual consultation on equal footing; and (5) mutual accommodation. These principles have been clearly embodied in both the joint communiqués between China and the Central Asian states and in their border agreements.

In the Sino-Kazakh joint communiqué issued on 28 February 1992, it was stated that 'The two sides have given a positive appraisal of the results achieved during the border negotiations between China and the former Soviet Union on the present section of the China-Kazakh border. Based on the present treaty concerning the Sino-Kazakh border, the two sides will, in accordance with the established principles of international law and in the spirit of mutual consultation on equal footing, mutual accommodation and mutual understanding, continue to discuss the border issues so as to find a fair and reasonable solution acceptable to both sides'.[9] The Sino-Kyrgyz joint communiqué of 6 May 1992 and the Sino-Tajik joint communiqué of 11 March 1993 both confirmed those principles in the Sino-Kazak communiqué for settling pending border disputes.[10]

In the last few years, negotiations between China and three Central Asian states have achieved many positive results. In the joint communiqué between China and Kyrgyzstan issued at the end of the Chinese Prime Minister Li Peng's visit to Kyrgyzstan in April 1994, it was stated that

> The two sides agreed to start work soon on drawing up a draft Sino-Kyrgyz border agreement, and meanwhile, continue to negotiate on sections where agreement has yet to be reached, so as to achieve satisfactory result at an early date.
>
> Pending a resolution on the border issue, the two sides will take measures to maintain the status quo of the border, in order to guarantee peace and stability in the border areas.

The most notable progress in negotiating for the bilateral settlement of disputed borders is the Sino-Kazak boundary agreement signed on 26 April 1994 by the Chinese Prime Minister Li Peng and the Kazakh President Nursultan Nazarbayev. The agreement finalized in principle the delineation of the 1700 km-long Sino-Kazakh borders.[11] The official Chinese press hailed this as 'a historical event of significance' in Sino-Kazakh relations and claimed that the Sino-Kazakh border would become 'a bond of friendly co-operation and common prosperity.'[12] The joint statement by the Chinese President Jiang Zemin and the Kazakh President Nazarbayev in September 1995 confirmed that both sides would soon start the survey and delineation of the borders according to the agreement of April 1994.[13]

What should be also mentioned here is progress in the Sino-Russian negotiations. On 17 October 1995, the instruments of ratification were exchanged in Beijing of the agreement between China and Russia on the Western section of their borders, which was signed on 3 September 1994 at the second Sino-Russian summit. This agreement delineated in a legal form 55 km of disputed border lines in the Western section of the Sino-Russian border. With this agreement supplementing the Sino-Soviet agreement on the eastern section of their borders, which took effect on 16 May 1991, for the first time in history the Sino-Russian borders were delineated in a legal form. The Russian Foreign Ministry hailed this agreement as a 'historical achievement', and declared it 'conducive to the stability of the border areas, and to the development of bilateral trade and economic relations, including trade in the border areas.' It also claimed that the agreement is 'a concrete expression of Russia's policy of developing a long-term constructive partnership with China.'[14]

Territorial disputes had been a thorny issue in the Sino-Soviet relations for many years. For the Chinese government, in post-Soviet Central Asia, the settlement of the border disputes with the newly independent Central Asian states has been one of the priorities of its foreign policy towards the region. It views such a settlement as an indispensable part of benign security relations with the Central Asian states. As argued above, China has successfully negotiated border agreements with both Kazakhstan and Russia respectively, and these accords have in principle settled border disputes between them. Although China has yet to sign full border agreements with Kyrgyzstan and Tajikistan, it is increasingly unlikely that border disputes would pose a major or serious obstacle in security relations between China and Central Asia in the future.

IV DEFENCE AND MILITARY CO-OPERATION

One important dimension of the new security relations between China and Central Asian states is the need to develop bilateral and multilateral defence and military co-operation. Such co-operation is mostly seen in enhancing confidence-building measures, reducing troops and military forces along the common borders, disarmament in the border areas, and increasing the transparency of border defence. The Chinese government has been actively promoting such defence and military co-operation between China and Central Asian states. It must be remembered that since their independence, the Central Asian states have been making efforts to build up their own defence and military forces and have been mapping out their defence strategies. They too are keen to engage in military co-operation with China. On the other hand, it must be noted that Central Asian states are still heavily dependent on Russia for their defence. Russia has therefore played and is still playing an important and indispensable role in the defence arrangements of Central Asia. In view of such a fact, a discussion of Sino-Russian military co-operation is not only necessary but also instructive in our examination of military co-operation between China and Central Asia.

The Five-Nation Military Confidence Building Agreement, 26 April, 1996

Perhaps the crowning achievement in defence and military co-operation between China and Central Asian states and Russia is the signing of the Five-Nation Agreement on Confidence Building in the Military Forces in the Border Areas on 26 April 1996 in Shanghai at a summit meeting among leaders from China, Kazakhstan, Kyrgyzstan, Russia and Tajikistan. Since the disintegration of the former Soviet Union, the Chinese delegation and the joint delegation of Russia, Kazakhstan, Kyrgyzstan and Tajikistan had held many rounds of talks on disarmaments and on confidence-building in the border areas. The Shanghai agreement, as claimed by the Russian President Yeltsin, was 'an epoch-making document' for the five countries involved, because by signing the agreement, they 'have undertaken very positive military and political obligations for the first time in history'. The Tajik President Rakhmonov, on the other hand, believed that the agreement 'is of inestimable significance'. The five countries concerned had travelled 'prolonged and complicated road of negotiation' of five years and 'achieved expected results'.[15]

Under the agreement, the military forces of both sides stationed along the border areas promise not to attack each other. The agreement rules out conducting military exercises aimed against each other. It also specifies that limits will be imposed on the scale, scope and number of military exercises on both sides of the border areas. The concerned sides should inform each other of any major military activities taking place in any area within 100 km of the borderlines. It further stipulates that the concerned sides will invite each other to observe the military exercises, and will prevent any dangerous military activities. It also stipulates that friendly exchanges will be strengthened between the military forces and frontier guards of both sides.[16]

Such a multilateral agreement is undoubtedly conducive to strengthening mutual trust between the Chinese military and the military of Central Asian states as well as that of Russia. It also increases the transparency of border defence on both sides. It is therefore an important step towards institutionalizing the security relations between China and Central Asia. More broadly, as the Kazakh President Nazarbayev stated, the Five-Nation Agreement 'lays a firm legal foundation for the sustained and effective development of bilateral and multilateral relations among the five nations'.[17]

Sino-Kazakh Military Cooperation

A good example that China has been actively promoting bilateral military exchanges and co-operation with Central Asian states is the case of Sino-Kazakh military co-operation. As early as 1993, a joint communiqué between China and Kazakhstan specifically stated that 'both sides agree to facilitate the contact and promote the relationship between their military and to conduct military exchanges according to international practice so as to enhance mutual trust and co-operation in the military field'.[18] In September 1995, the Chinese President Jiang Zemin and the Kazakh President Nursultan Nazarbayev issued a joint communiqué at the end of the latter's visit to China, affirming that

> In the sphere of military relations, links between the defence ministries of the two nations should be established and developed, and efforts at working out an agreement on reduction of military forces along the borders and strengthening the trust in the military field should be speeded up. Military technological co-operation should be carried out on the basis of mutual benefits and taking each country's international obligations into considerations.[19]

In 1995 and 1996, military exchanges were conducted between China and Kazakhstan on the regular basis. A Chinese military delegation from the garrison of the Xinjiang Uighur Autonomous Region visited Kazakhstan in August 1995.[20] In May 1996, both the Kazakh Foreign Minister and Defence Minister received in Almaty Fu Quanyou, the Chief of Staff of the People's Liberation Army (PLA) visiting Kazakhstan.[21] In October 1996, the Chinese Defence Minister Chi Haotian met with the visiting Kazakh Defence Minister Alibek Kasymov in Beijing and discussed co-operation between the two armed forces. The Chinese Premier Li Peng also received the Kazakh Defence Minister.[22]

Confidence-Building Measures Between China and Russia

As mentioned earlier, Russia is one of the signatories of the Five-Nation Agreement on Military Confidence Building in the Border Areas in Shanghai in April 1996. The initiation of military confidence-building measures between China and Russia, however, could be traced back to 1992, if not earlier. In December 1992, the Russian President Yeltsin visited China and signed a joint declaration on Sino-Russian relations. The declaration specifies some significant military confidence-building measures which include the non-use of force in bilateral disputes, reduction of troops in and disarmaments of the border areas, co-operation to promote nuclear non-proliferation and no-first use, and initiating military exchanges.[23]

In the last few years, China and Russia have signed some other important agreements on confidence building. In July 1994 the Chinese Defence Minister Chi Haotian signed an agreement with the Russian Defence Minister Pavel Grachev on the 'Prevention of Dangerous Military Activity' in Moscow.[24] In September of the same year, President Jiang Zemin and President Yeltsin issued a joint statement in Moscow, pledging that both sides would detarget their nuclear weapons at each other.[25] In February 1995, China and Russia reached an agreement on border guard co-operation.[26] There have been frequent military visits between China and Russia in the last few years, including a visit by Russian warships to

Shanghai and another by Chinese warships to Vladivostok, and exchange visits of local Chinese and Russian military forces and border guards. At the same time, both China and Russia are parties to the ongoing multilateral border talks which include three Central Asian states. Because of the dependence of the Central Asian states on Russia for their defence and because of the special role Russia plays in defending the external borders of Central Asian states, confidence-building measures between China and Russia help the military co-operation and confidence building between China and Central Asian states as well.

V CENTRAL ASIA AND MULTILATERAL SECURITY ARRANGEMENTS

To safeguard their national security, Central Asian states have been involved in a number of multilateral security arrangements since their independence. For analytical purposes, the multilateral security arrangements that Central Asian states have entered into could be divided into two categories: those within the CIS framework and those outside the CIS framework. Central Asian states' involvement in those multilateral security arrangements have various implications for their security relations with China and sometimes causes concerns on the part of China.

Multilateral Security Arrangements within the CIS Framework

In the last few years, CIS states have concluded a number of multilateral security agreements. On 15 May 1992, the fifth summit meeting of CIS States was held in Tashkent. One of the major agreements reached at this summit was the Treaty on Collective Security signed by Russia, Kazakhstan, Kyrgyzstan, Uzbekistan, Tajikistan, and Armenia. The signatory countries agreed that their security was indivisible. If one party to the agreement was subjected to aggression, that would be regarded as aggression against all parties to the treaty. Therefore, the other parties would immediately render the necessary assistance to the party which was the object of the aggression, including military assistance. The signatory countries also agreed to the principles of sharing responsibility for maintaining security; non-interference in internal affairs; collective defence; and making decisions on matters of principle with regard to safeguarding collective security through consultation. The agreement stipulates that some specific military bases and facilities of one member state could be stationed or deployed in other member states with the consent of the states concerned.[27]

The signing of such a collective security agreement among CIS states at the time was probably only natural. As far as the Central Asian states are concerned, they were extremely weak in military and defence capability. It would take some time for them to establish their own somewhat comprehensive military forces. Signing such a collective security agreement with Russia certainly enhanced the security of these countries. On top of that, the agreement also stipulates that parties to the agreement will not use force or threat of force to settle disputes among themselves. This clause undoubtedly reduced any possibility of Russia using force against the signatory countries. To Russia, the signing of such agreement gave the existence of CIS some substance. It could also reduce the political pressures (mostly from the Russian military) to withdraw the Russian troops from CIS states. At the same time, it helped secure Russia's special interests in Central Asia.

This collective security agreement signed by six CIS states was concluded without any clearly perceived outside military threat. Its conclusion had significant impact on relations among CIS states as well as on relations between China and Central Asian states. The fact that only six CIS states signed the agreement was an indication of the fragmentation or the regrouping of CIS states. It did not help the integration of the CIS states and was not necessarily conducive to the development of the CIS. This was so particularly in consideration of the fact that because of many existing border disputes among CIS states, relations among some of them were extremely tense. The collective security agreement may unnecessarily involve some signatory countries in unrelated conflicts. Besides, the emergence of such a collective security group with Russia at its core would inevitably put a good deal of military pressure on all the other CIS states outside this collective security arrangement.

More important and pertinent to our discussion here is the impact of such a collective security agreement on China. Of six signatory countries of the collective security agreement, four have common borders with China, namely, Russia, Kazakhstan, Kyrgyzstan and Tajikistan. As discussed earlier, in accordance with the agreement, any aggression against any one party to the agreement is regarded as aggression against all parties to the treaty. Under the agreement, the other parties should immediately render the necessary assistance to the party which is the object of the aggression, including military assistance. This is particularly significant in view of Russia's public pledge that 'the security of signatory countries is guaranteed under the Russian nuclear umbrella'. This indicates that the collective security system as envisaged in the agreement is not only based on the conventional military forces, but also on nuclear deterrence.

Although China has publicly expressed that it welcomes any international co-operation aimed at strengthening the security and stability of Central Asia, it has been watching very closely the evolution and functioning of this agreement, particularly the role and the engagement of Central Asian states in the agreement. China is especially watchful of any negative effects of this collective security arrangements on the security and stability in its Northwest.

It must be argued that this collective security agreement concluded in 1992 is not aimed at China. The existing and potential threat to Central Asia is not deemed as from China. In fact, it could be argued that this collective security agreement is rather defensive in nature and does not threaten any countries outside the arrangement. Indeed, it could be better seen as a mechanism to manage potential conflicts among CIS states. China should not feel uneasy about it and should not be too sensitive to it. It must also be noted that among Central Asian states, there is a different understanding of this collective security arrangement. Turkmenistan, for example, did not participate in the collective security arrangement. It rejected the idea of collective security among five Central Asian states, and emphasized instead its defence relations with Russia.

The other multilateral security arrangement within the CIS framework, which is worth mentioning here, further demonstrates the divisive nature of CIS states in their approach towards collective security. In May 1995, the agreement on protecting the external borders of CIS was signed by only seven states. Ukraine, Turkmenistan, Moldova, Azerbaijan, and Uzbekistan declined to sign.[28] Earlier in February 1995, at a Joint Meeting of the Council of Heads of Government and Council of Heads of States, a proposal of joint defence of the CIS's external border was seriously debated. Azerbaijan and Ukraine categorically opposed it. Many other CIS states would rather agree with Ukraine on 'mutual co-operation on the defence of borders' than participating in the joint defence of CIS external borders. One representative from Uzbekistan claimed that the proposed agreement by Moscow was opposed by many CIS states because 'the proposal to use common borders is only beneficial to Russia'. He also claimed that since the disintegration of the former Soviet Union, the Russian nuclear shield had become 'blind and deaf', because Russia could no longer use the radar and other communications systems installed in the former Soviet republics. Moscow's proposal was aimed at obtaining the signatory parties' support of Russia's nuclear defence system. Moscow, in his words, wanted to use the radar and communication systems in the CIS states concerned 'without spending a penny'.

Central Asia and NATO's 'Partnership for Peace' Programme

The so-called 'Partnership for Peace Programme' was first proposed by the US on 11 January 1994 at the NATO summit meeting. After the disintegration of the former Soviet Union in 1991 and the eventual dismantlement of the Warsaw Pact, Poland, Hungary and the Czech Republic and other Eastern European countries which had been previously in the Warsaw Pact expressed keen interest in the NATO membership as their security guarantee. While NATO was not necessarily averse to taking in some Central and Eastern European countries, Russia had been staunchly opposed to any expansion of NATO into Central and Eastern Europe, regarding such an expansion as a threat to the Russian security. In order not to provoke Russia unnecessarily and at the same time to accommodate Central and Eastern European countries eager to join NATO, a 'Partnership for Peace' (PFP) programme was launched at the initiative of the American President Bill Clinton at the NATO summit in January 1994 at Brussels as a compromise, aimed at establishing a new relationship between NATO and former Warsaw Pact countries. PFP is open to all North Atlantic Co-operation Council (NACC) states and other countries of the Organization for Security and Co-operation in Europe (OSCE) able and willing to participate on a voluntary basis. PFP lists a number of objectives to which participating states must subscribe, which include facilitating the transparency of national defence planning and budgeting processes; ensuring democratic control of armed forces; maintaining the capability to contribute to UN and/or OSCE operations; developing co-operative military relations with NATO, for the purpose of joint planning, training and exercise in order to undertake peacekeeping missions and humanitarian operations when called upon to do so. NATO will consult with any active partner that perceives a direct threat to its security. The consultations, however, would not involve extension to partners of NATO's security guarantee under Article V of the North Atlantic Treaty. At the time of writing, most European countries have participated in the PFP, including Russia and most former Soviet republics and Central and Eastern European countries. In Central Asia, Kazakhstan, Kyrgyzstan, Turkmenistan and Uzbekistan have participated in the PFP.[29] As a result, the political influence of NATO has in fact penetrated Central Asia as well as Russia and reached China's frontiers of the Northwest and the Northeast. China respects the choice of these countries in their foreign policy. China does not see their participation in NATO's PFP as unfriendly to China. Central Asian countries' participation in PFP so far has not affected China's relations with them, because China's relations with Central Asian states are regulated by a series of clearly defined agreements and principles. However, it would be advisable for China to study in an earnest manner the possible long-term impact on China's security of the penetration of NATO's PFP.

NOTES

1. *Renmin Ribao* (People's Daily), 18 August 1992.
2. *Renmin Ribao*, 2 August 1995.
3. *Renmin Ribao*, 30 September 1993.
4. *Reuters*, 22 February 1992.
5. Nazarbayev's talk to Italian journalist, *Za Mubezhom*, No. 13, 1992.
6. The United States also contributed US$ 80 million to Kazakhstan for dismantling its nuclear weapons.
7. *ITAR-TASS*, 25 April 1995. See also IISS, *The Military Balance*, 1995–6, p. 152.
8. *Renmin Ribao*, 9 February 1995.
9. *Renmin Ribao*, 29 February 1992.
10. For the Sino-Kyrgyz communique, see *Renmin Ribao*, 7 May 1992. The communiqué further affirmed that both sides would conduct negotiations on reducing military forces in the border areas and on confidence building. For the Sino-Tajik communique, see *Renmin Ribao*, 12 March 1993.
11. *Renmin Ribao*, 27 April 1994.
12. *Renmin Ribao*, 30 April 1994.
13. *Renmin Ribao*, 12 September 1995.
14. *ITAR-TASS*, 19 October 1995.
15. *Renmin Ribao*, 27 April 1996.
16. *Xinhua News Agency*, 26 April 1996.
17. *Renmin Ribao*, 27 April 1996.
18. *Renmin Ribao*, 24 October 1993.
19. *Renmin Ribao*, 12 September 1995.
20. *Reuters*, 7 August 1995.
21. *Reuters*, 13 May 1996.
22. *Renmin Ribao*, 24 October & 26 October 1996.
23. See *Beijing Review*, No. 52, 1992, pp. 4–5.
24. *ITAR-TASS*, Moscow, 12 July 1994.
25. *Renmin Ribao*, 7 September 1994.
26. *Reuters*, 13 February 1995.
27. See *Nezavisimozti*, 6 July 1994.
28. The other CIS agreement signed in May by most of CIS states is the Agreement on Creating a Joint Air Defence system.
29. Tajikistan is one of the few OSCE countries that have not participated in the PFP.

12 Central Asia and the World: Foreign Policy and Strategic Issues

Sergei Lounev and Gleryi Shirokov

I FORMATION OF STATEHOOD AND DOMESTIC CAPABILITIES

Central Asia became a geopolitical region after the break-up of the socialist form of statehood which united ethnic groups with a historically complex mutual relationship. As a result, historical antagonisms between the ethnic groups and former Soviet republics or their sub-regions began to show openly.

The break-up of the Soviet Union led for the first time to the formation of nation-states in Central Asia. Historically, Central Asia never had nation-states and lacked the process of modern nation formation in the region. The establishment of their statehood in real political and legal terms is not over yet. Since the boundaries between the republics were laid by the Soviet government in an arbitrary manner, the natural settlement divisions between the ethnic groups were replaced by administrative boundaries which, after the break-up of the Soviet Union, became state boundaries.

The incompatibility of these boundaries with the settlement areas of the large ethnic groups may lead in the future to ethnic conflicts between

- Kazakhstan and Uzbekistan;
- Kyrgyzstan and Uzbekistan;
- Uzbekistan and Tajikistan;
- Uzbekistan and the autonomous region of Kara-Kalpakia;
- Uzbekistan and Turkmenistan; and
- Russia and Kazakhstan (over northern Kazakhstan, where Russians are an indigenous population).

Independence has brought together into a state rather distinct national, religious and cultural entities. This potentially can become a fertile soil for a large-scale regional conflict, involving attempts to reconsider and redraw the existing borders.

When Central Asia was part of the Soviet Union it was treated as a common economic region. It was assigned a special role in the inter-regional division of labour with an emphasis upon raw materials supplies. Many vital resources and products were supplied to the region from Russia. This shaped the transport infrastructure, whereas economic ties did not take into account the administrative borders, which have now become state boundaries. Thus, the formerly common economic unit of the region does not correspond today to the status of the independent states.

Even in the Soviet period, the internal economic differentiation of Central Asia was quite significant. At the time of the break-up of the Soviet Union, Kazakhstan was the unchallenged economic leader in the region, with almost half of the regional GDP, whilst Uzbekistan had around one third of the regional GDP. The rest of the GDP was shared almost in equal parts by the other three republics. Now Uzbekistan has almost reached the level of Kazakhstan, largely owing to the fact that the industrial decline in Uzbekistan was in 1989–1994 the lowest in Central Asia at about 25 per cent,[1] whilst Turkmenistan is now slightly ahead of Kyrgyzstan (Kyrgyzstan experienced in the last four years an economic decline of 70 per cent)[2] and ahead of Tajikistan. In Tajikistan the economic decline in 1991 was 12.5 per cent in 1992, 33.7 per cent, and in 1993 and 1994 the economy nearly collapsed.[3] The damage caused by the civil war in Tajikistan was estimated at seven billion US dollars and the decline in the output of various industries between fifty per cent and eighty per cent.[4]

Taking for comparison 1991, which was a pre-crisis year for most of the republics of the Soviet Union, Central Asia generally demonstrated higher per capita results than neighbouring India and China, as well as Iran, Turkey and Pakistan. The Central Asian countries registered their per capita GDP as follows: Kazakhstan, US$ 3,185; Turkmenistan, US$ 2,270; Kyrgyzstan, US$ 2,030; and Uzbekistan, US$ 1,740.[5] In spite of the post-1991 economic decline, in most Central Asian states the per capita GDP rate is still higher than in most neighbouring countries.

As a new contender for an independent place in the world economy, Central Asia is not among the worst-placed areas. In terms of diversity of resources and volumes of natural resources extracted, Kazakhstan is the leader. Kazakhstan's raw material resources include a wide range of mineral resources available in the region (fuel and non-ferrous ore) with very high levels of extraction. The mineral base of the economy of other Central Asian states is as follows:

- Uzbekistan: gas and gold
- Turkmenistan: gas
- Kyrgyzstan: uranium
- Tajikistan: uranium.

However, the scale of Central Asian economies is not large. In 1991 Central Asia, with a population of 0.97 per cent of the world population, produced 0.4 per cent of the world GDP.

II THE DRIVING FORCES OF FOREIGN POLICY

The autochthonous urban population is basically the intelligentsia, skilled workers, tradesmen and service personnel. Some intellectuals were incorporated into the national elite mostly due to clan relations; and some others joined different national opposition movements and subsequently suffered repression. The majority, however, did not exert any significant influence on national policies.

The Central Asian authorities are quite wary of the local student movement, since in most places (with the exception of Turkmenistan), there is a sharp decline in the living conditions of the youth and an undulating rise of unemployment. For example, as a result of student unrest in Tashkent in the beginning of 1992, all non-local students were deported and new tertiary institutions were opened in administrative centres. The authorities are also watchful of the 'self-employed', such as small traders and shopkeepers, realising that they are a potential source of fundamentalism, as events in Iran in 1979 clearly demonstrated.

Rural population was a cause of even stronger apprehension. The most fertile areas of Central Asia are naturally the most densely populated. Northern Tajikistan has a density of 0.11 hectares per capita, while in the Fergana valley 300 people live on every square kilometer.[6] Meanwhile the increase in the population exceeds the agricultural growth. The single-crop feature (cotton) of these areas and the critical situation with water supply are to be noted as well. Therefore, mindful of a possible social explosion, the authorities are trying to limit the political activities of the rural population. For example, in Uzbekistan the Free Dekhan Party was refused registration.

Private enterprise is very underdeveloped in Central Asia. In 1994 only 50,000 people were involved in small and private business.[7] In almost all republics (apart from Kyrgyzstan), only those who have close connections with the state organs (government) and belong to clan-based elite can be successful.

So in real practical terms it is only the elite that matters in defining political direction. The 'construction' of the Central Asian elite is very specific: it is of a 'pyramid' shape; its proportion in the population is higher than in the 'European' republics of the former USSR; it is more diversified, and is based (in Uzbekistan to a lesser extent) on a patriarchal and clan system. As a result, the Central Asian elite is a single whole – from national leaders to low-level local leaders. A change of the elite implies complete replacement of leaders at any level.

Generally speaking, the non-communist opposition in Central Asia appears to be rather weak. Moreover, it is often divided into democratic and Islamic parts. While in Tajikistan (with reservations) and Kyrgyzstan the old elite was largely removed from power (though in some regions they have preserved it and are aiming at a revenge at a national level), in Uzbekistan, Kazakhstan and Turkmenistan the old elite remains in authority. However, in order to legitimize its position and receive support from below, the communist elite had to resort to nationalist ideas and principles.

In Uzbekistan, President Karimov was able to achieve a balance of leading clan forces, and regularly reshuffles personnel in different regions of the country. This helps on the one hand to ensure stability, (the civil war in Tajikistan is a vivid example of failure to balance the interests of the rival groups) and on the other hand to strengthen the power of the president.[8] In Kazakhstan the balance is not present: up to 85 per cent of the public service and the Supreme Soviet of the country are from the southern ('senior') clan. From this clan come D. Kunayev, the former First Secretary of the Communist Party of Kazakhstan and N. Nazarbayev, the incumbent president.[9]

In all the republics the strategic policies are shaped predominantly by the interests of the local elite. Tajikistan is overwhelmed by civil war, whereas Kyrgyzstan may be the only country moving towards a civil society where genuine market reforms with an absence of national discrimination (at least on the official level) are taking place. Unfortunately, the rift between the more developed north and the traditional south has recently widened. The southern elite more openly challenges the central authority, and many former local leaders are returned to power.

With paternalist and conservative regimes in power in most Central Asian states, there is no public control over the political course. The participation of the public in the political life can be termed as 'illusive'. Against the background of pseudo-democratic rhetoric and the existence of some democratic institutions, the population is formally engaged in the political process but has no say in it. The legislatures, as a rule, are also not empowered to control and co-ordinate the political course. The mass media is subject to tough censorship. In Uzbekistan, for example, no newspaper where the publisher is the editorial board or a 'physical person' was allowed to register. Only the authorities received such rights.[10] In many Central Asian states major Russian newspapers are banned, while Russian TV broadcasts are regularly suspended.

Only in Kyrgyzstan are the opposition parties not restrained in their activities. In Uzbekistan, the Birlik (Unity) party and the Erk Democratic Party, which represent genuine opposition forces, are suppressed. The presidential structures do not obstruct but rather support the creation of quasi-parties ('Progress of Motherland' and others) imitating political opposition. The Turkmen secret service has been making arrests of opposition figures even in Moscow with the collaboration of Russia's 'democratic' authorities. Activists of the opposition are often prosecuted in Kazakhstan as well.

The emergence of strong presidential power in practically all republics is facilitated not only by economic factors, the need for radical restructuring of the industry bridging the gap between traditional and modern sectors in the agriculture for example, but also by the intention of the national elite to consolidate and implement privatization in order to ensure its dominance under the new social model.

The most open authoritarianism is demonstrated by the presidents of Uzbekistan and Turkmenistan. Karimov clearly orients himself to a model providing minimal political rights with a maximum of economic rights. The Turkmen President Niyazov has introduced a personality cult and rejects, 'for the sake of stability', any claims to political freedom. The dissolution of parliament in Kazakhstan in March 1995, and extension of Nazarbayev's presidency to the beginning of the next century demonstrates that Kazakhstan has also chosen to strengthen the authoritarian regime. Only in Kyrgyzstan, where President Akayev is unsurprisingly nicknamed a 'dreamer', have no such attempts been registered.

At the same time, when analysing the power structures in Central Asia, it is important to take into account a lengthy period of 'collectivist' development in the region, as in the traditional East in general, as opposed to the individualistic West. From this perspective, authoritarianism stems not only from the specific cultural and ideological traditions but is also dictated by the requirements of the transition and the scale of the societal restructuring.

Uzbekistan is clearly aspiring for the leadership role in Central Asia. Her economic potential and size of population are notable. Already Uzbekistan renders economic assistance to the neighbours – for example, supplying gas to Kazakhstan at a price 20 per cent lower than the world price,[11] and the price charged to Kyrgyzstan is even lower. Uzbekistan also entered into a commercially disadvantageous agreement with Tajikistan for trade and economic co-operation in 1995, whereby government supplies from Uzbekistan exceed imports from Tajikistan by 80 million US dollars. Tajikistan's official debt to Uzbekistan (200 million US dollars) has been converted into a very favourable government credit.[12] The availability of indigenous engineering personnel and qualified working force,[13] large Uzbek colonies in all countries of the region, and political stability – all facilitate the realization of the Uzbek ambitions. In terms of religion and culture, Uzbekistan has an edge as well.

Kazakhstan, being less Islamized, with no centres on its territory of historical and cultural importance for other Central Asian states, with 40 per cent of Kazakhs not fluent in their own language, and with a negative impact on the Republic of the departure of Russian and Russian-speaking population, can hardly achieve a leadership role in spite of its intensive diplomatic efforts.

Currently Uzbekistan is trying to contain the rise of tension in the region. It is known, for example, for its role in defeating the 'Islamic and democratic' coalition in Tajikistan. Uzbekistan's decision to be directly and militarily involved in the civil war in Tajikistan was dictated by apprehensions about the rise of fundamentalism in Central Asia, the exodus of Uzbeks from Tajikistan, and increased demands by Uzbek Tajiks for reunification with Tajikistan. At the moment the Uzbek regime is the main shield against the spread of fundamentalism and this cannot but be appreciated by the world powers. However, Uzbekistan's possible use of force in order to ensure its leading role may cause a negative response from neighbours and the international community at large. It has to be noted that the neighbouring countries have a very powerful leverage over Uzbekistan in view of its extreme dependence on water. Rivers that flow in Uzbekistan begin in Tajikistan, Kyrgyzstan and Afghanistan.

With the break-up of the Soviet Union the post-Soviet space is characterized by the emergence of states with diverse political orientations. While in Russia the regime has a non-communist (or anticommunist) nature, in the Central Asian states, with the exception of Kyrgyzstan, the traditional communist elite has preserved its power. This potentially could have led to a conflict situation. But initially, the government of independent Russia was rather indifferent to the processes evolving in the Central Asian region. It was even trying to distance itself from them. Later on, the countries of the region came to a better appreciation of the possibility of conflict with Russia, though only Kazakhstan has a common border with Russia. Nationalist postures which had to be displayed by the old elites started causing tension between the Central Asian states.

Uzbekistan's relations with Turkmenistan and Tajikistan sharply deteriorated recently. Their cooling is caused not only by Uzbekistan's attempt to subjugate the neighbouring countries to its control, but also by its steps aimed at influencing their foreign relations (including relations with Russia) and preventing the spread of Islamic fundamentalism from West Asian countries.

These attempts, however, have met with serious resistance. As for Tajikistan, Dushanbe is not rejecting Uzbek support but relies more on Russia for the preservation of its statehood and the restoration of the economy destroyed by the civil war. Uzbekistan responds by putting more pressure on Tajikistan, demanding from Dushanbe more concessions to its opposition forces, initiating autonomy movement (or outright secession) by the most developed Khojand region of Tajikistan.

In view of the structure of its economy (such as large reserves of hydrocarbons), the ethnic factors (for example, one third of Turkmens reside in Iran) and its geography (with the shortest and easiest access to world markets being through Iran), Turkmenistan is relatively isolated from other Central Asian countries and orients itself predominantly towards developed countries and West Asian states. Moreover, with the completion of the railway between Tejen Serakhs and Meshked, Turkmenistan is able to influence the foreign trade connections of the Central Asian region.

Initially the Uzbek and Turkmen presidents exchanged rather tough mutual accusations. In September 1995 Turkmenistan accused Uzbekistan of excessive use of the Amu-Darya waters which, according to Ashkabad, disrupted the water consumption in Turkmenistan and damaged the ecological situation in the Aral Sea area. It is likely that Turkmenistan may demand that the usage of water in the area be reconsidered, which would be fraught with serious economic consequences for Uzbekistan.

Until recently, Uzbekistan's conflicts with Tajikistan and Turkmenistan were evolving parallel to and not intersecting with each other. But since the autumn of 1995, the President of Turkmenistan has been supporting Tajikistan and has promised Dushanbe material assistance and, amongst other things, has undertaken to build a railroad which would allow the bypassing of Uzbekistan. In other words, tension has become more noticeable. From the end of 1995 and the beginning of 1996 it has become latent but could explode at any time.

III CENTRAL ASIA AND THE OUTSIDE WORLD

Central Asia does not occupy a priority place in the interests of world powers and neighbouring countries. The US and Western Europe are predominantly interested in the political stability in the region, and the development of co-operation in oil and gas exploration, essentially with Turkmenistan and Kazakhstan. But it is too early to refer to considerable economic interests of these leading world centres, not to mention their political and strategic interests. China obviously pays special attention to the Asia-Pacific region. India's priority are the North and Japan, and Pakistan is overwhelmed by its relations with India, whilst Turkey is more interested in Europe.

The Central Asian states are very keen to attract foreign investment and ensure markets for their goods. Their initial expectations, linked with Turkey and other Muslim countries, have not been realized so far, mainly due to the limited economic capacity of Ankara and other interested parties. The West, on the other hand, not only lacks understanding of the region, but is critical of the slow pace (or absence) of economic and political reforms here.

Most of the political elites believe that for the sake of political stability, opposition movements have to be suppressed. The lack of elements of democracy, on the other hand, disturbs the US, Western Europe and Russia, where leaders persistently emphasize the need for respect of basic human rights, even though they are violated from time to time in their own country. Fundamentalist movements in all of the Central Asian states are substantially restricted, with the ruling elites justifiably considering them a threat to their power and to political stability. These measures are welcomed by the US, Western Europe, Russia, China and India but cause friction with Iran and Saudi Arabia.

The task of ensuring an appropriate place in the international community dictates the need for consolidating independence and adding general elements to the external attributes of independence. This conflicts with other set tasks. Central Asian states, for example, are trying to distance themselves from Russia, although this contradicts the task of ensuring normal domestic functioning. Turkey's excessive activity, based on Ankara's expectation of an easy take over of the region, has provoked a much more watchful attitude from the regional countries.

This diversity of tasks implies a skilful manoeuvring between the US, Western Europe, Russia, China, Turkey, Iran and other Muslim countries. The large number of organizations chosen by Central Asian states to join or to co-operate with is notable. Apart from the UN and the Council for the Security and Cooperation of Europe (CSCE), they include the CIS, the Commonwealth of Central Asian States[14] and the Organization for Economic Co-operation (OEC).[15]

The security threats to Central Asian states originate primarily from inside the countries (the Tajikistan example is quite vivid) as well as from neighbours and from each other. The fact that the overwhelming majority of countries – Russia, China, US, Western Europe, Turkey, for example – are currently interested in political stability in the region helps to ease tensions there. However, in future the situation may change as a result of geopolitical developments and domestic turbulence. At present the most serious threat comes from Afghanistan, especially in view of the existing fundamentalist focus in Central Asia. All the governments in the region, most prominently the Uzbekistan and Tajikistan governments, treat it very seriously and are trying to prevent it by all possible means.

The most valuable partners for Central Asia are probably Russia and the CIS, China and India, the closest major Islamic countries (Turkey, Iran, Pakistan and Saudi Arabia) as well as the developed countries making up the core of world economy, such as the US, Western European countries and Japan. Most interested in using or controlling the Central Asian resources are Turkey and Iran, which lack their own resources; large economies like China and India, which could only partially meet their resource needs; and Russia, which has traditional industrial links with the region as well as a transport system to support integration moves.

For Iran, co-operation with Central Asia is to a lesser extent related to resource needs. Saudi Arabia and the developed countries' dependence on them is even smaller. The economic policies of developed countries towards Central Asia are linked to and dependent upon their global economic strategy more than on economic needs of the regional countries.

Nevertheless, all of the above countries here in one way or another have demonstrated their interest in developing economic relations with Central Asia. At the same time, the governments of Central Asian states have stated that all of the above countries are desired partners. Trade between the above countries and Central Asia is expanding, and as it does so, other economic and political ties develop as well. However, when analysing the process of the search for partners by Central Asian states aimed at finding their niche in the world economy and political community, it is appropriate to refer to those countries as potential partners, in view of either geographic or cultural proximity, or powerful economies, or both. However, the process of mutual search for partners is not complete yet.[16]

China's main interest in Central Asia is to ensure political stability and prevent fundamentalists coming to power. This great power has reasons to be apprehensive of growing problems in the Xinjiang Uighur Autonomous Region (or even in Tibet) if fundamentalism is on the rise in Central Asia. Already in 1991 the Uighur community in Central Asia boosted its activities, and groups calling for the independence of the Xinjiang Uighur Autonomous Region started emerging. China had to rush to strengthen its borders and tighten the entry into the autonomous region.

At the same time China is interested in enhancing its influence in Central Asia and expanding the local market for exports from Northwest China which, due to their quality, are hard to promote elsewhere. China is increasing trade with the regional countries: for example, 42 per cent of Kyrgyzstan's trade with non-CIS countries was with China.[17] In most Central Asian countries China is amongst the three leading foreign countries which have established joint ventures. In 1995 in Kyrgyzstan one in every five joint ventures was with China,[18] and by 1994 China had established seventy joint ventures in Uzbekistan.[19] Under consideration is the construction of a gas pipeline to China from Turkmenistan. During Li Peng's visit to Turkmenistan in 1994 it was decided that the two countries' experts would start work on the project.

China had territorial claims with Kazakhstan, Kyrgyzstan and Tajikistan when the republics were part of the Soviet Union. The Central Asian governments are concerned about any possible resumption of the claims. China, it must be noted, has refrained for quite some time from making public statements on the issue.

The Central Asian states accentuate their friendly feelings towards China. President Akayaev even sued the 'Blue Mountains' paper, the official organ of the Kyrgyz parliament, for 'persistent outrageous attacks against China'.[20]

India has similar interests in the region. In a case of confrontation between Islamic fundamentalism and the international community, South Asia may become its main battleground. In view of its basic contradictions with Pakistan and the presence of one hundred million Muslims in India, New Delhi is extremely wary of the possibility of Central Asia becoming an ally of the fundamentalists or of Pakistan. It is not accidental that at any talks with Central Asian states, India would seek their assurances of averting the rise of fundamentalism.

In trying to obstruct the emergence of a broad fundamentalist bloc, India resorts not only to diplomatic but economic steps as well. Even at the time of perestroika in the Soviet Union, India was attempting to develop economic co-operation with the region through construction projects, training of local cadres, and trade deals, among other things. But until now this has not materialized into anything substantial, mainly due to political instability in India itself and New Delhi's limited economic capacity.

In the same period, Pakistan has significantly enhanced its presence in Central Asia by sending clergy and representatives of special services. Once the independence of Central Asian states was proclaimed, Pakistan started rendering economic assistance, even though the per capita income in Pakistan was substantially lower then that in former Soviet Central

Asia. Pakistan immediately offered them credits. In August 1992 Tajikistan was offered a loan of 500 million US dollars to build a hydroelectric power station.

The landlocked Central Asian states are highly interested in connecting their railways with Pakistan, which would give them access to the Indian Ocean. Already in the beginning of the 1990s, plans were drawn for the construction of roads connecting Kyrgyzstan and Kazakhstan with the Karakorum highway in Pakistan, as well as connecting Uzbekistan with Karachi. Talks started on building a gas pipeline from Turkmenistan to Pakistan via Afghanistan. However, feuding problems have not been resolved yet. The closest route via Afghanistan is dangerous, whilst the route lying through China and Iran is too expensive. Uzbekistan is promoting the idea of transferring the waters of the Ind River into the region which would require the construction of a 2,600 km channel through Pakistan, Iran and Afghanistan.

Pakistan's relative weakness does not, however, allow Islamabad to become a major partner of Central Asian states. Because of that, Pakistan is trying to assist regional co-operation between the Islamic countries, and to use Turkey, Iran and Saudi Arabia for strengthening its own presence in Central Asia. Pakistan's main task is to form an alliance of friendly states helpful in confronting India, and making Pakistan a strong regional power, recognized by the main world power centres. Pakistan does not hide its aims. In April 1992 Prime Minister N. Sharif stated that the victory of the mujahedin in Afghanistan created favourable conditions for the formation of a new regional body, consisting of Pakistan, Iran, Turkey, Afghanistan and the Central Asian states. Pakistan has considerable influence over a number of Afghan factions which cannot be ignored by the ruling elites in the region. The Central Asian authorities, especially the Uzbek regime, accentuate their good relations with Pakistan but probably do not have high expectations of Islamabad. The international community is perturbed by Pakistani-Afghani co-operation in the drug business and by the active search by drug dealers for reliable partners in Central Asia.

Challenges relating to the acquisition of nuclear weapons are also a cause for concern. American Senator L. Pressler pointed out that if a Confederation of Islamic states was formed, it would have nuclear weapons. According to Indian sources in the beginning of the 1990s, there were more than two thousand nuclear warheads in the Central Asian republics. Indians were also convinced that Pakistan was trying to purchase uranium from Tajikistan through the Afghani mujahedins, which could be used in its military nuclear programme.[21] There were concerns that through Central Asia Pakistan could get access to sophisticated Soviet arms and nuclear technologies for military use.[22]

Pakistan's support of Islamic fundamentalists is a separate issue. The Uzbek Foreign Minister S. Safayev publicly denounced in 1993 the Pakistani Islamic party Jamaat-I-islami for supporting the Tajik fundamentalists.[23] The Pakistani press acknowledged that the Pakistani missionaries in Central Asia were inciting the local believers against the 'pro-communist' authorities.[24] The Pakistani authorities deny any involvement and note that such actions are taken only by Islamic movements.

Afghanistan is the obvious potential base for the growth of fundamentalist forces in the region, through its Tajik and Uzbek populations. Uzbekistan has succeeded in establishing relations with General Dostum, which ensures that the Afghani-Uzbek border remains calm.[25] Meanwhile, the Tajik opposition has found asylum in Afghanistan and the Tajik-Afghani border has become a place of regular confrontation. At the same time, Uzbekistan and Tajikistan cannot fail to foresee the possible break-up of Afghanistan and the formation of new states, such as a Tajik-Uzbek state or separate Uzbek and Tajik states. In that case the ruling elites would find it difficult to resist the strong temptation to expand their territories, which would be at the expense of domestic political stability. It should be noted that if Afghanistan breaks up, the region will be inevitably taken over by Iran, which would provoke a tough reaction from the West.

Iran has been clearly attempting to become an ideological and political leader of the Central Asian states. In the economic spheres, its strengths are in convertible currency (petrodollars), and transit routes through its territories, including gas and oil pipelines. Iran at the same time lacks sophisticated equipment and technologies. At the moment, the US is putting enormous pressure on Iran's partners in order to isolate Tehran, and so far Iran has been able to establish significant economic ties with Pakistan only. Iran has also committed itself to building a railroad to Ashkabad. Ideologically, however, differences remain on a civilizational basis between the Turkic population of Central Asia and the Iranians (only the Tajiks are the Iranians' kin), and between the predominantly Sunni Central Asia and Sh'ia Iran. Not surprisingly, Iranians have developed intimate relationships only with the Tajik opposition.

The Iranian model is not very attractive to local elites. It is not a coincidence that it was only at the end of 1993 during Iranian President A. A. Hashme-Rafsanjani's visit to Uzbekistan that the countries agreed on the opening of an Uzbek embassy in Iran.

From a cultural point of view Turkey fits in the role of regional leader much better. Turkey's secularism is also appealing to the Central Asian ruling elites. Immediately after the proclamation of independence by the Central Asian states, Turkey started showing keen intent. During Prime Minister S. Demirel's visit to Central Asia, loan agreements were signed for the sum of US$ 600 million. Uzbekistan alone was promised US$ 700 million.[26] Ankara also started its radio broadcasts to the region which have reached 33 hours a day.[27] Dreams of restoring the Ottoman Empire have started appearing in Turkey. Turkish State Minister O. Kilerjioglu openly wished to see the crescent extending from Central Asia to the Adriatic Sea, with Turkey in the middle.[28]

However the major powers in the region like Uzbekistan and Kazakhstan, as mentioned above, are themselves aspiring for the leadership role and therefore want to distance themselves from Turkey. Uzbekistan, for example, rejected the idea of drawing together the Turkic and Uzbek languages. It proposed instead to work out a new regional language – the 'Ortaturk' language. Pan-Turkism is not a popular idea at the grass roots level either. Turkey is not capable of forcing Russia out in the economic sphere, not to mention the military and the political. The Central Asian elites must have realized Turkey's relative economic weakness back in 1993, and since then they have ceased referring to the Turkic model.

At the same time a considerable growth in Turkey's cultural influence is very likely as more and more young people from Central Asia receive their education in Turkey. Turkey may well become the main source of scientific and technical education, whilst co-operation in the areas of transit and trade will continue to grow.

The West is generally supportive of Turkey's claims in Central Asia, considering Ankara as an alternative to theocratic Iran.[29] This stance is quite contradictory. Supporting 'secular Islam', the West neglects the fact that in Central Asia it may acquire a very different form and meaning. There is an understanding by Western Europe, however, that Turkey's relations with Central Asia may lead to economic and political difficulties. These could include the possible re-export to Europe through Turkey, and with Turkish labels, of raw materials from Central Asia as well as the eventual military and political involvement of the West in regional events if Turkey, a NATO member, is engaged there.

The idea of an Islamic alliance even under Turkey's leadership does not appeal to the West either. But in principle the West treats Turkey as a more acceptable alternative to Iran. The conservatives see Turkey as an alternative to Russia as well. Japan does not conceal its stance on this issue. Announcing the granting by the Japanese Export-Import Bank of a loan for the construction of the Kokdumalak oil and gas complex in Uzbekistan, Tokyo pointed out that it was imperative to help the Central Asian states dependent on Russia to become self-reliant.[30]

Western liberals do not oppose Russia's close relations with Central Asia and even encourage them. They believe that Russia's involvement in the southern and southwestern tier of the CIS will lead to diminished Russian pressure on Ukraine, the Baltic states and Eastern Europe.

In the economic sphere the Western countries are interested mostly in the excavation and refining of oil and gas, as well as of rare and precious metals. They are also concerned about the safety of their investment. Not surprisingly, these two items are almost always mentioned in government agreements between Central Asian and developed countries.

A considerable part of assistance from the West is directed to financing the structural changes and the balance of payments. In absolute terms Uzbekistan is the leader as a recipient of economic assistance. By March 1994 Uzbekistan received US$ 1.2 billion of credits,[31] and in 1995 received up to US$ 500 million.[32] In per capita terms the leader is Kyrgyzstan. However, as a result of this, Kyrgyzstan's foreign debt reached US$ 500 million,[33] while the instability of the som, the Kyrgyz currency, undermines the country's exports.

Whereas Western Europe is more interested in containing fundamentalism, the US, treating it as an abstract issue, focuses on human rights. Unfortunately from time to time it also shows double standards.[34] There is a slightly growing trend for isolationism in the US with regard to regions which are not seen as vital to the US. The American policy towards Central Asia has been characterized generally by multiple aims which may be summarized as follows: politically, supporting political stability in the region with muffled criticisms of regional authorities for lack of genuine political reforms and human rights violations, and countering the spread of Islamic fundamentalism; strategically, dismantling all nuclear capabilities from Central Asia and curtailing the growth of the military-industrial complex (in Kazakhstan in particular), preventing the expansion of Iranian influence (first priority) and possibly as well as that of China, accepting the region as the sphere of influence of Russia (accompanied by constant criticism of Russia's 'imperial policy'); and economically, supporting Western oil companies, and assisting Central Asian states' transition to a market economy. American policy will also aim at securing the co-operation of Central Asian states in the fight against global problems such as ecological deterioration and drug trafficking.

In the medium as well as the long term, therefore, foreign policy changes in Central Asia are likely to depend first of all on domestic factors and corrections in the balance of power between the various clans and elites, as well as on domestic situation in Russia and global trends.

NOTES

1. Starchenkov, G., 'The Glitter and Misery of Sovereign Uzbekistan' *Asia and Africa Today* No. 6, 1995, p. 10.
2. Starchenkov, G., 'Kyrgyzia: Life Without the "Elder Brother"' *Asia and Africa Today*, No. 2, 1995, p. 28.
3. Olimova, S. K. and Olimova, M. A., 'Independent Tajikistan: Difficult Path of Change' *Vostok*, No. 1, 1995, p. 141.
4. *Segodnya*, 15 April 1995.
5. Caculated on the basis of *International Financial Statistics: Supplement on Countries of the Former Soviet Union*, IMF, Washington, 1993.
6. Maklai, O., 'Russia and Central Asian States', *Asia and Africa Today*, No. 4, 1995 pp. 3–7.
7. Olimova, C. K. & Olimov, M. A., 'Independent Tajikistan: Difficult Path of Change', *Vostok*, No. 1, 1995, p. 143.
8. It is to be noted that the tribal system in Uzbekistan is much more eroded than in other republics.
9. 'It is remarkable that the legitimacy of the leaders of other republics is also largely determined by their descent. Thus, A. Akayev is a direct descendant of the last Kyrgyz ruler, the Shabdan Khan, while S. Niyazov comes from the Teke tribe which in the past always "supplied" the Turkmen leaders.' *Moscow News*, No. 15, 10–17 April, 1994, pp. 8–9.
10. *Segodnya*, 11 January 1994.
11. *Moscow News*, No. 3, 16–23 January 1994.
12. *Segodnya*, 12 January 1995.
13. Only Uzbekistan is able to replace to some extent the fleeing Russian-speaking cadres by the local ones. Uzbeks are the only ethnic group in the region which had access to European education from the end of the 19th century from the Kazan University, much earlier than other ethnic groups.
14. The Commonwealth of Central Asian States includes Uzbekistan, Kazakhstan, and Kyrgyzstan. It provides for a customs union and aims at establishing a common economic space.
15. The Organization was founded by Turkey, Iran and Pakistan not only for promoting their economic ties but also to aid the Central Asian states and Azerbaijan.
16. In 1991–1992 Central Asian states had higher expectations of Turkey, than of Iran and Saudi Arabia, later China and again Russia. From 1993 in Uzbekistan, for example, references to the 'Turkish' or the 'Chinese' model have been dropped.
17. Alishbaeva, A., 'Foreign Economic Policy of Kyrgyzstan', *Evraziiskoye Soobshestvo*, No. 1, 1995, p. 13.
18. Ibid.
19. *Segodnya*, 21 April 1994.
20. *Rossiskaya Gazeta*, 23 August 1995.
21. *Izvestiya*, 2 October 1992.
22. *The Times of India*, 23 June 1992.
23. *Izvestiya*, 19 March 1993.
24. *Segodnya*, 20 August 1994.

25. In 1994 Dostum's planes even bombarded several times the Tajik refugee camps not far from the Afghani town of Kunduz. See *Segodnya*, 18 May 1994.
26. Starchenov, G., 'The Glitter and Misery of Sovereign Uzbekistan', *Asia and Africa Today*, No. 6, 1995, p. 8.
27. In comparison, Iran broadcasts 12 hours per day, and Pakistan, 5 hours.
28. *Pravda*, 19 January 1993.
29. In 1992, the EU granted US$ 700 million to the region, emphasizing that Turkey was going to play the role of the bridge. See *Pravda*, 19 January 1993.
30. *Segodnya*, 15 April 1995.
31. Ibid.
32. Ibid.
33. Starchenkov, G., 'Kyrgyzia: Life Without the "Elder Brother"', *Asia and Africa Today*, No. 2, 1995, p. 27.
34. The US, for example, was critical of S. Niyazov's extension of his term without holding elections. The State Department spokesman referred to it as a 'departure from democracy'. See *Segodnya*, 18 January 1994. At the same time Bill Clinton supported President N. Nazarbayev's move to dissolve the Kazakh parliament. See *Segodnya*, 16 March 1995.

Index